A People's Collector in the British Raj
Arthur Galletti

Brian Stoddart is an Emeritus Professor at La Trobe University,
Australia, where he also served as Vice Chancellor and President.
Now he works as an international consultant to higher education
reform programmes funded by the Asian Development Bank,
the World Bank and the European Union. His doctoral work
was on South Indian nationalist politics. Later he created an
international reputation for his extensive work on sports
culture, including *Saturday Afternoon Fever: Sport in the Australian
Culture* and *Sport, Culture and History*. However he maintained his
deep interest in South Asia throughout and has done numerous
research projects in the field. Prof. Stoddart has also done
extensive work for the press and electronic media, including a
remarkable career as a radio commentator and collaborator on
television series.

A People's Collector in the British Raj
Arthur Galletti

Brian Stoddart

Readworthy
New Delhi

First published 2011

Readworthy Publications (P) Ltd.

Editorial and Regd. Office	**Sales Office**
B-65, Mansa Ram Park	4735/22, Prakash Deep Building, Ground
Near Master Palace	Floor, Ansari Road, Daryaganj
New Delhi–110 059-07	New Delhi–110 002
Phone: 011-2533 3244	Phone: 011-43549197

Email: info@readworthypub.com
Web: www.readworthypub.com

Cataloging in Publication Data--DK
Courtesy: D.K. Agencies (P) Ltd. <docinfo@dkagencies.com>

Stoddart, Brian.
   A people's collector in the British Raj: Arthur Galletti / Brian Stoddart.
      p.   cm.
   Includes bibliographical references (p.   ) and index.

ISBN 13: 978-93-5018-041-9   ISBN 10: 93-5018-041-3

   1. Galletti, Arthur, 1843-1967. 2. Municipal officials and employees--India, South--Biography. 3. Tax collection--India, South--History--20th century. 4. India, South--Politics and government--20th century. 5. India--History--British occupation, 1765-1947.   I. Title.

DDC 352.1409548   22

Printed at Salasar Imaging Systems, Delhi-35

Preface

I cannot remember exactly when first I encountered Arthur Mario Agricola Collier Galletti di Cadilhac's name but it was in the Tamil Nadu State Archives in Madras, now Chennai, while rummaging through files researching my doctoral thesis on Congress politics in the early 20th century Presidency. Most records came from the government side, the Madras Secretariat gathering intelligence from its representatives in the *mofussil,* the rural districts where the Collector was the most important Raj representative. I was interested primarily in the evolution of Indian nationalism and the activities of Congress in south India but grew curious about the Indian Civil Service, men come from Oxford and Cambridge and the British middle and upper classes to the far reaches of Provincial India. They ruled great stretches of land and sometimes millions of people, the heart of British administration in India. For the most part their dispatches from 1920s and 1930s rural Madras Presidency displayed similar views, ideas, attitudes and suggestions.

One man soon stood out, though. First, there was his name—in a sea of Englishness leavened by the odd Irish, Scots, Welsh, sometimes Indian and even white Dominions slant, "Galletti" was like a lighthouse beacon. Who was he and how did he come to be there? That question recurred when I read some of what he wrote, because again he was very different from the rest. As my broader research deepened I began looking out for 'Galletti material', putting it away for future reference. The search for Galletti was on.

That search has lasted a long time. I became involved in another field of research as soon as I finished the thesis, spending several years writing and teaching in the new area of sports studies but still retaining my deep interest in India. Then I strayed into university management and spent several more years trying to change systems and people. Along the way, though, I never forgot Galletti and that initial question: who was he and why was he there?

In idle moments I reviewed the material, followed up obvious historical leads, and on rare occasions strayed into Galletti archival *cul de sacs* whenever possible. One piece of detective work led finally to his daughter, Emma, and on a cold winter's morning in a small Italian town she greeted my wife Sandi and me off a bus, opening the hatch of her small Fiat to reveal what would be the first of many Galletti treasures. That spurred me on, and even though I still had another "career" for several years my Galletti files grew.

One of the greatest pleasures in preparing this book has been the archival work taking me from the Tamil Nadu State Archives, the Andhra Pradesh State Archives and the National Archives in India to the India Office Records in the British Library, and libraries all over the world in India, Australia and the United Kingdom. In all those places I have had the most wonderful assistance, amidst the normal archival frustrations, and Galletti would not have emerged but for that support from librarians and archivists in Perth, Canberra, Melbourne, London, Oxford, Cambridge, Delhi, Hyderabad and Chennai among others.

Similarly, several universities over the years have supported my research financially and I remain grateful to all of them: Western Australia, Curtin, Canberra, Australian National, New England, RMIT, and La Trobe. I owe a particular thanks to Vice-Chancellor Nick Saunders and then Deputy Vice-Chancellor (Research) now Vice-Chancellor at Charles Darwin University, Barney Glover, who appointed me as a Research Professor at the University of Newcastle immediately after I left La Trobe—that allowed me to complete the research and write the book alongside some other work at Newcastle and I am deeply indebted to both of them.

Along the way particular friends and colleagues became as fascinated by Galletti as I did and never let me forget my "mad Italian", encouraging me to keep going and to write the story even while I was doing vastly different things. One highly important influence came from the man who introduced me to India at the University of Canterbury in New Zealand, Ian Catanach. He was an outstanding teacher, relentless and ruthless marker, and was the major contributor to any skills I now have as a social historian. Sadly, he will not see this book as he passed away during 2009, a great loss to South Asian scholarship. Robin Jeffrey, Peter Reeves, Dipesh Chakrabarty, Gyan Pandey, Auriol Weigold, John McGuire, Boria Majumdar, David Washbrook and many, many others in their own ways over the years have helped me develop Galletti. Suvam Pal very helpfully traced some materials in India for me and Richard Bosworth, Australia's great biographer of Mussolini amongst many other achievements, provided many insights into the Italian sources.

By far the greatest source of support, however, has been Arthur Galletti's family. Led by the remarkable and redoubtable Emma, they have done everything possible to help me write a warts and all story of a remarkable, difficult and puzzling man. Emma has constantly made available the trove of family photographs, papers and publications, as well as her inimitable memories of her parents and India. Emma's son Pascal Ricketts and his wife Sally (themselves with strong memories of and connections to India), along with their daughters Beatrice and Anna have made the *Casacce* freely available to Sandi and me to the point where we are treated like family, a great privilege as well as great fun. More importantly, they shared the family papers openly, traded family secrets directly and were generally so trusting–it was humbling to benefit so much as an historian and biographer from their open and welcoming interest.

From Arthur Galletti's other children we have come to know David Galletti, Ian Galletti, and William de Bruyn who lives just a few kilometers away from our Australian home, such is the reach of this remarkable family. Antoinette Moat, Galletti's grand-daughter and her husband John Moat have been marvellous supporters, affording us time and space in their wonderful home in the wilds of South Devon. Antoinette has also generously provided many splendid photographs of her grandfather and his family. Clara Muzzarelli, the family archivist, was most helpful and even commented on some early drafts. Cynthia Salvadori has become a great email correspondent from Kenya, while in London Elizabeth Skinner recounted many Galletti fabulous tales.

This has been an historian's wonderland, in other words, not the least because of a breathtaking moment in the *Casacce* library when some files appeared that helped solve the final jigsaw. Historians dream of such moments. That was mine, and I owe it to Arthur Galletti's family who are all themselves wonderful and extraordinary people.

Outside my own direct family, by far my greatest supporter and inspiration was my long-time friend, Indianist par excellence and devotee of the curious, Ken McPherson. He read all the drafts, asked excellent questions, provided insightful background, and shared my interest in the "different" Madras that Galletti represents. We met in 1971 and he was on hand when Galletti discovered me. Through the subsequent years Ken encouraged my pioneering work on sport as I encouraged his on the Indian Ocean. We shared the excitement of research discoveries, the professional and personal highs and lows and prompted each other's extravagances in books, antiques and art. As Galletti neared completion, he was as pleased as I was at how it came together.

Sadly, Ken cannot share in the delight of seeing this book appear because early in 2009 he was stricken with a brain disease that prevented him from reading and/or debating, the two greatest routine pleasures in his life apart from chocolate and marzipan. I was able to spend his last few months helping him and, hard though it was, it was no price to pay for everything he gave me. Ken McPherson died on 29 March 2010, and scarcely a day passes when I don't wonder what he might have made of something or other.

I miss him deeply, and one small consolation is that I was able through late 2009 to edit his book on the Tamil Muslims, and then to see it to press. It is a testament to a scholar who always thought differently and was prepared to take another path, an inspiration to me and others.

Throughout all this, though, my greatest support has come from Sandi who became as fascinated as I was by Arthur and Clara Galletti, came to love their family and the *Casacce* and to develop her own interest in the story. In some ways I do not have to thank her, because she had as much fun and maybe even more than me in running the story to earth. Nonetheless, I am deeply grateful to her for the love and support she gave me throughout the subject and has done throughout our lives together. So, too, am I grateful to our girls, Laura and Kirsten who had the frustration of their parents going off to Italy and the United Kingdom to "work", allegedly, on a book they heard too much about. I am proud of both of them and thank them for putting up with me.

Brian Stoddart
"Selkirk"
Kyneton
13 January 2011

Contents

1

Prologue

An Imperial Moment

Empire Day, 24 May 1918, was wet, windy and miserable in Horsleykonda, an insignificant little town over 3,000 feet up in south India's Nilgiri Hills. Before the later 19th century emergence of neighbour Ootacamund, forever known as 'Snooty Ooty', Horsleykonda hosted most Madras Presidency elite civilians during the hot season. Now it saw only those from Chittoor District and immediate surrounds.

With the end of World War I still unknown months away, this Empire Day was more than usually significant for India's ruling caste and local supporters. 'King and Empire' signified loyalty and continuity, especially when imminent constitutional reforms threatened to further dilute direct British control over India. Horsleykonda's principal celebrations were consequently solemn and serious despite their small scale: an 'at home' staged by local missionaries where a hardy few tackled target shooting and an outside treasure hunt while most others huddled inside; and a later dinner hosted by the District's Acting Deputy Collector. Alfred nicknamed 'Imperial' Tampoe was a gaunt, moustached, sober figure, the first Singhalese-recruited member of the Indian Civil Service to which entry was prized both 'at Home' in Britain and in India. Rarely numbering more than one thousand members the 'Steel Frame', as it was known, anchored British administration as a conservative, conventional, clever but clubby corps.

Earlier heavy showers sprang leaks in the original tent erected for the dinner so it was replaced by a smaller one, camp tables forming an H-shaped setting for seventeen guests:

- Alfred Tampoe;
- Mrs Tampoe;
- Robin Tampoe, their son;
- Mr. Eddie Tampoe-Phillips, Tampoe's nephew lawyer visiting from Singapore;
- Dr. T.T. Thomson, a medical missionary for the London Missionary Society in south India since 1906;
- Mrs. Thomson;
- Reverend G.H. MacFarlane, an LMS representative in south India since 1881;
- Mrs. MacFarlane;
- Mr. C.E.C. Fischer, an Indian Forest Service senior officer, leading botanist of south India and later Kew Gardens resident expert on Indian botany;
- Mrs. Fischer;
- Reverend S. Nicholson, another LMS minister in India since 1897, now head of mission in nearby Cuddapah District and an amateur anthropologist;
- Mrs. Nicholson;
- Mrs. Gooch, wife of F.W. Gooch, the district *abkari* and salt tax officer who was absent on duty but also on the verge of retirement;
- Clara Galletti, wife of Arthur Galletti, the District Collector;
- Arthur Galletti junior, a 12 year old student at the Europeans-only "High Class Boarding" Breeks School in Ootacamund;
- Robert Galletti, 11 years old and also at Breeks; and
- Arthur Galletti, Collector of Chittoor and prime local symbol of the Raj.

These people knew each other well meeting regularly for dinner, tennis, snooker and bridge at the Club or in each other's homes, so close was official district life. Clara Galletti hosted the same crowd to tea a week earlier and just before Empire Day the missionaries staged yet another tea, itself preceded by a tennis tournament won by Clara Galletti and Mr. Fischer with Mrs. Fischer and Dr. Thomson runners-up.

Clara Galletti thought the Empire Day dinner went well despite the poor weather. Discussions about the War, however, raised extreme passions in these microcosmic imperial settings. At an earlier function Clara was accused of being 'pro-German' because she criticised the war and its senseless carnage on both sides–in a recent letter she doubted that Germany alone caused the conflict.[1] Questioning publicly Britain's 'rightness' in the conflict was unwise, no matter a person's private views.

Seated near Arthur Galletti during dinner, Mrs. Fischer and Mrs. Thomson asked him to declare that he represented the King alone in these trying times, that he had no other loyalties. Was he not the King's servant completely? Galletti replied that he served India and its people rather than the King. Scandalised, the two women and others questioned how Galletti drew the King's pay while holding such outrageous views. Galletti was a striking figure: 180 centimeters tall, weighing about 80 kilograms, energetically athletic, eloquent and well-spoken, intellectually dominant and, at 41, still reckoned handsome. Vigorously, loudly, even aggressively the Collector assailed the gathering with what were later described as his "republican", anti-monarchist ideas. The mood in the tent turned tense and uneasy, even resentful.

Toward dinner's end, Alfred Tampoe asked Galletti to propose "The King's Health" from his prime place at table marked as it was by a Crown and Union Jack fashioned from local seeds

---

1   Clara Galletti to Mother, 22 May 1918, Galletti Papers.

by the Tampoe servants. Seething still from the earlier exchange Galletti replied angrily that he would propose no such toast. The assembly was shocked because, as "leading man", Galletti should have officiated.

What happened next had even greater consequences. In the confusion following Galletti's refusal, Mr. Fischer proposed the toast and all, bar one, stood and raised their glasses. The exception was Arthur Galletti. He remained seated and, according to most observers including his remarkable wife, *did not drink the toast*, a clear snub to King and Empire from someone paid to represent, serve and defend both in India.

Wild and conflicting reports about "The Horsleykonda Incident" spread rapidly through ICS and Madras Presidency social circles. It became "official" several months later when irritated and exasperated senior Government of Madras officials saw opportunity to curb the brilliant, erratic and flawed Anglo-Italian Cavaliere Arthur Mario Agricola Collier Galletti di Cadilhac. The controversial career of the self-styled "People's Collector" and Government of Madras scourge was blighted terminally that day, but the episode captured the personality and beliefs that stood him apart from his ruling colleagues in the midst of great social and political change.

2

Becoming Arthur Galletti

Throughout his thwarted career critics suggested Arthur Galletti's personal and professional problems emerged as much from his 'different', multicultural heritage as from his complex personality. Others thought the two aspects linked inextricably, his rich and intertwined family history determining his character and behaviour. Given that, almost the only straightforward fact about Galletti's life was his birth at his maternal grandfather's country property near Great Dunmow in Essex on 25 March 1877. Even then, the birth certificate reflected the cultural complexities. His father was listed as Arturio Antonio Gaetano Mario Galletti di Cadilhac, "Captain Royal Artillery in the service of Italy" with his mother being Margaret Isabella Galletti di Cadilhac, residence Bigod's Hill.[1]

Galletti's mother was the Honourable Margaret Collier, only daughter of Sir Robert Collier and his wife Isabella nee Rose who herself descended from a tough Scottish line. Robert Collier, son of a successful businessman, magistrate and alderman become a Member of Parliament, was educated at Plymouth Grammar School then Trinity College, Cambridge, before finally taking a degree and being called to the Bar in 1843, then working as a barrister around Devon. His early reputation came from a successful 1845 defence of Brazilian pirates who killed a British

---

1   According to family records Galletti's father was named Antonio Maria Gaetano Arturo. The family histories that appear here have been collected through discussions with family members and by a search of all available literature. However, I owe a great debt to Simon Gooch who most generously shared the findings of his genealogical research commissioned by the Collier family.

seaman. One family descendant later wondered if Robert Collier shared 'fellow feeling' with the pirates, given his restless character. There was, in fact, a pirate Collier, Jonathan who lived during the 17th century and eventually became respectable. Many wondered even later whether Arthur Galletti shared all those 'fellow feelings' and restlessness.

Robert Colliers's legal reputation grew alongside his political aspirations. Earlier proposed as a Whig parliamentary candidate because of his Anti-Corn Law League activities, he succeeded his father in 1852 both as Liberal MP for Plymouth and Deputy Lieutenant of Devon. During Palmerston's second Whig government from 1859-65, Collier became Judge Advocate of the Fleet then Solicitor General, and was knighted in 1863. Continuing as Solicitor General in the brief Russell Government that followed, Collier later became Attorney General in the first Gladstone government. Collier was a reformist. In 1867, he argued that the £10 rate threshold for gaining the vote be abolished, because it divided electorates into "two classes of superior and inferior, more and less respectable voters". In 1869 he sought to abolish jail terms for bankrupts.

His later career was controversial. Resigning from Parliament to take a lucrative Devon legal post, Collier then reneged, returning to Westminster and the centre of a patronage/corruption row. Many believed Gladstone appointed him to the superior court position simply so that he might be qualified for admission to the Judicial Committee of the Privy Council. In 1885, Collier was created Baron by the outgoing Gladstone government, and took the name Monkswell from his former Devon home.

The now Lord Monkswell's wife, Isabella Rose, was the daughter of the High Sheriff of Warwickshire whose wealthy family held substantial lands. One brother lived in New Zealand for some time before returning to England, another was shattered by his Crimean War experiences.

Lord and Lady Monkswell had three children. Robert, born in 1845, became the second Baron Monkswell at his father's death in 1886. After Eton and Cambridge the younger Robert, too, became a lawyer. He was a Liberal in the House of Lords and a Radical Club member active in London city politics, becoming Chairman of the London City Council in 1903. He held that post as a progressive, a group blending radical Liberals and nascent trades unionists. Condemning the existence of London sweatshops, he held similarly progressive views on several issues. His career withered before his death in 1909, his House of Commons ambitions unrealised. Robert Collier junior was a perennial Galletti mentor, enabling his nephew's access to education, the ICS and influential social and political networks.

The second Lord Monkswell's brother, John Collier, was born in 1850 and attended Eton but left at 16 complaining education there was pointless. He travelled to the continent joining, among other things, a Heidelberg dueling club at the University. After brief stints as a Foreign Office clerk and city commercial man, he turned to painting. A star Slade School of Art student, the Royal Academy first hung his work in 1874. After a doomed love affair with his brother's sister-in-law Collier married Marian Huxley, daughter of Professor T.H. Huxley, the eminent 19th century scientist who became President of the Royal Society and ardent Charles Darwin follower.[2]

The couple were quite the bohemians in later 19th century London but Marian, herself a talented painter, was almost certainly schizophrenic and her increasingly erratic behaviour was a constant family worry before her 1887 death. Jack Collier then married Marian's sister Ethel in Norway because "wife's sister" marriage remained illegal in England until 1907. His painting career flourished as he moved between the arts and more conventional circles—he did an excellent and important

---

2   Collier portraits of Huxley and Darwin hang in the Athenaeum Club in London.

portrait of Rudyard Kipling in 1892 soon after the writer's return from India.[3] Some of Collier's more adventurous works puzzled, even disturbed the critics. Jack Collier worked in the Foreign Office during the latter stages of World War I, but kept painting until his death in 1934.

Jack Collier also mentored Arthur Galletti throughout his life, even though he considered that the object of the advice ignored most of what was offered. Through the Collier and Huxley lines Galletti accessed a radical, progressive and intellectual strain normally denied ICS members.

Margaret "Madge" Collier, Galletti's mother born in 1846, grew up in London sharing the political, liberal/radical and artistic atmosphere created by the extended family. She received no formal education, was tutored privately, and experienced freely all the family dramas. In her early 20s she fell in love with a British army officer but the affair ended badly. Margaret went to Italy to recover and while in Rome met Arturo Galletti di Cadilhac, marrying him there in 1873. The personalities, experiences and backgrounds brought to the marriage helped form Arthur Galletti's outlook, attitudes and behaviour.

Arturo Galletti, born in 1843, was the son of Bartolomeo Galletti and Anna de Cadilhac. Anna was born in 1825, the daughter of a French family escaped to Italy during the French Revolution. A renowned beauty, her 1842 marriage to Bartolomeo was a scandal. fourteen years older than her he was the handsome, wealthy but illegitimate son of a spice merchant, and a political liberal who supported Italian unification. Commissioned a colonel in 1848, Bartolomeo joined Garibaldi to defend Rome against the French, becoming a general and decorated hero. Anna nursed injured troops and became as equally famous. When Rome fell Bartolomeo left for a Paris exile but Anna stayed to protect family commercial interests. When Garibaldi united

---

3   This is in the National Portrait Gallery, London.

Italy in 1861, Galletti marched with the victorious army but was then sent off to suppress provincial brigands rather than becoming a key player in the new state. Anna visited the new capital, Turin, seeking a more influential role for her husband but while there had an affair with King Victor Emmanuel II that produced a daughter, one of his many illegitimate children.

Bartolomeo and Anna separated. She spent her life seeking recognition for her illegitimate daughter. He retreated to Rome, and in the mid-1870s embarked on a two year theatre troupe world tour, going as far as Australia with the renowned Italian actress Adelaide Ristori and her husband.[4] Bartolomeo, Arthur Galletti's grandfather, died in Rome in 1887 and Anna, his grandmother, in 1896.

Bartolomeo and Anna's son Arturo, father of Arthur Galletti, also joined the military, was reputably among the most handsome of Italian men, and was deeply interested in politics. After he married Margaret Collier, the couple moved from Rome to the Marche on the Adriatic coast. They bought a 200 hectare property called *San Venanzo* at Torre San Patrizio, south of Ancona and north of Ascoli Piceno, spending money and time to transform it from a modest dwelling to a notable home. Margaret Collier turned writer, publishing *The Camorristi* in 1882 and *Our Home by the Adriatic* in 1886. In 1887 came *Prince Peerless*, a book of fairy tales illustrated by her brother Jack Collier. That year she also produced the novel *Babel*, a romantic but dark, Adriatic-set story depicting an English woman's troubled life with an Italian husband. The husband dies at the hands of a local peasant, and the wife realises she still loves him despite all the problems.

---

4   Tony Mitchell (ed.), *High art in a Foreign tongue: Adelaide Ristori's 1875 Australian tour—Selections From Bartolomeo's around the world with Ristori and Australian reviews of Ristori's performances* (Brisbane, Australasian Drama Studies Association, 1995)—the Galletti diary is in the State Library of New South Wales in Sydney.

The marriage was as troubled as *Babel* suggested. Arturo was violent and had several affairs. The marriage failed finally because he created a second family with an Italian house servant—one story has a son from that liaison going to America bearing the name Cadilhac, soon to become Cadillac. A variation has Arthur Galletti, late in life, demanding from the Cadillac board a new car in compensation for unauthorised use of the name! The real origins of these stories probably lie with the fact that Antoine de la Mothe Cadillac (1658-1730), another ancestor, was an early settler of Detroit in 1701.

Margaret spent long spells back in England, her family supporting her through the separation difficulties. In 1889, she asked brother Robert to meet her immediately in Naples because she had left the husband who 'ill-treated' her, as Arthur Galletti put it years later.[5] In 1891 she was in London living with Jack and Ethel Collier in their Marylebone home near Lords Cricket Ground. The marriage staggered on until 1899 when formal separation was agreed and protracted discussions began over *San Venanzo* ownership. Margaret Galletti spent the rest of her life between the Continent and England before her 1928 death. Arturo, meanwhile, entered the Italian Parliament in 1892 where he remained until 1909, splitting his time between Rome and the Marche. His affairs were highly complicated at his death in 1912 and Arthur, his son, took almost two years leave from India to return to Italy and sort them out.

Arthur Mario Agricola Collier Galletti di Cadilhac, then, was born at his grandfather's Essex country house but grew up in a household where English, Italian, French and German were spoken freely (the last by his Swiss German governess). He learned them all. When his mother moved to Naples because of her marriage problems, Arthur attended a school run by Germans for whose language and culture he developed a lifelong passion. Liberal political outlooks marked both sides of his family,

---

5   Arthur Galletti to Beatrice, 21 January 1963.

the reformist Colliers and the Garibaldian patriotic Gallettis producing a progressive outlook that later marked him as a radical among his ICS colleagues. His parents' unhappy marriage and his resultant cold upbringing created rigid views on love and marriage that would trouble his future wife. From his Collier grandfather Arthur Galletti inherited the conviction of always being right and not easily contradicted, from his Galletti one a love of travel and intrigue. The two extended families helped him access socially well-connected quarters in England and on the continent, but he always preferred the open European outlook to what he considered the Anglo 'closed' one. A Collier Quaker background came out in him as a literal, intellectual, clinical religious belief that later caused severe friction inside his own family.

Galletti's fictionalized memoir, a mixture of fact and fantasy, has his father describing him as "a queer fish" who, from an early age, set his own course and took his own counsel.[6] While quite young he developed a confidence in his own abilities that verged on arrogance. Cool, bright and self-possessed, he was as interested in games as in the academic work at which he excelled. As his daughter Emma later suggested, his apparent superiority complex undoubtedly sprang from his upbringing. With little of a family life during his early years, and seeing volatility rather than stability in relationships, Galletti relied on his own achievements and abilities to succeed. He sought little support or approval from elsewhere, and was not practiced let alone skilled at accommodating others or working collaboratively.

He was 'unusually intelligent', both in his own estimation and that of observers.[7] In Naples he topped his class, even in German against native-speakers. At 12, he determined to get

---

6   India 1878-1922, or, God or Beast? By Elizabeth Smith, Relict of the late John Smith, I.C.S. This is in the Galletti Papers and is subsequently referred to as the Galletti memoir.

7   Galletti to Beatrice, 21 January 1963.

an English education and enter the ICS, but lacked the money to do so because his family was now poor as well as fractured. While his uncle Rob was in Naples helping his mother, Galletti sounded him out on possible scholarships. Monkswell obliged and as soon as Galletti reached England he entered a Welsh Prep School directed by a Collier cousin. He won an £80 scholarship to Cheltenham, a leading public school, where he was further supported by Collier money. He won several Cheltenham prizes, mostly for languages but also in mathematics and classics, and those prized books remained forever on his library shelves, leather bound with Latin inscriptions and bearing the Cheltenham crest.

Passionate about sport, Galletti considered himself more "all rounder" than specialist at games like cricket that he thought required particular hand-eye co-ordination gifts. His favourite sports were rugby where he played as a fullback, rowing (he claimed to have stroked the school boat), hockey, fives and tennis. There were no tennis courts at Cheltenham but there were at his home where he lived (but was "not loved", he wrote later), being a day-boy rather than boarder. His tennis was so good, he claimed, the school would determine its champion and only then call him to play that person. Tennis remained a lifelong passion. So did his taste for the outdoors, such as climbing the Tintern Abbey ruins while on a school day trip, alarming boys and staff alike.

Throughout his life, Galletti considered himself a David against Goliath. His school recollections devote several pages to a 'mill' (fight) provoked with a bigger, stronger, older boy. Galletti challenged him over a slight, the whole school attended, masters watched discreetly from windows, the plucky Galletti won using superior spirit and tactics. That victory won him universal admiration and respect, according to his story. Similarly, Galletti recorded that a school friend later ran into serious problems with the police. Galletti travelled from Oxford to London to help the friend, blind to whatever sins the man had committed. That independent, "defend the underdog" attitude characterised Galletti's life and caused most of his later professional travails. His then mentor/hero was Reverend H.A. James, Cheltenham Headmaster from 1889-1895 (Galletti's period) following a similar post at Rossall and preceding his headship at Rugby from 1896-1909. From 1909 until his 1931 death James was President of St. Johns College, Oxford, and corresponded regularly with Galletti who admired him greatly. Galletti viewed the 'Pot' (James' Cheltenham nickname, he was 'Bodger' at Rugby) as much friend as headmaster because the older man admired the boy's independent, liberal view. James, for example, threatened to close all school sweetshops, but Galletti argued a particular widow would then lose her livelihood. James cancelled the proposal. The headmaster was apparently impressed when Galletti chose the Cheltenham classics rather than modern side because, instead of following a guaranteed route to an officer's commission via Woolwich, he chanced entry to Oxford then the ICS. A. Jame's letter shows that Galletti's mother was pushing her son towards an Italian military career, but the headmaster persuaded her on Oxford.[8]

While much of this early life account is Galletti's retrospective reconstruction, he was strongly independent from an early age. He was intelligent and well read. His father was largely absent from his life, so male mentors came from the Collier side and from figures like James who encouraged individuality and liberalism. That showed out in a story concerning his final school year. Galletti greatly admired Gladstone whom he met with his parents, courtesy of the Collier connection, while the statesman was on an Italian holiday—many years later Galletti recalled the graciousness with which Gladstone gave time to talk with a young boy.[9] In his memoir Galletti writes to the local newspaper just before the 1895 general election, criticising

---

8   H.A. James to Margaret Galletti, 6 December 1894, Galletti Papers.

9   [A. Galletti], Letter to the editor, *Times*, 10 June [1933], Galletti Papers.

a conservative Cheltenham master who attacked the liberal Gladstone. Galletti's comments reputedly attracted wide support for which he was upbraided by James' conservative replacement as Headmaster. There is, however, no evidence of the letter appearing in any local Cheltenham paper.[10] From an early point, then, Galletti considered himself a Liberal, or liberal at least, and he maintained that stance throughout his life.

Interestingly, Galletti's memoir also describes what he considered to be Cheltenham's pronounced homoerotic atmosphere. Renowned younger "conkys" (concubines) were courted regularly by older boys, he argued. While most of this was platonic rather than actively physical, he thought, there was a small group of conspicuous homosexuals. Galletti considered himself the centre of attention for many boys because he was good looking. However, he declared himself oblivious to all blandishments because of his cold, unfeeling attitude towards people. Clearly alive to the nature of his character Galletti repeated that view throughout his life, especially later in relation to his wife.

Galletti went to Trinity College, Oxford, on a £150 annual scholarship ('Pot' James believed it was £80), but tutored other students to earn needed additional funds. His main claim to Oxford fame was in becoming 'Gordouli', the figure who remains the centre of the feud between Trinity and adjoining Balliol College.[11] Traditionally, Balliol students taunt their neighbours by singing over the dividing wall:

> Gordouli
> Face like a ham
> Bobby Johnson says so
> And he ought to know

---

10 The story, however, was forever important to Galletti–Galletti to Clara, 9 February 1902

11 For the Trinity background, see Clare Hopkins, *Trinity: 450 Years of an Oxford College Community* (Oxford, OUP, 2005).

This began in the mid-1890s when Galletti was at Trinity, initiated at a Balliol dinner attended by (later Sir) Robert Johnson of New College who became Deputy Master and controller of the Royal Mint. During dinner some of Johnson's Balliol friends referred to a Trinity man nicknamed 'Gordouli' because of his impossibly 'foreign' name, 'Gourdouli' borrowed from a popular cigarette brand. Bobby Johnson claimed to know the foreigner: "he's the fellow with a face like a ham'. This 'fellow' had Trinity rooms overlooking the Balliol quadrangle so the party raced there, delivered the new song that immediately became the set piece for a created inter-college rivalry. By World War I the ritual was marked by competing songs, shouted obscenities, stone-throwing and prankster raids, invariably fuelled by alcohol.

Gordouli was Arthur Galletti even if he later told his son, Robert, he had no such nickname-Robert took a scholarship to Balliol where he, too, was immediately dubbed Gordouli. Some questioned the connection because Galletti definitely did not have "a face like a ham", being instead a "strikingly handsome young man". Bobby Johnson was not good looking so his companions may have been ridiculing him as much as Gordouli. Galletti's rooms were near the wall, though, and he was a rare 'foreigner' in Trinity.

The latter point is ironic, given Galletti's later career. Under Benjamin Jowett as Master, Balliol admitted many Indians during the later 19th century, several of whom later entered the ICS. In 1931 Balliol hosted Gandhi during his Round Table Conference visit to England, and the College retained a liberal stance. By Galletti's time Trinity, in contrast, was far less progressive than Balliol, resisting India office attempts to enrol greater numbers of Indian students. In fact, Trinity admitted none but white students until 1951 and even produced its own song to counter Balliol's:

Balliol, Balliol
Bring out your black men
Jack Johnson says so
And he ought to know

Jack Johnson, of course, was the controversial early 20th century African-American world heavyweight boxing champion. Underlying the superficial humour of the Trinity-Balliol exchange lay seriously divided attitudes towards race and progress, exacerbated by Trinity's long-term practice of drawing heavily from the public schools and, therefore, the "better classes" socially.

The liberal Galletti was essentially on the wrong side of the wall. That explains his abiding admiration for Balliol and his unbounded glee when his son Robert gained entrance there during the 1920s. Galletti regarded Balliol's academic achievements highly but its liberal stance even more so, while his own College's social narrowness made him an obvious outsider.

According to his memoir, Galletti spent as much Oxford time on sport as on academic work. Significantly, the Galletti of the memoir entered Balliol rather than the Trinity. He claimed to have played rugby, including for the University but there is no record of that, as well as tennis in addition to creating the first bridge four ever to appear in Oxford. Similarly, he suggested the Oxford University Dramatic Society sought him out, attracted by his good looks. He claimed significant friends. Raymond Asquith was the son of Herbert Asquith, the British Prime Minister who was also a Balliol man. Raymond Asquith, a brilliant lawyer, became a Fellow at All Souls before being called to the Bar where, among other cases, he was junior counsel at the sinking of the *Titanic* inquiry. The younger Asquith was mentioned as a certain Liberal MP, but the war intervened and he died on the Somme in 1916. Galletti liked the son, but despised the father's politics much preferring Gladstone's "sincerity".

Galletti wrote that he mixed with (later Sir) John Simon whose reform Commission visited India in the later 1920s, and F.E. Smith later the Earl of Birkenhead who would become Secretary of State for India. Galletti heard both speak in the Oxford Union and liked the former more. Another friend was

E.J. Palmer, a Balliol tutor who joined the church and served as Bishop of Bombay from 1908 until 1929. Galletti claimed that his greatest influence, however, was the historian A.L. Smith who became Master of Balliol from 1916-1924. Smith, he claimed, was fascinated by his outlook, tastes and sharp mind that all stood out among other undergraduates.

The Master of Balliol in Galletti's time was Edward Caird, a philosopher who followed Hegel. Hegel was one of the few things German Galletti disliked and he did so intensely, preferring Kant and Schopenhauer. Galletti had a similarly deep dislike for John Stuart Mill whose works dominated ICS examination papers.

Amidst sport and study he found time for considerable travel in England and on the continent. This came through two avenues. The first was his family connections, because one of the Colliers came to Oxford to be with Galletti instead of going to Cambridge. The second involved the funds he generated as a tutor to the well-off. There was a curious twist here. He claimed this tutoring was organised initially by a Balliol Fellow who lusted after him homosexually but whose overt advances, essayed in Rome on a trip to see the Pope, soon retired into friendship.

Among the travel was a claimed presence in Constantinople while Turks were killing Armenians in the streets. The Galletti of the memoir intervened and almost lost his life. The political Liberal was always in evidence—during a discussion with H.A. James y in the Boer War, the old headmaster hoped the war would end quickly and Kruger be executed. Galletti opined that Kruger might die of natural causes before the war ended, because it was no certain victory for England. Those views soon hurt him when declared publicly.

By now Arthur Galletti had met Clara Salvadori-Paleotti, three years his junior. *In Our Home by the Adriatic*, Margaret Collier describes how early on in her Marche life she surprisingly received "a little note written in English". This led to her friendship with "an Anglo-Italian colony" living a few miles away from *San Venanzo*. That colony became her social lifeline, adding further richness to an already complex family structure. Margaret Collier described this group as the female line of an English family that settled in the area 50 years earlier, the daughters all marrying local men. As usual with the Galletti circle, it was not that simple.

Adlard Welby (1776-1861), a wealthy Lincolnshire landowner, had eight children with his wife but added a further 11 with the family's governess! An English future for the illegitimate children bleak, Welby sold up in Lincolnshire and shifted the new family, including five unmarried girls, first to Ancona then to Porto San Giorgio. The five girls caused a local stir, even if their Protestant faith provided a small marriage bar, overcome easily with a £1,000 dowry each.

In 1837 a French doctor, Pierre Jourdan, was in Ancona at the time of a cholera outbreak. Hearing two English girls were afflicted he rushed to assist. Sadly, Lydia Susan Welby died but sister Joanna survived to marry Jourdan. Their daughter Emma grew up in Paris, but returned to the Marche to marry her cousin Alfredo Salvadori-Paleotti. That couple's daughter, Clara, became the object of Arthur Galletti's affections. There was even more family social interweaving: Arthur Galletti's older sister, Giacinta known as Cynthia, married Clara's cousin Guglielmo 'Willy' Salvadori-Paleotti, a philosophy professor whose Albanian ancestors had reached Italy in the 15th century. Cynthia and Willy moved to Switzerland after he was almost killed by the Fascists in 1924, and their son Max became a leading anti-Fascist and internationally renowned intellectual.

Among Clara's many interesting cousins was Tommaso Salvadori. His mother, another Welby clan sister who married a British diplomat, Tommaso trained as a doctor then joined Garibaldi's Sicilian venture medical staff before unification.

Transferring his interests to zoology, he became a leading international ornithologist and served as Vice-Director in Turin's Natural History museum. He later joined the British Museum's natural history division, reorganizing then publishing their catalogues on parrots and pigeons. An expert on exotic (to European tastes) fauna, his name lives on in the Salvadori Pheasant, a now-rare bird found on the Indonesian island of Sumatra, and in the Salvadori Monitor, an extremely large lizard present in Papua New Guinea.

In Arthur Galletti's memoir he meets his future wife in 1891, which would have been on his way through Porto San Giorgio en route from Naples to Cheltenham when he was 14 and she 11. Later, though, he was encouraged to consider Clara as a wife by her aunt Adele, the mother of Willy Salvadori and his sister's later mother-in-law. Galletti described Clara in his memoir as a girl who loved music, religion and him equally! He added, perhaps more with hindsight than contemporary evidence, she was "self-willed and would not yield up her individuality". In the early 1880s some Collier family members visited the Salvadori clan of which Clara was part and described them as 'wild beasts'—their hair was all over the place but they spoke English very well if with funny accents. Early Clara pictures show great beauty, and the wild hair.

Having set himself for the ICS, Galletti had to undergo the ordeal of the open examination. Hilton Brown, a Galletti ICS contemporary, described it later in one of his novels:

> A solid month of answering the hardest questions skilled torturers can devise with the knowledge that a single inadequate answer may ruin your chances for life.[12]

This occurred in Burlington House along Piccadilly and Galletti duly presented himself there, most successfully as it turned out, gaining one of the highest aggregate marks in the

---

12   Hilton Brown, *Dismiss!* (London, Methuen, 1923), p. 17.

history of the examination. That immediately made him one of the best and brightest and he might have nominated himself for any of the leading Indian provinces. He, however, chose Madras and for a young man in his position, with a glittering career ahead, that was unusual to the point of unique.

By 1900 when Arthur Galletti entered the ICS, it was *the* sought after English civil services branch attracting the best and brightest candidates.[13] As Great Britain reorganized its Indian administration following the 1857 uprising shock, the ICS provided "The Steel Frame" for Britain's subcontinental presence and remained so until independence in 1947. During the later 19th century ICS entry became strictly competitive through public examination. Older hands thought that made successful entrants too "bookish", but most observers considered the new system superior to the earlier one that trained men at Haileybury College, their entry won through social connection rather than ability. The new approach emphasised intellectual achievement, so successful entrants often had more trouble passing equestrian tests than language ones.[14]

British India was at its apogee around the turn of the 20th century. There was little if any thought about substantial political power transferring to the Indian people. The Indian National Congress was founded in 1885 by well-educated if politically moderate Indians who, mostly, sought a share in running their own country rather than complete political independence. British

---

13 The epilogue, "De-romanticizing the Indian Civil Service" in Bradford Spangenberg, *British bureaucracy in India: status, policy and the I.C.S., in the late 19th century* (Delhi, Manohar-South Asia Books, 1976) is a corrective to the normal view of the ICS as the civil service destination of the period, but is not entirely convincing.

14 Gilmour David, *The ruling caste: Imperial lives in the Victorian Raj* (New York, Farrer Strauss Giroux, 2005) provides an excellent overview of the ICS and its evolution until the turn of the 20th century. An earlier account is the equally excellent Philip Woodruff [Mason], *The men who ruled India: Vol. II the guardians* (London, Cape, 1971 edn).

administrators expected India to remain *ad infinitum* the Jewel in the Crown of Empire, and that was demonstrated symbolically in the great Durbars of 1905 and 1911 even if the seeds of change were already sown. In London, the India Office commanded by the Secretary of State was the only civil service department devoted to the affairs of one imperial member, demonstrating the subcontinent's importance to Great Britain. For senior officers in that department and their emissaries to India as Viceroys or Governors, India's future was firmly established as a paternalistically run offshoot of Great Britain. They assumed India needed Great Britain, because Indians were incapable of running the country. India must be 'improved', and improvement had a long way to run before any possible transfer of power might be contemplated. Those already in or entering the Steel Frame along with Galletti held that view strongly and almost universally.

These bright young men espoused the ideals of Empire and service while displaying a strong commitment to India, its people and its progress. For some that involved intellectual discovery about their new country. Alan Butterworth, for example, became a leading authority on the Madras Presidency's ancient stone and metal inscriptions. Others became experts in language, history and culture, like H.H. Dodwell who later set up the Madras archive office. He took leave at the height of the early 1920s Non Co-Operation movement to study British Library and India Office records systems, and later wrote for the massive Cambridge history of India series. J.C. Molony and Hilton Brown became writers in and of Madras, including its history. Some maintained intellectual interests outside India. A.Y.G. Campbell, a Galletti *bete noir*, became Chief Secretary and was a published mathematician as well as, with his brother, writer about Irish folk tunes.

Collectively, the ICS was conservative, mirroring generally its members' origins and backgrounds, even if individually those members remained strong-minded producing rivalries, differences, arguments, envy and even hatred. As Woodruff and

Gilmour point out, there were spectacular political exceptions to the conservative rule, like Allan Octavian Hume who left the later 19th century ICS to help shape the Indian National Congress. The Eric Blair better known as George Orwell story also demonstrates the point. By the 1920s another former ICS officer in Burma, Bernard Houghton, was writing so radically the special branch in Delhi opened a file on him.[15] While few went that far, ICS men held quite different views about how best to steer Indian progress. Clive Dewey demonstrates how F.L. Brayne, an Evangelical, thought Indians needed saving from themselves while Sir Malcolm Darling, a humanist, regarded Indians as so imaginative and innovative that they possessed more answers than did their rulers.[16] Galletti was entering a service where divergent social and political views existed, but where debate occurred within a highly bureaucratic framework and an over-riding set of political assumptions.

Madras was always 'different' within administrative and ICS circles across British India. Philip Woodruff noted wryly:

> To the last, the Government of Madras preserved a separatism of their own and were inclined to regard the Government of India as a rather vulgar late-18th century innovation.[17]

Bradford Spangenberg spotted "the quintessential example of administrative reform sabotaged by inter-governmental conflict" in Madras' late-19th century refusal to reorganize its districts in line with all-India changes.[18] Madras developments and ideas were frequently ignored inside India and at 'Home' where it was automatically assumed the South would oppose

---

15 See Bernard Houghton, *Bureaucratic government: a study in Indian polity* (Madras, Natesan, 1921).

16 *Clive Dewey, Anglo-Indian attitudes: the mind of the Indian civil service* (London, Hambledon, 1993).

17 Woodruff, p.116.

18 Bradford Spangenberg, pp. 96-99. Symbolically, 'Madras' does not even appear in his Index.

change.[19] Its pedantic, pedestrian reputation preceded it and the Presidency was the least popular choice among those joining the ICS. W.O. Horne, Chief Secretary early in Galletti's time, was allocated to Madras in 1882 because he was the second lowest candidate in the entire examination ranking list—he had no choice in the posting, the lowly ranked invariably landed in Madras.[20] J.C. Molony, who joined in 1900 with Galletti, recalled his relatives were so concerned by his Madras appointment they urged him to request a transfer. Had he done so, he thought, Government "would probably have put him in the Tower".[21]

It was harder and took longer to get promotion in Madras where districts were far bigger than elsewhere, the result of the 1870s reform failure. A Madras District Collector had the same or greater responsibility than a man controlling several divisions in a province like Bengal. Vizagapatam district in the Presidency's north, for example, occupied 17,000 square miles and contained over three million people, all controlled by one Collector and his staff. The Madras Presidency Collector, uniquely in British India, reported directly to the Government of Madras and not to an intermediary officer.[22] The benefit was that the officer had direct access to government thereby, theoretically, streamlining decision-making. The disadvantage was that Collectors often considered themselves more important than they really were, provoking argument with Secretariat superiors who were dismissed too easily as 'desk-wallahs'.

---

19 See, for example, the paucity of references to Madras in L.S.S. O'Malley, *The Indian civil service, 1601-1930* (London, Murray, 1931 and London, Cass, 1965).

20 W.O. Horne, *Life and sport in the old I.C.S.* (London, Blackwood, 1928), p.8.

21 "Civilian"[J.C. Molony], *The civilian's South India: some places and People in Madras* (London, Lane Bodley, 1921–Delhi, Asian Educational 2004 edn), p. 14.

22 Sir Edward Blunt, *The I.C.S.—the Indian Civil Service* (London, Faber, 1937) gives an excellent outline of the machinery of British Indian administration, and shows how Madras was 'different' in many aspects of that administration.

Other Indian jurisdictions considered Madras methods and procedures slow, cumbersome, even reactionary. Administrators elsewhere in India harboured suspicions that Madras lacked urgency, a consequence of being untouched by 1857 events. That attitude, developed first in Calcutta then New Delhi as the successive centres of British Indian power, meant far fewer Madras men gained entry to all-India governmental levels than did those from Punjab, United Provinces, Bengal or Bombay. As Horne put it, "for an ambitious man, it was hopeless" being in Madras. Madras was dubbed the 'benighted Province', signifying its low status as a career destination and, later, as an obstacle to political and constitutional change.

Galletti, though, chose Madras deliberately, precisely because of the responsibilities given a Collector there. Even before he joined the service he was set on Madras where he thought he stood greater chance of being the benevolent leader of a big district and a big population, effectively in isolation from central control. He would lead his people to progress, improve their services and life opportunities and, over a long period, help them prepare to run their own affairs. Even at this point, then, he demonstrated a capacity for individualism rather than collective action, and a concern for the welfare of 'his people' that was essentially paternalistic.

On his first journey towards the "benighted" Presidency where he would become that "big" leader, Arthur Galletti stopped in Italy and travelled by train from Rome to Gubbio in Umbria on a personal mission. Alfredo Salvadori, Clara's father, had purchased a small *castello* and its lands a few miles outside the beautiful medieval town and shifted his family there in the late 1890s. The *Casacce* was and remains a stunning property, the house standing atop a hill surrounded by larger hills and fertile valleys, and looking away towards Gubbio. This was Galletti's first visit to what would later become his home when Clara inherited the *Casacce*.

He was despondent before this mission, though. Clara's mother, Contessa Salvadori, was distinctly cool towards his pursuit of her daughter, and her written response to his request for permission to attend was 'not reassuring', as he wrote. Clara herself needed considerable persuading. However, Galletti replied, he would pursue his quest for Clara as a "wife whom you respect for herself and whom others respect you for winning".[23] When he left to continue towards India he was far more cheerful because, somehow, he won agreement to the engagement from Clara and her parents. It would be a long and troublesome one.

Galletti sailed from Rome and reached Bombay on 7 December 1900. His 'difference' emerged quickly. In the first of his letters to Clara, whom he did not see again for six years, he reported that almost every passenger was 'very cross' at returning to India and they were all 'full of prejudice' snobs.[24] An archdeacon's wife was especially full of herself, he reported, openly declaring disdain for Italians. Galletti chided her. She suggested he learn how to deal properly with senior officials' wives because they, not their husbands, determined promotions. At Suez, Swami Vivekananda joined the ship and also Galletti's religious discussion with the archdeacon and a Central Provinces ICS man. Swami Vivekananda was the first Hindu sage to mesmerise the West by introducing Vedanta philosophy and yoga, and founded the Ramakrishna Mission in Calcutta. Galletti thought him "exceedingly well read" but an 'awful humbug'.

Galletti gladly left the ship at Bombay on the morning of 7 December 1900. Later that day he left by train (very comfortable, he thought) for Madras which he reached on 9 December, and reported for service on the morning of Monday 10 December. His great Indian adventure had begun.

---

23   Galletti to Contessa Salvadori, 7 November, 1900.

24   Galletti to Clara, 11 December, 1900.

Galletti reached a Madras that, according to one local guidebook, was "a large straggling congeries of suburbs and villages".[25] Another contemporary account suggested the city "presents a disappointing appearance and possesses not a single handsome street".[26] As J.C. Molony put it, "It is a vexed and open question whether Madras is the most charming place in the world or the most utterly wearisome".[27] Horne found the town 'rather withered' when he arrived there in 1882. Even the big firms occupied tumbledown buildings while Mount Road, the main thoroughfare, displayed a mixture of thatched bazaar and shabby stucco bungalows. The hotels were 'simply unspeakable'.[28] Alan Butterworth thought Madras more 'country' town than city in the mid-1890s just prior to Galletti's arrival.[29] Hilton Brown has one character recall a first sight of Madras:

> A place of interminable and spacious vistas of open land, threaded here and there by lost and wandering roads to which fragmentary buildings clung desperately, holding out a promise—that was never fulfilled—of some sort of a cohesive town to come.[30]

Galletti observed the city's European quarter had no streets, just 'country roads'. Then among the largest of Asian cities with almost half a million people in 1900, Madras retained a country town feel because, away from crowded central areas, suburbs were open with large grounds for large houses. An unplanned city its roads, streets and laneways meandered across almost 30 square miles, most road surfaces unsealed. Footpaths

---

25 *Higginbotham's guide to Madras* (Madras, Higginbotham, 1903), p1.

26 *The asylum almanack for Madras and Southern India,* 1900 Madras, Asylum Press, 1900), p. 572.

27 Molony, p.44.

28 W.O. Horne, pp. 9-10.

29 A. Butterworth, *The Southlands of Siva* (London, Lane Bodely, 1923), p. 44.

30 Hilton Brown, *Dictators limited: a novel without Incident* (London, Allen & Unwin, 1923), p. 123.

were rare outside main streets like Mount Road. Mount Road appeared first in 1795, and from the 1860s featured the newer Indo-Saracenic-Arabic architectural style enabled by a previously unknown stone quarried in Cuddapah district. That innovation influenced newer public buildings to be built during the later 19th century, giving Madras a more distinctive presence.

Other than on Mount Road most people walked along the middle of unmade streets competing with donkey and bullock carts, rickshaws, bicycles whose numbers exploded during the 1890s, and the slowly increasing numbers of cars and trucks. An electric tramway appeared during the 1890s, while the railway system connecting Madras to the rest of the Presidency and India was also relatively new.

Madras originated as a port city, even if the state of the port symbolised the Presidency's slow growth. The Madras coastline was open to the Indian Ocean so there was no 'natural' port, just a site at a river mouth open directly to the sea. Traditionally, ships 'stood off' and unloaded into lighters, often with great difficulty.[31] Crew on ships carrying horses from Australia during the late 19th century, for example, simply dumped the animals overboard and encouraged them to swim towards shore. From the later 19th century onwards government spent money and time creating an enclosed port not fully completed until the 1920s. That meant Madras trade and commerce often suffered because major companies favoured more efficient sea transport centres, with even major city firms finding it more convenient to have goods shipped to Colombo in Ceylon for onward transport to Madras by train.

Behind this 1900 port-in-progress stood Blacktown, a crowded commercial centre whose innumerable small business traders dealt in all possible commodities from their one-storied buildings with cattle wandering through them.

---

31 Allister Macmillan, *Seaports of India and Ceylon* (London, Collingridge, 1928) contains an excellent and detailed description of Madras. Ken McPherson added greatly to my understanding of Madras as an Indian ocean port city.

Galletti spent hours exploring Blacktown's narrow, crowded streets that spilled into similarly crowded neighbouring quarters. In the middle of Blacktown stood the packed and deafening main fruit and vegetable market spreading over several acres. Chetti traders dominated most of southern Mint Street, a main thoroughfare. They yielded to Gujarati and Marwari traders in the street's central sections. Govinder Naicker Street contained mainly commercial premises, Godown and Bunder Streets hosted Muslim merchants trading piecegoods and cloth, while in Broadway the new electric trams added to traffic congestion, noise and confusion. First and Second Line Beach streets hosted the leading shipping and commercial companies. From 1906 Blacktown, so named originally because it was the "native" quarter, became Georgetown named after Prince George who visited Madras that year before becoming Prince of Wales soon after then King George V in 1911.

J.C. Molony highlighted the rich contrasts seen in Madras: "here they chaffer for *ghi* and *dhal*, haggle over the rice and chillies and cardamons and gingelly and turmeric."[32] While playing tennis the ICS man could hear "the maddening Indian music of pipe and horn and tom-tom". The people were fascinating, he thought, describing the young clerks and students now seen along the Marina:

> Attired in what is apparently going to be his modern dress—a *dhoti*, that is to say a cloth, a tweed jacket of sporting cut, with buttons on the pockets and a distinct 'yoke' at the back–the sort of thing no one but a professional golfer would venture at home–long wispy black hair, and top of all a most distressing little round pork-pie hat.[33]

Molony however, thought Europeans more misplaced in Madras than these *modern* dressers.

---

32 Molony, p.53.
33 *Ibid.,* p. 48.

From Georgetown the suburbs spread a little way north but mainly south and west. Predictably, the suburbs developed special characteristics, dominated by particular social groups. Vepery, in the north, was largely Eurasian, abutted by Purusawalkam described as 'squalid'. Nearby lay Kilpauk, a predominantly European suburb with park-like properties containing huge houses reflecting the elite, wealthy end of Madras society. Egmore was similar but not as exclusive with some of its quarters still crowded areas of 'native' housing, as local parlance had it. Stretching towards the south lay Nungambakkam, Teynampet and Adyar, all exclusive European suburbs sacrificing proximity to worksites closer in for comfort, space and separation.

Madras ICS officers had two main worksites. The Secretariat in Fort St George stood on an 'island' between two river outlets immediately south of the port. Entered via a narrow drawbridge guarded by English soldiers, the Secretariat was "the outward and visible sign of the inward and spiritual Government."[34] Molony depicted the love/hate relationship many officers had with the Secretariat: "All Civilians despise the Secretariat and would not accept employment in it for anything; and many are called but few refuse." The second site was the old palace of the Princes of Arcot further south in Chepauk that now housed the Board of Revenue. The Board, forever the focus of Galletti's reforming zeal, directed the collection of Presidency taxes and was headed by the four, later three Members in charge of specific areas. Becoming a Member was a career aspiration for most ICS officers because salaries were significant, the prestige and influence more so.

Stretching along the water from Chepauk lay a string of suburbs occupied by specific local social groups. Muslims lived mainly in Triplicane. A little further south lay Mylapore, dominated by successful Brahmins who were mostly lawyers. The suburb was home to south Indian art and culture, especially

---

34 Molony, p.45.

Carnatic music. Mylapore was also the centre of considerable local political activity with several inhabitants among the local Indian National Congress leadership.

British social life revolved around two institutions. The Madras Club in the centre of town dated from 1832 since when it was the preserve of the senior civil services, especially the ICS, and the military. In the late 19th century its membership expanded to include acceptable European members of "civil" society, particularly the city's commercial and professional elite. No women were admitted, strict behavioural codes prevailed, seniority was prized and respected, but the odd eccentric could be found. The aspirational model was that of the leading London clubs, so the Club was proud its kitchens were organized on English rather than Indian lines. The food was good, alcohol plentiful and J.C. Molony thought the atmosphere "St Jamesian".[35]

The sprawling and spacious Adyar Club, several miles south and located on the banks of a river offered a golf links, a riding track and provided rowing as well as tennis and racquets, along with bridge and billiards indoors. Molony liked Adyar because of its spectacular sunsets and its resident kingfishers patrolling the river.[36] Importantly, it was open to women so most European families moved between it and the Madras Club. Adyar was odd, though, because the suburb also hosted the world famous Theosophy centre run by Mrs Annie Besant who was still in residence and would be until the 1920s. The Theosophists had an uneasy relationship with the more straight-laced Madras and Adyar Club denizens. That sprang mainly from the Theosophists' unconventional beliefs, but also because they included and mixed freely with Indians, many of whom were professionally

---

35 *Ibid.*, p.52.

36 *Ibid.*, pp. 50-1.

and commercially prominent. Otherwise, prominent Indians joined the Cosmopolitan Club, established to facilitate controlled social mixing between Europeans and leading Indians.

Eurasians or Anglo-Indians were socially isolated. As late as 1921, when the Madras Cricket Club played an Anglo-Indian XI the latter players were simply allocated a few chairs at one end of the hosts' clubhouse, nary an MCC member approaching a guest.[37] Alan Westlake, a prominent Madras ICS man, was told by an early 20th century north India club colleague that while his future Anglo-Indian father-in-law was certainly a fine chap, being 'just 12 annas in the rupee' made him unwelcome.[38]

By 1900 Madras had several banks, insurance companies, trading houses, professional offices and specialist retail shops for those who lived and worked there in the services and allied industries. There were over 200 telephone subscribers with all clubs and most senior trading houses connected. There were many churches, reflecting the Indian interests of European, American and British missionary societies, all headquartering their Presidency activities in Madras though most evangelical work occurred in district locations like Coonoor. The Madras weather theoretically ranged between 70-90 degrees Fahrenheit, but at times humidity was extremely high and in summer months the heat was intense, provoking government's annual relocation to Ootacamund and the hills. Cholera and smallpox were prevalent, and not long before Galletti's arrival fever and influenza killed a greater number of people than normal. Two years later Murray Hammick, a high ranking Galletti contact, lost his 10 month old son to fever.

Madras, then, was a 'senior', long-standing British Indian province but considered 'benighted' by potential recruits and officials elsewhere in India. It was conservative, even by

---

37   *Madras mail,* 16 December 1921.
38   Alan Westlake Papers, CSAA.

British India standards, had different ways of doing things, was administratively hidebound, had very large districts over which a Collector must rule, and was generally more 'difficult' than other jurisdictions. Critics of Madras frequently had their views confirmed by developments such as a solemn Government Order issued in 1909. When deciding whether officers were entitled to a *punkah-wallah* at government expense, superior officers should consider the applicant's status, nationality, habits and constitution, and whether or not they were accustomed to having a *punkah-wallah*![39] A few years later, Richard Tottenham recalled the stir created by a 'cad' who turned up for an evening walk along the marina beachfront dressed in shorts and a shirt instead of the obligatory full dress![40] While there was substance to this negative view of Madras, by 1900 it was weakening but most recruits still avoided the Presidency and went there reluctantly when assigned. It was rare for highly ranked candidates to go there, so Galletti's request for appointment was unusual.

For any ICS newcomer like Galletti the first and worst ordeal was 'calling'. The Chief Secretary supplied the recruit with an enormous list of names and addresses of wives to be 'called upon' so that the 'griffins', as they were known, could be admitted to 'society'. Given Madras geography, this took days and considerable travel, mainly by expensive horse and buggy. Calling hours were between 12 and 2, then 4 and 6 adding to the logistic nightmare, especially in warm weather. If a woman was 'not at home' the newcomer placed his card in a box left on the front verandah then scurried off to the next address. However, if the woman was at home a servant would accept the card on a tray, carry it in, the lady would admit the caller then conduct

---

39 GO 221 Financial (Press NP), 5 June 1909, P 8253, IOR–a *punkah-wallah* was an Indian servant employed to sit outside an office, pulling the end of a string attached to a fan above the head of the European officer inside in order to make it work.

40 G.R.F Tottenham Papers, CSAA; see also Sir Sidney Wadsworth Papers, CSAA.

20 minutes of desultory discussion. "Calling" required full dress in 1900, even heavy 'London' suits in a completely unsuitable climate, although the rules had been relaxed recently so that top hats were not obligatory. Galletti closed one letter to Clara saying he was dressed in full frockcoat and tall hat, heading into the hot sun to renew his calling duties.

Leading wives redrafted the Madras 'calling' rules in 1893. British society in Madras was close and even closed, so newcomers had to be incorporated formally and fully if they were to be included in its affairs. It was an initiation ceremony, really, one hated by most newcomers. Sir Richard Tottenham considered it 'barbaric'.[41] Arriving a few years after Galletti and just before World War I Sidney Wadsworth recalled a hot, sticky, oppressive and rigid society. Social demarcation lines were observed fanatically, 'old' merchants and senior ICS men ruled the roost. Social occasions were taken very seriously, 'dressing for dinner' required men to wear a swallowtail coat, wing collar and white tie. Senior men arrived at the Secretariat even then in a carriage and pair, lesser men travelling by buggy or bicycle. Wadsworth risked his reputation by travelling on the electric tram because he could afford neither buggy nor bicycle.[42] As late as 1919 Lady Willingdon, wife of the new Governor, thought Madras 'society...past belief'.[43]

At the turn of the 20th century official Madras was rigid, layered, and textured.[44] From the late 19th century until World War I, cold season entertainment was lavish and no young man could afford socially to decline the many invitations to dinners, balls, plays, recitals and outings. That increased the newcomer's living costs substantially, adding more anxiety in the strange new environment. Social division was sharp. Old hands 'watched'

---

41 G.R.F. Tottenham Papers, CSAA.

42 Sir Sidney Wadsworth Papers, CSAA.

43 Lord Willingdon to Sir Edwin Montagu, 15 April 1919, Eur D 523/19, IOR.

44 W.O. Horne, pp. 18-23 is good on all this.

newcomers closely, placing them in an impossible position. New ICS men were generally thought to have opinions and self regard well beyond any achievement, so were criticised for putting on 'side'. If the newcomers did not assert themselves, however, locals thought they lacked the 'character' necessary for promotion. The ICS and merchant communities regarded each other suspiciously, the commercial group itself riven by ranking–merchant house men looked down upon retailers, the latter not admitted as Club members until shortly before the war.

This was the Madras ICS realm and milieu into which Arthur Galletti pitched. By his own contemporary admission he was intolerant with those who could not follow reason, he himself open to persuasion based on logic and reason.[45] This Anglo-Italian liberal, intellectually minded, opinionated, outspoken and emotionally detached 23 year old was about to encounter the conservative, formal, bureaucratic and inward-looking world of civilian south India.

---

45   Galletti to Clara, 27 December 1900.

3

Rising Star, 1900-1906

From Madras railway station Arthur Galletti swept off in a carriage belonging to Sir Murray Hammick, seventh son of the second Baronet and a Jack Collier acquaintance, to the Branch Elphinstone Hotel on Mount Road, more large country house than hotel where guests' personal servants outnumbered house staff. A.R. Knapp, Secretary to the Board of Revenue, provided the addresses at which the newcomer should leave his 'card', and Galletti bought tents and two Australian horses for Rs.1,000 in anticipation of going to the *mofussil* (up country). He was immediately alarmed by the escalating set-up costs.

Uncle Jack Collier knew another useful senior ranking ICS officer, H.V. Cobb. A rare exception to the Madras Rule, he shifted successfully to the All-India Political (Foreign) Department handling relations with the princely states. Having just become British Resident at Jaipur in Rajasthan, Cobb. was well-placed and influential. He recommended Galletti to the Madras Governor's Private Secretary, two Board of Revenue Members and two senior Collectors. They all stood ready to help, an unusually senior welcome for a griffin.

Those connections worked immediately. Knapp (whom Galletti nicknamed 'Nap') proposed posting Galletti to Chingleput district adjoining Madras. Even then, it was more Madras suburb than district. Coveting the prestigious South Arcot district, though, Galletti begged a posting there from the Chief Secretary, Sir Gabriel Stokes. The Private Secretary to the Governor, a Cheltenham man like Galletti, and Lionel Bradley, a Collier Board of Revenue contact, told Galletti the highly regarded South Arcot Collector was appointed the next Private Secretary to the Governor and the quality of his successor not guaranteed. Wanting to serve an influential Collector, Galletti asked for Godavari in the Telugu-speaking country where J.J. Stuart was prominently in charge. That request was approved directly by the Governor, Lord Ampthill.

All ICS newcomers met senior people upon arrival—joining numbers were small, after all, only eight besides Galletti in 1900—but Galletti gained unusually good access. He was already 'known' to influential and soon-to-be influential Madras ICS men. Stokes, Knapp, Bradley, Wynch and his first Collector, J.J. Stuart all attained very senior appointments, and all figured prominently in Galletti's professional life. In a close, even closed atmosphere Galletti had a sensationally good career platform, courtesy of his family connections.

For all those senior men and other ICS members, however, Galletti was immediately 'different'. For a start, he brought his sister Cynthia to Madras and she stayed for several months. That was why they first chose Chingleput for him assuming, wrongly, Cynthia's presence meant Galletti had substantial private means to fund a lively social life uninterrupted by work. On the contrary, Cynthia accompanied Galletti because their mother's marriage problems meant money was short. The family thought it cheaper to keep Cynthia in India, funded from Arthur's service pay. Cynthia considered it a test case for Clara's benefit: could two people live on an ICS salary?

The situation was simple. Galletti had to repay his uncles for financing his education, assist his mother financially and support his father. Dispatching Cynthia to India allowed the family time to build her dowry while settling matters financially. There was talk but no certainty yet of Cynthia marrying Willy Salvadori, Clara's cousin, so India might yield other marriage opportunities—she was virtually a member of the 'fishing fleet' of women come to India in search of husbands, and was regarded so by Madras society. That, too, made Galletti 'different'. He was building a reputation for the unusual, and that stood out in a rigidly ordered society.

Madras lifestyles disappointed Galletti deeply. He thought the city expensive, stylised and silly. He disliked most Madras wives and believed they misunderstood India and Indians, imagining they were still in England, revering gossip, and running their husbands' business affairs.[1] Galletti described a garden party hosted by Lord Ampthill where guests bowed reverentially to the great man who reciprocated. While Galletti respected Ampthill, a very tall man who rowed for Oxford, he considered him unauthoritative and unworthy of the deference, even the post. Another garden party honoured the touring Viceroy, Lord Curzon, whom Galletti encountered later in Simla. Curzon was only in his early 40s but already a great traveller and former Foreign Secretary. Galletti considered him a fine speaker and impressive person.

Sir James Thomson, a bluff and direct senior Madras ICS man appreciated Galletti speaking his mind where many others did not—"what I think is not always what they want me to think," Galletti wrote. Ampthill asked Cynthia if 'Italians' always immediately declared whatever was going through their minds. Galletti took the comment and the label as a personal warning against being too outspoken and too noticeable.[2] Sir Murray Hammick, his mentor, flinched at Galletti's constant pronouncements on politics, India, religion and everything else. Hammick, an old Balliol rower and son of an ordained priest-baronet, was a staunch churchman and conservative thinker. Galletti claimed to shock Madras European society by walking rather than riding everywhere. He met 'real' people that way, he said, and began understanding their 'mind'. In the Connemara Hotel he met a retired army captain whose 'Chi-Chi'

1   Galletti to Clara, 20 December 1900.
2   Galletti to Clara, 20 December 1900.

(Anglo-Indian) wife was despised by mainstream European society. Galletti befriended them and challenged local sentiment, convinced his liberal views were right.

Before leaving for Godavari Galletti observed a social characteristic he ignored, to his cost, throughout his career. He joined the ICS Christmas dinner at the Madras Club. The 'Club', home to the city's administrative and commercial elite, was arguably the best in India and one of the largest in the world where members gathered daily to gossip about city, Presidency and Indian affairs. Galletti marvelled how quickly knowledge of all kinds travelled through the Club and out into 'society'. He reckoned his own 'eccentricities' quickly became general knowledge. Had he remembered that, later experiences might have been less painful.

His first posting, Godavari was physically larger than Wales and one of the Presidency's premier districts. A huge mid-19th century Krishna-Godavari river delta irrigation scheme improved agricultural production markedly, creating a canal system that connected the region directly with Madras markets. The new commercial opportunities increased landholder prosperity substantially.[3] There were silk and cotton weavers, sugar and tobacco producers along with several rice and oil mills. The population, it was said, were highly superstitious and heavy smokers. They also took in large amounts of opium to ward off fevers caused by high temperatures and humidity—Godavari *averaged* F82 degrees. All but the Brahmins who dominated local life were fanatical about cockfighting while women played board games and boys flew kites. Puppet shows were a main source of entertainment.[4]

---

3   *Land, Water, Language and Politics: the Evolution of Andhra as an Indian Region From 1850.*

4   There are good descriptions of Cocanada and Godavari in 1901 in F.R. Hemingway, *Madras District Gazetteers: Nellore* (Madras, Government of Madras, 1907); *Madras asylum press guide and almanack* (Madras, Asylum Press, 1901), and the entry on Godavari [written by Galletti] in *Imperial gazetteer of India: Madras vol.1* (Calcutta, Government of India, 1908), pp. 268-298.

Cocanada, the main town, had over 50,000 citizens including European merchants clustered on the flat sandy plains barely above sea level. Once an important port, silting made it now less so with ships standing off 4 miles and discharging cargo into lighters. The town was the district headquarters, connected by two canals to the massive waterways threading throughout the district. There was little real industry apart from a light steel works, three rice mills and five printeries. There were several mercantile groups of varying sizes, and enterprises like J. La Rive and Co. whose principal combined ships chandlery with auctioneering and service as the local French consul. One prominent local trader, J. Innes, had as his partner a local man, Komireddy Suryanarayanamurthy, showing at least some interaction between Europeans and Indians.

Having chosen the district because of the Collector, Galletti soon observed that Stuart thought highly of himself and little of others. That was wonderfully ironic coming from Galletti, given his newly minted Madras reputation for being opinionated.

Once in Cocanada Galletti received from the principal clerk a list of tasks ordered by Stuart. Galletti would learn Telugu three hours a day, hear at least three court cases a week, read and understand all standing orders by which government worked, hear petitions from the aggrieved and write draft rulings on those petitions. Stuart was mostly absent, conscientiously touring his large district to meet its 2.2 million inhabitants.

Galletti lived in a large tent for several weeks, then moved into a small bungalow in the Collector's compound. Finally, he moved into a large 'European' house. His landlord owned at least 100 houses in Cocanada, indicating how some local Indians flourished under British rule. By early April it was 95F in the shade, but Galletti reported himself unbothered by the weather because it was just like Italy (given the humidity difference, a challengeable claim). His 'European' house was comfortable and well suited to conditions. The wide verandahs and spacious rooms in the house lowered the heat. Of the six large rooms, four had attached bathrooms. There were separate living quarters for servants, stables and storage areas, and a coach house. Galletti employed the *punkah wallah* (fan puller) supplied to him at government cost. ICS officers lived well in district India, even though Galletti complained constantly about costs.

He quickly promoted his social reformer credentials shocking local sentiment, he said, by sacking one servant and making another carry a heavier workload. Similarly, his regular servants transported furniture he bought at a sale—they would normally hire additional labourers. Galletti proudly upset local views, ideas and practices: "the path of the reformer is always a stony one," he wrote. Nonetheless, he loved the country and its people and enjoyed district life.

Despite his reformist zeal he had a large staff as did all *mofussil* ICS and non-official leaders. Within weeks Galletti had a butler, a butler's understudy (the *chokra*), a cook, the cook's assistant, two horse attendants (the *syce*), two grass cutters, a waterman and a sweeper girl. The wives of the cook and butler, too, went on the payroll and, as a result, Galletti constantly worried about his finances. He bought his horses and tents under a Government of Madras loan, and after repayment deductions from his salary he had Rs. 246 per month on which to live. Consequently, he travelled by road rather than train whenever possible—if he travelled more than 20 miles by road in a day he received an additional allowance. On one trip he earned Rs. 7 profit and considered it a significant sum, even though he had to ride his bike and Cynthia his horse for the 20 miles.[5]

Much of Galletti's district life involved being on camp which he enjoyed immensely throughout his career, considering it the main chance to meet 'real' people, hear their aspirations and serve their needs. His earliest letters described the revenue

---

5   Galletti to Clara, 14 April 1901.

assessment work undertaken while on tour. Where government had direct control over the land, peasants paid both land and water tax. In areas where *zamindars* (or landlords) controlled the land peasants paid land tax to them, and tax to the government for irrigation water. Crops were taxed by type according to their commercial value.

During the early 19th century, the British conducted a massive survey of land and people to determine what tax rates should be imposed. The original surveys, completed in Madras by 1896, defined who owned what land, whether that land was wet (irrigated) or dry (subject to natural rainfall), what soils were involved, the quality and type of crops grown, the production costs averaged over 20 non-famine years, cartage and merchant fees and other variables. The tax level was then set at up to 50 per cent of the net profit. Some resettlement (or resurvey) occurred, notably in the Krishna-Godavari region to account for post-irrigation conditions, but camp work now mainly involved annual *jamabandi* checks into the accuracy of the records on which taxes were levied. The *karnams*, or local village accountants, were the main sources of information but government, a long time earlier, established a system to verify the *karnam* records.[6]

On one of his first camps Galletti discovered a *karnam* had listed one crop as rice when it was really saffron, saffron taxed at Rs. 10 per acre and rice Rs. five The ploy was obvious– the *karnam* assessed the peasant at Rs. 5 per acre instead of Rs. 10, the peasant then paid a share of the windfall as commission to the *karnam*. Similarly, crop sizes were underestimated frequently, the peasant again paying a lower tax in return for a commission. That was why fields were re-measured frequently, touring officers supervising the slow and tedious work—Galletti calculated it took surveyors four hours to measure 25 acres. This

6   The full, massive detail of this is explained in *Manual of standing information for the Madras Presidency, 1893* (Madras, Government Press, 1893), Chapter 4.

work occurred all over India, providing British revenue through land, water and crop tax. Understandably, resurveying and reassessment became major political issues between government and landholders, major weapons for the Indian National Congress when raising constitutional reform campaigns.

In Madras, rules and regulations accumulated in the Board of Revenue's Standing Orders dictated revenue work. Those orders, developed over a century or more, were controlled by Members of the Board of Revenue. Galletti claimed to have begun a campaign to abolish the Board in 1902. While the Board was needed a century earlier, he argued, the District Collector could now deal directly with peasants and collect their taxes. The Board was costly and unnecessary. Its Members, he claimed, were highly paid but unproductive, filling time by altering orders unnecessarily and complicating work for field officers like him.

He ran this campaign against his own interests, he said, because in due course he would be promoted to the Board. When that time came, if the Board still existed he would refuse to join. The Government of India should abolish it and save Government of Madras funds. To nudge the Government of India towards that decision he initiated the 'Board Must Go' (BMG) theme he maintained throughout his career. Even newly arrived in Madras he claimed to have outlined the scheme to Board Members who were unimpressed! In return, Galletti claimed, he was branded "a seditious agitator, anti-English, playing to the native gallery... regarded as a blackleg and a traitor."

Undaunted, he publicised the anti-Board campaign. In 1904, for example, 'A Correspondent' wrote to the *Madras Mail* suggesting massive structural administrative reform.[7] Several upper layers of Government of Madras bureaucracy should be removed to create better balance, stability, and cost efficiency. That would ensure remaining Secretariat and Board 'big officials'

---

7   "Madras District Administration", *Madras Mail*, 1 January 1904.

shared the pressure currently endured by hard working *mofussil* men. The Board did good and necessary work during the mid 19th century, but was now redundant. Members invented tasks simply to occupy themselves. Districts were physically too large, Collectors prevented from knowing the people under their care. Monies saved through reform could fund personal assistants to support those Collectors. ICS members who heard and read him regularly on the subject undoubtedly identified Arthur Galletti as 'a Correspondent'.

There was substance to this argument, as with many of the issues he took up. Heavy district workloads preoccupied Madras ICS men and many shared Galletti's thinking. In 1908 L.M. Wynch, the Collector of Tinnevelly, reported working at least 10 hours a day just to discharge routine duties. That left no time for contemplative work, future planning or building stronger local relationships. The situation must be corrected, Wynch argued, given increased political work brought on by Indian National Congress activities. Perhaps the Sub-Collector rather than Collector might conduct all revenue work? Alternatively an experienced personal assistant could be assigned to each Collector.[8]

Galletti, then, had support on several issues. However, when his 'memoir' version of events is compared with other evidence, he frequently claimed to begin campaigns at points earlier than those at which they appeared! That served his self-image as a reformer, a champion of the Indian people. Had he aired those organizational reform views with Board of Revenue Members late in 1900, he would not have gained preferential posting treatment. He might well have been dismissed. Meanwhile, he kept touring Godavari, dismayed that the average peasant required 10 pairs of oxen and several hired ploughmen to cultivate just 40 acres. Workers were feeble, oxen stunted—men like him must lead India towards social change and improvement.

---

8   Wynch, L.M. Memo in Lionel Davidson to Chief Secretary, 12 June 1908, GOM GO 604, 27 July 1908, P/7981, IOR.

When not in camp, Galletti was in Cocanada where club life differed radically from that in Madras. One Sunday morning he found several merchants drinking heavily at the club following a rowing expedition during which some were already so drunk they fell in the canal. He spent the day with them hunting jackal, all the while thinking them vulgar and lower class. In district, he thought, one must mix with all classes to ensure having any 'society'. The most pleasant people he met were the Bank of Madras branch manager and his wife. The husband was a devotee of Mrs Besant's Theosophy and mysticism, other European women disliked his wife who returned the favour. They considered her snooty, she like Galletti thought them vulgar. This was district India station life: the pretence of unity and purpose papering over suspicions and enmities wrought by class, income, and parentage.

Unlike Madras, district club membership was more inclusive, relying heavily upon non-official members because Cocanada was the chief district town but hosted few senior officials. Several were stationed at Rajahmundry: the District Judge, the District Superintendent of Police, the Sub-Collector, the Superintendent of the District Jail and the Government College Principal. That was a Galletti bonus: he became an important figure in Cocanada. Besides the bank manager, the British India Steam Navigation company agent was the leading non-official. Cocanada being an important commercial port, BISN was a significant commercial entity. The agent, a man named Brown, had a Eurasian wife so mixing with him would have been a social disaster in Madras. Here in Cocanada, however, according to Galletti most women married to Europeans were Eurasian, while single men either kept Indian women or visited prostitutes. Most merchants ran minor businesses; one had an Indian business partner, another was a French Eurasian.

Galletti complained that Cocanada's European Club happily included French Eurasians and others uncountenanced in Madras, but refused entry to Indians. The Club split over the issue years earlier, and had reunited only recently. The Collector was President during the row, but other committee members rejected his reforms so he resigned and now avoided the Club. Stuart pressured his assistant, Morris, to boycott the Club as well but Morris refused because it was the only social outlet available. Galletti refused, too, going there daily to play cards or snooker when in town.

Galletti's merchant friends disliked Stuart and were only slightly less contemptuous of Morris who threw a glass at one during an argument. The merchants advised Galletti against becoming 'superior' like Stuart and Morris. When Stuart left Godavari in April 1902, the official farewell attracted few non-officials, the one merchant present becoming drunk and instructing the Collector on the shortcomings that made him so unpopular.[9] Galletti mixed with the merchants continuously despite fighting one called McKenzie who was drunk. McKenzie was still a good fellow, Galletti thought, the pair singing together in church the day after the fracas.

Galletti learned quickly that Presidency behavioural and social codes were rigidly structured. He bought a dogcart, he reported, because European women like Cynthia should not walk around town, they must travel by carriage.[10] Then, Godavari contained several *zamindari* landholdings where peasants paid their rents to a local landlord, the *zamindar*. The *Zamindar* of Kirlampudi befriended Galletti who found him pleasant and intelligent. When Kirlampudi praised Sir James Thomson, Galletti passed the comments to his mentor. Thomson thanked him, but reminded Galletti not to invite the *zamindar* to dinner, it was not the done thing. Galletti was astonished, and angry:

---

9 Galletti to Clara, 30 April 1902.

10 Galletti to Clara, 14 April 1901.

English people out here think it is a mistake to treat native gentlemen as equals; they must be made to feel that they belong to a subject race.[11]

Rejecting that attitude, Galletti seized every opportunity to meet local notables like Kirlampudi. Galletti and Cynthia were frequent guests during their first three months in Godavari and Galletti was fascinated: the *zamindar* had his own circus complete with performing horses and acrobats, and gave Galletti a five-day old fawn as a pet. [12]

Galletti's quest to find India and 'real' Indians took another form. Discovering that street and market Telugu differed greatly from that taught by his Brahmin clerk, he conversed with everyone he could—cleaners, clerks, traders, washermen, to hear and learn from 'real' people. That way, Galletti claimed to learn in six months all the Telugu needed to pass his language examinations. According to official records, though, he still took the normal two and a half years to pass those tests formally. Galletti also convened an assembly of learned Telugu speakers, he claimed later, discussing in their language his grand federal scheme to reorganise Indian government into language-based provinces, local people holding transferred powers.

Even at this early stage Galletti separated himself from mainstream official life, lined up with the Collector's opponents, and advocated the need for Indian political reform. He was on the brink of his first major confrontation with his superiors and it was a serious one because, for his colleagues, it questioned his loyalty to Britain.

By 1900 the Boer War in South Africa was well under way, and during 1901 campaigns there went poorly for British forces. India's European community was concerned, calling frequently for India to be allowed to do its 'bit' for Empire. European-owned

---

11   Galletti to Clara, 14 April 1901.

12   Galletti to Clara, 7 April 1901.

newspapers like the *Madras Mail* and the *Madras Times* were full of loyalist war articles. As a war reminder, they published regular reports from the three Boer prisoner-of-war camps in the Presidency, especially about the Boer officer who escaped, disguised himself as an Indian and reached Madras.

One particular newspaper focus concerned the role played by European nations, especially Germany, in supporting the Boers. Early in 1902, the *Madras Mail* published an article condemning Germany for its anti-British and pro-Boer position, listing a series of alleged examples. One particularly colourful claim had Boer forces bribing German journals to publish anti-British materials.

A few days later, under the heading "Anglo-Phobia in Germany" and signing his name, Arthur Galletti confronted the correspondent.[13] He spent two years in a German school, he wrote, had many German friends and was in Germany less than two years earlier. Continental people, he suggested, remarked routinely that they could not discuss the War with Englishmen who invariably flared up, felt insulted and assumed anti-British sentiment. Italy's *Tribuna* newspaper, he continued, had commented that in England:

> The vulgar were still anxious to manufacture heroes out of the most unpromising material.

That comment arose, he said, because General Sir Redvers Buller claimed Spion Kop as a victory when clearly it was not; because welcoming parades lauded Buller when all evidence suggested he gave his position away incompetently; and because England welcomed General Sir William Gatacre home warmly despite his abject failure.

It was true, Galletti commented, that Continental papers reported Boer successes rather than British ones, because the 'unexpected' interested Continental readers far more! Yes, he

---

13 Arthur Galletti to the editor, *Madras Mail*, 6 February 1902.

confirmed, Continental papers did report British successes as 'alleged' ones, because English authorities controlled war reporting so tightly that authenticity could not be proven. German papers reported accounts of British atrocities received from Boer sources, not just Boer ones reported by the English press—that is, German reporting was even-handed, the English equivalent not. In Galletti's view Continental journals became suspicious, even skeptical because British correspondents had overplayed the extent of successes at the beginning of the war. All that, he concluded, was confirmed by the South African Commission 'fiasco's. The Commission of Inquiry into the War in South Africa was a spectacular failure, yet Austen Chamberlain retained his appointment while Cecil Rhodes was patently guilty but remained unpunished. The Continental mind, as Galletti called it, resented these wrongs and sympathised with the Boers.

Though more pro-German than pro-Boer, the letter angered every Madras European social group, outraged his ICS colleagues, and rendered his superiors incandescent. He questioned British conduct of the war. He questioned British political and military leadership, capacity and wisdom. He questioned the honesty of British war reporting. He questioned British capacity to analyse honestly the course of the war. He questioned Britain's slavish commitment to the war. By implication, he questioned the validity of the war itself.

The article portrayed an author with divided loyalties at best, anti-British at worst. Given the nature of Madras society, all Europeans knew this Arthur Galletti as a junior ICS officer working in the Telugu country, allegedly representing the very King and Empire his letter called into question.

Galletti acted deliberately: "I have caused a little stir in the official dove-cotes."[14] He recalled that in 1895, when he publicly criticised his housemaster's views on Gladstone, his uncle Robert

---

14   Galletti to Clara, 9 February 1902.

Collier advised that in India such actions would be professionally fatal. "Now I have done it", he declared, provoked by rabid press articles and sentiments expressed daily by Europeans in clubs and workplaces. The English were ill-disposed towards Europeans and that nuanced Boer War commentary, he argued. People disliked being instructed by their juniors, of course, and 'idiots' would construe his remarks as pro-Boer, but he wrote to honour his values and beliefs. He could have written anonymously, he said, but no-one would have read it so he signed his name. He wrote the article carefully to avoid expressing directly his own views and so contravene ICS rules, but he 'sailed rather close to the wind'. There were specific dangers in commenting on the War Commission, he recognised—his Governor, Lord Ampthill, had been Austen Chamberlain's Private Secretary so was an interested party.

Defensively, Galletti wrote an explanation to a "high official" in Madras [probably Thomson] and asked it be passed to Ampthill. The Governor admitted to the 'high official' he was 'startled' by the published letter, and asked that Galletti be 'much more careful' in future.

A few days later, a *Madras Mail* editorial revisited the Anglophobia it thought gripped the Germans, referencing Germany's aggressive efforts to create an empire that fell far short of Britain's civilising improvement of peoples everywhere.[15] Galletti ignored the bait. Shortly afterwards, however, 'A.G.' responded to a correspondent who belittled German horsemanship. A friend now serving with distinction in South Africa, said Galletti, was a hopeless horseman until tutored by a German riding master who made him a leading cavalry officer. Galletti concluded that 'we' Europeans (in the broadest sense) must learn, understand and appreciate each other far better than at present.[16]

---

15   *Madras Mail*, 22 February 1902.

16   A.G. to editor, *Madras Mail*, 7 March 1902.

Madras Mail readers would have identified 'A.G.', adding to his earlier image as a pro-German, anti-British figure that of an opinionated young man lecturing his betters on the need to better understand Continental Europe. The episode marked Galletti out within the ICS as someone to be watched, not in the usual anticipation of a bright career but as one to be regarded warily. For his superiors and colleagues, Galletti was regarded already as a highly intelligent man and an obviously loose cannon.

Galletti escaped punishment but was reprimanded severely by Sir James Thomson, advised to be more cautious about future public statements and actions. He was a bright man with a big future, but these outbursts marked him for life. His uncle Sir John Collier agreed: "try and add to your very considerable intellectual gifts that of a little common sense." Collier could not fathom why Galletti was so 'perverse', it would cost him his career. People should confront and accept their shortcomings, Collier agreed, but Galletti should not be the one highlighting those deficiencies. He was a junior man, should know his place and hold his tongue. As Galletti described himself in his memoir, however: "He was never wanting in contempt for the intelligence of others or confidence in his own'.

Thomson, Galletti's main local mentor, went further. He doubted Galletti would take advice from anyone unless it matched the advice he gave himself![17] Presciently, he warned Galletti his actions confirmed a reputation as 'not one of us':

> The present is *not* a time to air cosmopolitan sentiments unnecessarily; our people don't want instruction of the sort at present and will not admit any right or propriety in *your* offering it.... if your conduct and opinion *seem* to favour the foreign element more than the nation whose bread you eat you need not be astonished if you are looked at askance and your loyalty made matter of question.

---

17   Thompson to Galletti, 26 March 1902, Galletti Papers.

Thomson reminded Galletti he began Indian professional life with the 'deadweight' of another nationality: "You ought not be where you are", Thomson advised Galletti, if his heart and loyalties lay elsewhere.

All this weighed heavily with J.J. Stuart, the Collector of Godavari, who hounded Galletti over the pro-Boer letters. Galletti sent Stuart other letters on the subject that the Collector thought so "cheeky" they might ruin his junior.[18] Had he not been so good-natured, Stuart suggested, he would have suspended Galletti. Stuart revered 'loyalism', so Galletti was now treated suspiciously by his superior officer who had to file regular reports about his progress as part of normal career development procedure. Galletti believed Stuart would "continue to tell other people I ought to be kicked out of the service as a traitor." Stuart went further, like Collier and Thomson, suggesting Galletti's 'absurd ego' would ruin him if uncontrolled.

Galletti shrugged it off, suggesting Stuart could not use the letters because they were 'unofficial'. Making fine distinctions between letters as unofficial, demi-official and official became a Galletti hallmark, and exasperated many superiors over many years. While outwardly insouciant, during the rest of 1902 Galletti conspicuously applied himself to work, becoming well regarded by his superiors. In August 1902 the Governor, Lord Ampthill, noted: "Mr Galletti seems to have been spending his time well since he gave up writing pro-Boer letters to the Press."[19] In January 1903 the Acting Collector of Godavari reported Galletti's work in the Division as exemplary. His revenue work showed "marvellous energy and seeking to gain information wherever possible." Galletti had 'great confidence in himself' and was 'quite prepared to accept responsibilities'. The reporting

---

18   Galletti to Clara, 6 April 1902.

19   Comments in this section drawn from GOM Public 1063 Confl. 25 November 1903, TNA.

officer observed that the Galletti 'edge' remained, though, his magistrate's court work sometimes seeing him at odds with the prevailing code:

> This is probably not to be wondered at as Mr. Galletti is as much Italian as British—in some respects more Italian than British—and the views of the two countries on procedure and evidence vary.

Years later Galletti claimed to have brought with him to India a grand 'federation' constitutional reform scheme, language-based provinces to be self-governing under a (British) Government of India umbrella. There were two essential elements. First, the national level would be British-dominated for an extended period as Indians learned to run their own affairs. Second, at provincial level popularly-elected governments would be guided by British Governors (called Presidents), aided by sympathetic men like Galletti given enhanced status as Divisional Commissioners (overseeing several Districts, each with an Indian Collector). In limited respects, this resembled the 1909 then 1919 reform proposal contemplations of restricted policy transfer to Indian supervision.

Galletti's proposal was different because provinces would be based on linguistic rather than the prevailing, arbitrary, geographically-determined British Indian boundaries. So, Madras Presidency would be divided into the Tamil, Telugu and Canarese-speaking regions with other significant language groupings, like the Oriya-speakers in Ganjam assigned to other language-based provinces like Orissa. This looks remarkably like present-day federated India and it is clear that, even if he did not bring it with him from Europe, Galletti promoted the idea well before World War I.

His argument was simple, logical and sensible. Language differences reflected different traditions and practices in culture, literature, social relations, organizational politics, land practices and religious ones. He overstressed the point, but it was significant. After all, he argued, even within the Madras ICS officers specialised in one language (Telugu in his case) even if they must have proficiency in another (for him, Tamil). Accordingly, officers were posted mainly to their specialist language regions because their skills gave them insight into local practices. They were the key administrators. Given that the current Madras Secretariat was overblown, an unnatural administrative artifice was imposed on otherwise distinctive political entities with their own cultural impulses. He argued for a reallocation of resources from Madras city (the Secretariat and the Board) to the *mofussil*. In principle the idea had considerable merit. In practice, it discounted the power structures created by Madras organizational history and the weight of the bureaucracy emanating from that history. His idea was strong, then, but underrated the sheer scale of structural change and mental realignment required for implementation.

Galletti's ideas were stimulated further by his Telugu studies and discovery of Tanguturi Veerasalingam, the great 19th century Telugu social reformer. Veerasalingam, acknowledged intellectual founder of the modern Andhra Movement for a separate language-based state, invoked memories of past great Andhra empires like that based around Hampi, home to the Vijayanagara rulers between the 14th and 16th centuries AD. According to Konda Venkatapayya, the Andhra movement leader and Congress boss who confronted Galletti later in Guntur, Veerasalingam's Telugu literature and prose revival was *the* vital precursor to the first regional discussions in 1894. Venkatapayya and his Congress colleagues successfully linked Gandhi's *Swadeshi* (traditional goods) and national education campaigns with the Andhra drive, so the two were linked by 1913 when the first formal pro-Andhra group met. Venkatapayya forwarded Andhra representations to both the Morley-Minto and

Montagu-Chelmsford reform commissions.[20] Andhra supporters claimed government favoured Tamil-speaking regions over Telugu ones, that Andhra was underdeveloped educationally and economically-a separate state was the only solution.[21]

Galletti's language-based reform scheme allowed no Congress role. Significantly, he appears nowhere in any pro-Andhra literature as one of the movement's great originators or supporters. He may have wanted his views hidden from government to avoid trouble, but that would have been out of character. Alternatively, Andhra Movement leaders might not have wanted to recognise a European leader, but that also seems unlikely given the propaganda value in having an ICS figure like Galletti as an ally and supporter. The question remains about whether his ideas pre-or post-dated the formal rise of the Andhra Movement, but he was unquestionably by many years the first ICS member to promote language-based provincial organization.

Galletti's early support for Indian self-development sprang from an acerbic view of prevailing British attitudes. In early 1903, for example, India marked Edward VII's accession to the throne with the great Delhi *durbar* celebrations in miniature across the country. Galletti unhappily and sourly orchestrated fireworks displays and other entertainments in Cocanada. According to him 'The English' staged the celebrations simply to convince themselves 'natives' were completely loyal.[22] He saw things differently: "The government is to them [the people] a number of Collectors like me who raise millions in taxation." Because little of that tax appeared to support new roads or other services, the 'natives' believed Collectors shared the profits.

---

20   Konda Venkatapayya, *The Andhra Movement* (Madras, Andhra Mahasabha, nd [1928]).

21   *The Andhra Movement* (Guntur, Radha Press, 1915).

22   Galletti to Clara, 5 January 1903.

Despite all evidence to the contrary, he continued, the English were convinced India had the world's best government, and that ICS men were there not for money but the opportunity to serve Indians. This mordant view captured Galletti's early ideas and attitudes, and would soon be displayed at all-India level.

Early in 1903 the Government of Madras informed Galletti he was transferred to the Government of India for training in legislative drafting. He would be in Simla, the hill station to which Delhi officials retreated in summer. Sir Murray Hammick and Sir James Thomson engineered this, seeing Galletti as a 'coming man' despite his eccentricities. A spell in Simla over the summer season, socialising with the right people, would set him for future promotion.

With just two weeks notice, and surprised by the offer, Galletti travelled via Calcutta where he spent a few days, reporting it a more 'open' city socially than Madras. In Calcutta, he reported, Europeans walked about or travelled in trams without losing social status. Madras was more 'closed', liberals like him misplaced in a city that needed sweeping social reforms. His memoir letters from this period, based on actual ones but altered strategically, reflect his self-image: a renegade reformer scared by none in authority but supervised by dull, stupid people blind to his real worth. Galletti considered himself a man of the 'people' in conflict with an unyielding, unthinking bureaucracy. Some evidence was stretched to accommodate that view. He claimed, for example, to ride his bicycle 60 miles uphill to Simla, defying official orders prohibiting such unseemly activity. He certainly cycled a long way, but no such orders existed.

Galletti encountered in Simla a world very different again from that in Cocanada or Madras. He wore 'London' clothes including a stiff shirt with matching wing collar, special riding clothes, and was obliged to 'dress' (in dinner suit) every night. He stayed initially in a hotel then shifted to the Club. His main Simla preoccupation was playing bridge to supplement his income because he was living beyond his means. He earned £400 per year, he said, but spent £800 in Simla so bridge income was vital. Galletti played successfully, but upset colleagues with his 'professional' card play.

Legislative Department senior officers had anticipated a very different sort of man, so Galletti's appointment created friction between Simla and Madras.[23] The Department sought someone with 10 years service and experience as a fully-fledged District Judge, not a junior like Galletti. 'As the departmental head put it, they expected a man who had eaten his dinners in London' [at the Inns of Court]. 'Not being that person, Galletti was marked immediately. 'The Department asked Madras formally why he was sent. The Simla Secretary suspected, correctly, that Galletti 'knew' the Madras Chief Secretary who placed him in Simla as a favour.

Simla upbraided Madras, suggesting Galletti "had no special aptitude for legal studies and no desire to become proficient in legislative drafting." Madras senior officers countered that the remarks slurred Galletti himself, so the Government of India had to withdraw the allegation. Legislative Department officers like H.W.C. Carnduff and Thomas Raleigh (a former Madras man) agreed Galletti had a 'legal turn of mind' and could grasp a 'fine point'. Conceding he had no *inclination* rather than no *aptitude* for the work, they considered Galletti an innocent victim of Madras posting incompetence and did not wish to return him south with a 'black mark'.

Galletti saw opportunity in the situation, asking to be excused from the Higher Examination components he had yet to complete to reach his next career level. The Government of India saw through his ruse, passing the question back to Madras where senior officers criticised his opportunism. Galletti also

---

23   See GOI, Notes, Judicial–A. June 1903, No. 288; October 1903, Nos. 173-174; November 1903, No. 127, NAI.

informed Simla superiors he was 'completely surprised' by the posting, that Madras had not discussed it with him, and that he preferred executive to legislative service. Those declarations reached Madras, upsetting and alienating supporters who thought he undermined them.

Thomson was particularly displeased: Galletti was gifted a marvellous opportunity from which he should have benefited greatly, but chose to betray his Madras seniors:

> He is opinionated and chock-full of conceit, and I dare say these in him, as a learner, have been too much for his teachers.[24]

Thomson decided Madras should explain its position carefully, express dissatisfaction with the Government of India's attitude, and blame the fiasco 'on Galletti himself'. Within three years of arriving in India, Galletti had upset very senior officials in both Madras and Delhi/Simla, displaying a highly independent attitude towards Indian development and views too easily interpreted as anti-British.

Galletti reported that he and his four Scottish lawyer colleagues faced little work in Simla, and that no-one knew why he was there. Nevertheless, he set to diligently and, according to him, impressed both the Secretary and the Law Member of the Legislative Council, Thomas Raleigh. Galletti mixed early on with H.A. Stuart, another Madras man currently Secretary to the Commission of Inquiry into the police, and Stuart introduced him to Sir Andrew Fraser who chaired that Commission. He was meeting the right people. Simla social life was highly active in "season" and Galletti thought there were at least 180 "women of prey" (the "fishing fleet") seeking husbands, so he was busy. He spent time with Sir William Meyer, seconded from Madras to

---

24 J. Thomson note, 26 July 1903, GOM Public 727-8 Confidential, 17 August 1903, TNA.

edit the massive Gazetteer of India for which Galletti wrote the Godavari entry. Galletti also began work on his English-Telugu dictionary that appeared after he left India over 30 years later.

Like many other senior officials Meyer warmed to Galletti at their first meeting, and did the junior man a favour. Reluctantly, Madras agreed Galletti should sit his Telugu examinations in Simla rather than returning to Madras specially. Meyer, a good Telugu speaker, was appointed examiner. He passed Galletti, but senior Madras officials suspected the test was not as stringent as normal. Meyer reported 'Galletti fluent in Telugu', though 'not with a good accent', and 'considerably less' fluent in Tamil.[25] The pass put Galletti into Assistant Collector grade but influential Madras figures thought he reached it unfairly, yet another early mark against him.

After several months in Simla Galletti was returned to Madras, in reality because he was unsuited to the work but in his mind because he upset the Viceroy, Lord Curzon. His story was based on fact, but embellished. Galletti now disliked Curzon despite the earlier Madras impressions, yet the Viceroy was someone he might have supported. Curzon wanted to prosecute Europeans guilty of mistreating Indian servants. Galletti, surprisingly, claimed Curzon hated Indians and played the reformer simply to antagonise the European community. Galletti thought Curzon, widely nicknamed the 'Imperial Bounder' a dull, vain, ambitious and vicious man. This circular logic stemmed from Galletti's view that he was intellectually superior to the Viceroy but lacked Curzon's social and political connections—otherwise, Galletti would have been Viceroy.

Galletti's version of his downfall starts with Curzon reading an accurate Calcutta newspaper report of the Viceroy's confidential plans to award himself and colleagues huge salary increases. The Secretary of State having already vetoed the proposal, Curzon

---

25 See GOM Public GO 746, 21 August 1903 in P/6659, IOR.

was deeply embarrassed by the public revelation. Summoning the Secretary of the Legislative Department, he demanded the editor be prosecuted under the Official Secrets Act. Galletti drafted the first response, advising little chance of successful prosecution. Other departmental members agreed, Curzon was distinctly unimpressed.

Then Curzon read about an Assam case where a European planter killed a servant. At trial the European-only jury found the man guilty of 'hurt' rather than murder, fetching him just a six months prison sentence. Curzon was furious, demanding an appeal be drafted by the Legislative Department. Galletti again made the first assessment, and considered the evidence so poor it was unlikely the man would serve even the six months. Galletti reported that to his Deputy Secretary, Secretary and Law Member. All agreed.

Curzon exploded. He demanded the Chief Commissioner of Assam appeal but that official refused, citing the grounds rehearsed by Galletti. Curzon urged the Legislative Council to appeal. The Law Member and the Senior Executive asked Galletti to scour international law codes in search of any precedent for an appeal being run when, effectively, the case was acquitted. Galletti declared there was no such precedent, Curzon provided with that interpretation.

According to Galletti's version, Curzon then asked the Law Member to identity this impudent jackanapes draftsman. The Law Member replied it was a bright young chap from Madras. Curzon immediately ordered the bright young chap back from whence he came. Shortly before leaving Simla, Galletti claimed to have met Curzon at a garden party where the great man stared him up and down, wordlessly. In Galletti's mind, his all-India career foundered because he acted correctly but was victimised by a vindictive Viceroy. That confirmed Galletti's view the system must be reformed by people like him.

Several family stories have Galletti clashing directly with Curzon. One has Curzon and Galletti riding in a carriage. The Viceroy asks the origins of the big palaces they were passing. Galletti replies they belong to 'Indian gentlemen' to which Curzon retorts he was unaware that 'Indian gentlemen' existed! It is a great story, but more likely apocryphal than authentic.

The overwhelming evidence is that Galletti was returned to Madras early because Simla officials resented his being foisted upon them, because his attitude towards the work was uncompromisingly critical, because he did not cultivate his senior contacts assiduously enough, and because his political views were substantially at odds with the mainstream. It was a major career opportunity, Galletti could not exploit it fully, and he never returned to the all-India level.

The Simla social scene had similarly serious repercussions, particularly for his later marriage. He was there during the summer season when many women were prowling for husbands and/or, according to him, sex. He reported being propositioned by a homosexual member of his Department, but threatened to throw the man over the balcony! According to his memoir and other writings Galletti resisted all Simla temptations-bar one.

In his memoir, Phoebe Williams arrives from Lahore as lady-in-waiting to a Colonel's wife. She lodges in Galletti's hotel, in an annexe where a dozen rooms opened onto a common verandah, each pair of rooms connected by an unlocked door. Phoebe occupies the room next to Galletti. She notices him, pays him attention, flirts outrageously then, one morning opens the connecting door to reveal herself sans frock and wearing little else. Galletti admires her body, says it is inappropriate to do anything in the morning but they can cuddle that night, in bed. That duly occurs, she asks him to take her virginity, he does, and they conduct a highly passionate affair because, according to him, she has a healthy sexual appetite. The affair requires elaborate organization because Phoebe shifts rooms and is at constant command of and check by her employers, while Galletti must schedule his income-generating bridge!

In this account the woman makes the overtures, Galletti grants her wishes. He considers it a healthy but purely physical affair, she commits the cardinal sin of 'falling in love'. Throughout his life, Galletti maintained strong views that separated what he termed 'sacred' and 'profane' love. 'Profane love', sex, he considered a purely physical act unrelated to "sacred love" existing between married partners. Sex was healthy and produced preferably large families, but must not be confused with 'love' that was based more in intellectual realms. 'Sacred love', moreover, was dominated by the male who was more gifted intellectually than the female.

Phoebe—actually a woman named Nancy—sent him several letters confusing sex and 'love', in his view. Galletti put her off, telling her he was engaged already and she left Simla never to be seen again. In the memoir Phoebe dies in 1923, murdered by her husband who had just learned of the Simla dalliance, and Galletti discovers the death in the *Civil and Military Gazette,* the iconic north Indian newspaper on which Rudyard Kipling worked. However, no such incident appears in the paper around the period specified. It seems certain the affair happened, then, but that some aspects of it were embellished. Whatever the full truth, the Nancy/Phoebe ghost came to haunt Clara.

Galletti returned to Madras and a Secretariat posting in November 1903 and lived in the Club. He preferred being a divisional officer with an independent and influential *mofussil* life, but recognised the career benefits of being at headquarters.[26] Galletti knew being in Madras would help restore his reputation, but he disliked the social rigidity. Early in 1905 he left a Governor's dinner party early, before the dancing finished—the whole thing

---

26   Galletti to Clara, 11 November 1903.

was much too dreary, he said.[27] That broke protocol, convention being that no-one left before the Governor's wife gave the signal and that always followed the end of dancing. Such actions made his professional rehabilitation just that little bit more difficult.

Galletti lived in a double-storied block for single men, senior men occupying separate bungalows. Office hours were from 11 am till 5 pm so he had plenty of time to hunt, row, play cricket and tennis and billiards, shoot, and join the card tables. He wrote for the *Madras Mail* and the *Madras Times* and fulfilled social duties like 'calling'. The Italian Consul in Calcutta asked him to be part-time Vice-Consul in Madras but his superiors refused, considering the position too demeaning for an ICS man. Galletti did the work unofficially and was later awarded the title Cavagliere that he used rarely.

The Secretariat occupied Fort St George, home of British power in south India from earliest days, handling higher level policy issues and decisions. The Board of Revenue ran day-to-day matters and resided in Chepauk Palace, former home of the Nawabs of Arcot. The physical separation heightened tensions between the two arms, and helped Galletti mature his BMG (Board Must Go) campaign. Board Members were like Ministers, while in the Secretariat ICS members of the Governor's Council fulfilled a similar role. Powerful Secretaries, four in the Secretariat and two in the Board, reported to those seniors. Reporting to the Secretaries were the Under Secretaries whose ranks Galletti joined, beneath them literally hundreds of clerks and other officials. It was a vast, complex bureaucracy that over many decades developed its own ways of doing things, most of which Galletti derided. He was not alone. Alan Butterworth, later Chief Secretary, dismissed his Secretariat time as "burning

---

27   Galletti to Clara, 12 January 1905.

incense to vanity."[28] Butterworth also recalled his time as an Under-Secretary as a period when they had "a joyous tiffin at which we criticized our seniors, ragged playfully, and fed the kites ...ever wheeling and whining about the Fort."[29] Galletti enjoyed the same experience.

Galletti was Under Secretary to several departments like Finance, and Political that regulated relations with princely states inside Presidency borders. Because of his Simla legislative draft training, he composed initial draft bills for several other departments. Predictably, he claimed this work had great influence, such as a monetary scheme for India that attracted Finance Department attention in the Government of India where he was wanted as Secretary.

His political activities developed, too, especially his views on freedom for India. Shortly after his return, around Christmas 1903, he claimed to have attended the Madras session of the Indian National Congress, one of only two Europeans there. Because that was unusual, he said, he was invited onto the platform and that was reported in the local press. That upset his superiors who had the Chief Secretary reprimand him privately. His on going newspaper publications did not help his cause, Galletti added.

Had Galletti attended the Congress meetings he would certainly have been unpopular with his superiors. Lord Ampthill, the Governor, was apprehensive about the sessions being conducted in his city and took Curzon's advice on their management. In passing, Ampthill lamented that 'the native press saddens and nauseates' in its political affairs coverage.[30]

---

28 A. Butterworth, *The Southlands of Siva: some reminiscences of life in Southern India*, (London, Lane Bodley, 1923), p.44.

29 *Ibid.*, pp.48-9.

30 Ampthill to Curzon, 5 July 1903, Curzon Papers F111/194, IOR.

If Galletti attended sessions and was reported doing so by that press, it would have been noticed.

Galletti dismissed the Indian National Congress and its leadership's quest for political concessions. The "natives", he argued, simply sought more power for themselves. A tolerant government should be unconcerned about these activities that pleased activists but bothered no-one. In his view, Congress members shared only a command of the English language. Otherwise, the organization was a 'Tower of Babel' with a plethora of languages, customs, cultures and beliefs cross-marked by caste differences and Hindu-Muslim divisions. Congress members publicly aspired to a nation, he thought, but privately argued a corner for their particular educated class interest group. In effect, they were semi-English as confirmed by the appointment of Lal Mohun Ghose, an unsuccessful 1880s English parliamentary seat candidate, as Congress President in 1903. Given all that, Galletti declared, Madras proceedings were predictably uneventful.

There is no formal evidence that Galletti attended the Congress sessions that were disrupted by heavy rains at the conference site in the Teynampet Spring Gardens complex.[31] Some subjects he mentioned were discussed, and the President was Lal Mohun Ghose from Calcutta. There was one Madras European there, though, Eardley Norton, a well-known, almost notorious Madras criminal lawyer who attended Congress first in 1887, and was regarded as reverently by Congress members as Alan Octavian Hume. Norton came from a well-known Madras liberal family, and was invited onto the Madras stage to second the nomination of Ghose as President. Galletti drew on Norton's profile to help depict his own liberal outlook, and to put himself among those few Europeans who assisted the rise of Congress.

---

31 *Madras mail,* 28, 29, 30 December 1903.

Galletti's then tolerant attitudes towards Congress policies differed substantially from his later stance on fighting for the rights and goals of 'real' Indians. However, those views played to his preferred model for future Indian political organization, the grand 'federal' scheme with linguistic states like Andhra, Orissa and Karnataka. Even so, even this early period reflected Galletti's building distrust of the Presidency's Congress political leaders. He thought they put self-interest first and the mass of Indians a distant second. Galletti maintained that view throughout his career, eventually insisting India's accession to political freedom be supervised by benevolent Viceroys and Governors rid of a self-serving ICS and an equally self-serving Congress. A curiously paternalistic position, given his background and intellect, it stranded him between Congress and Raj.

That Congress episode was followed early in 1904 by a speech he claimed to deliver at Presidency College, a leading Madras higher education institution. He responded to a lecture on the course of the Italian Risorgimento delivered, he said, by Professor Dodwell. Galletti drew comparisons and contrasts between pre-unification Italy and current British India, highlighting the need for political change and the growth of responsible patriotism. He claimed some of his superiors were present and thought his remarks seditious, so sought official action against him. The Governor put it down to youthful enthusiasm and took no action, but senior service members suspected him and his views from then on.

If it was a response to H.H. Dodwell, the speech must have been delivered a few years later. Dodwell arrived in Madras as Acting Professor of History at Presidency College only in 1909 before being appointed Keeper of the Records in 1913. In 1924 he became Professor of Indian History at the School of Oriental and African Studies in London, where he stayed until his death in 1946. If Galletti debated Dodwell, it must have been around 1909-10, and that would match some of the other difficulties he encountered then.

If there is uncertainty about his claims on Congress and the Presidency College speech, there is none about his letter writing. Late in 1903 he published in the *Madras Times* poems intended to convey 'information' to that 'ignorant person Lord Ampthill' touring Godavari to hear grievances personally even though he did not understand Telugu.[32] On 1 January 1904, 'A Correspondent' wrote on 'Madras District Administration'.[33] It can only have been Galletti. The 'Board Must Go' mantra was absent, but the prose echoed Galletti's campaign. The 'big officials' at the Board, argued the correspondent, should assume some of the pressure carried by officers slogging it out in the *mofussil*. Districts were too large, Collectors and their assistants carrying too much work. The Board was necessary and productive in the early 19th century but had outrun its worth, Members interested only in protecting their own interests and position. Eliminating those positions would increase efficiency and productivity, helping fund Personal Assistant to the Collector positions that should be established in heavy districts.

Galletti wrote on more than administrative matters. A few days later 'Truth' contributed a letter commenting on an article about the Pope and his supposed role in seizing 'treasure'.[34] Again, it can only have been Galletti given the access to Italian newspapers and information on which the case was based. *Tribuna* was cited, for example, a paper to which Galletti subscribed for years and that he quoted regularly.

His colleagues knew the identity of "A Correspondent" because Galletti broadcast his views regularly to all in sundry, especially his seniors. After Simla, the pro-Boer issue, his pronounced affinity for Congress and Indians, and his attack on senior Board officers who were overseers of ICS discipline and

---

32   Galletti to Clara, 16 December 1903.

33   *Madras mail,* 1 January 1904.

34   *Madras mail*, 13 January 1904.

behaviour, Galletti was difficult to defend, even for sympathisers like Sir James Thomson.

Throughout these years and professional travails there continued the long-distance, by-correspondence relationship and engagement with Clara Salvadori. Early exchanges were predictably and conventionally normal, Galletti declaring he loved his fidanzata, she was the only girl in the world for him and he awaited her letters with breathless anticipation, deploring separation and 'the dreariness of waiting'.[35] The separation and extended engagement came only from financial constraints, his devotion to duty, and his career development.[36] Portentously, before the Simla affair, he asked Clara to quiz him on his past because things should be transparent between lovers, especially if anything 'discreditable' existed.' He had nothing to hide.[37] He meant those things. Clara, meantime, was learning Tamil and Telugu, trying to understand India from a distance. Having her present as a wife would clearly add a supportive dimension to his life.

Over time, however, the correspondence grew querulous, even combative and Clara seriously contemplated cancelling the engagement because some Galletti propositions upset her so much. She was not alone in her doubts. Galletti's father disapproved of the match, and Galletti thought Lord Monkswell's support lukewarm—the latter doubted his nephew's sincerity.[38] The root cause of this emerging difference became the biggest dividing line between them throughout their lives: the extent to which two individuals entering marriage retain or yield their individual outlooks and characters inside a new set of obligations to each other.

---

35 Galletti to Clara, 20 December 1900.

36 Galletti to Clara, 7 April 1901.

37 Galletti to Clara. 1 January 1901.

38 Galletti to Clara, 11 December 1900.

During 1903 Galletti informed Clara he preferred they marry in India or Aden—Egypt became a later preferred site. The reason was simple. He did not want to marry in Italy with no provision for divorce. It was unlikely they would want to divorce, he said, "but marriage without a possibility of divorce strikes me as indecent and improper."[39] Clara's reaction was predictable, and her family became concerned at the time taken for the marriage to occur. Late in 1903 he wrote a long letter to Clara's mother explaining the delay as purely financial. At his insistence, he said, his mother had taken a loan from his uncles to help her survive and assist his educational development. In return, the uncles must now get transferred ownership of *San Venanzo* following his parents' divorce, rental fees from peasants going to his mother as income. Eventually, he would repurchase the property but, meanwhile, must establish himself in Madras, pay off the loans and be responsible for family members including Cynthia and his brother Clemens.

Differences peaked during 1905 when Clara told Arthur she wanted to break the engagement. She doubted her 'worthiness' to become his wife, doubting they had the true feelings necessary for a good marriage. Galletti responded bluntly.[40] He was firmly committed, even if people like Clara mistook his cool detachment for cynicism. Any doubts she had sprang from her own low self-esteem rather than any fault of his. She must confront that low self-esteem to improve herself. He returned to his key belief, arguing she had false views about the enthusiasm, passion and devotion necessary in marriage. Why should he let her faults and inadequacies go unremarked and unchallenged simply because she was his wife? She would remain a person like any other, only married to him. He would be considerably inconvenienced if she

---

39   Galletti to Clara, 6 August 1903.
40   Galletti to Clara, 9 August 1905.

cancelled their agreement—he had considered himself "bound" for five years (clearly not counting Simla) so had not surveyed the market for other eligible women.

Clara responded angrily. Two weeks later, from the Nilgiris Club in Ootacamund, Galletti sent her what can only be described as a brutal letter.[41] He attacked her 'angry' letter that criticised his philosophy on their imminent relationship. There were in life, he declared, commonly accepted conservative social propositions that must be rejected. One was that the sole aim in and purpose of life was marriage. The second was that marriage then should produce mutual and unquestioning admiration between partners, an absorption with each other that excluded all other people. Galletti railed against both propositions. The purpose of life, he argued, was to lead a good and happy existence by "loving" everyone and improving things everywhere possible. That was not a religious 'good', it was a social and a service one. Logically, married people should maintain active and committed lives outside marriage in order to do 'good service'.

While his logical position was defendable, Galletti continued provocatively. It was 'immoral', he proclaimed, to exalt the marriage partner above all others and have no other interests whatsoever. In fact, it was unjust. Individuals should "exalt" the most worthy and most deserving, and any marriage partner would likely be neither. No person should automatically, blindly devote themselves to someone to whom they were married.

Clara's views were 'utterly worthless', he continued, because she was ignorant about India and what awaited her. His comment belittled, even dismissed her language studies and constant search for information about her impending new country. British India was full of 'busy men and idle women", he declared, she must fit in 'if and when' she came to live with

---

41   Galletti to Clara, 29 August 1905.

him. His official work and general activities were important, hers not. A busy husband like him was a poor companion at the end of the working day, and that work included Club and social commitments. A myriad of servants would serve them and their children, Clara would have little to occupy her days and evenings. By definition she would need other European company. Her musical skills and interests in 'light literature' would help, but she must establish social circles outside marriage.

He finished by accusing Clara of blackmail. He had suggested they marry in Egypt. She could travel there alone, they could combine the honeymoon with sightseeing and learning about another great culture. Clara had refused, nervous about how things were developing, reconsidering the engagement and intended marriage. What, she wondered, would happen to her reputation if she travelled to Egypt, discovered herself exploited and abandoned? She wanted to be married at home, she said, to ensure the outcome. Galletti took exception: his writing might not contain normal love letter 'flattery' but he was not devoid of affection for her. He was simply being direct in stating his mind.

Somewhere in all this Galletti made a strong point—social life in British India was an important part of the ruling fabric, and women had to find ways to occupy themselves because servants discharged most daily routine matters. However, the unfeeling, unyielding and unsympathetic way in which he made the point, especially to a woman who was his fiancé, was harsh, bordering on cruel.

Somehow, though, he convinced her to proceed with the marriage, despite the agitated late-1905 correspondence. When in early 1906 Arthur Galletti finally married Clara Salvadori, in Porto San Giorgio and not in Egypt, she must have anticipated he would be a difficult, unpredictable husband. By his memoir account, some of that difficulty appeared during the honeymoon that included a stay at the Gritti Palace hotel in Venice—he claimed they stayed in separate rooms. Clara herself much later declared that aspects of the memoir relating to her were "half lies". In his view, he came to the marriage with a very different outlook from Clara. He claimed never to have 'loved' any one person—he considered that selfish and unnatural. He 'loved' everyone from an interest and character point of view. So-called 'romantic love' was simply a version of lust he did not possess–he had a naturally healthy animal appetite for sex, but not lust. Arthur underlined that view in an early letter where he argued that only in the West did social restriction (marriage) prevent the exercise of a natural function (sex) immediately upon people reaching maturity.[42] Any man of above-average intelligence should have sex to produce as many children as possible for the good of the world, but intertwining sex and love, he thought, was false and misleading.

Clara disagreed strongly, thinking it entirely natural she focus her effort and attention on the one person she had chosen to be with and to have his children, but also to have his undivided affection. That she never got. From a very early point, Arthur ruled they occupy separate rooms because that would enable them to continue developing their individual personalities. They would come together for sex, with companionship scheduled around meals and visiting the club for exercise and social activities.

Galletti was aware he could be cold to the point of being harsh, even cruel towards his wife. At various points he remarked that he hurt her deeply by saying he 'loved' other people more than her. He meant the word in his sense, but Clara naturally saw it differently, especially when applied to other women. Man was driven by both libido and self-assertiveness, he thought, so a wife took care of the first while the man concentrated on developing the second through work and career, and by dominating others.

---

42   Galletti to Clara, 1 January 1901.

He cared deeply for Clara in his own way, but from the start she was never fully convinced. Arthur Galletti's memoir character selects his wife clinically—he had known her a long time, she was slim and athletic. Her breasts were small but firm, her hips right for childbearing. Like a Giotto Madonna she had an aquiline nose, dark brown hair and deep brown eyes. An accomplished musician, she was not a scholar but understood light literature. She was a perfect mate, even if he did not 'love' her. That described Clara physically. Intellectually, however, it was wildly off the mark because she was extremely intelligent. That made his treatment the more painful because her intelligence was accompanied by extreme sensitivity. Given her constant self-doubts and those she held about Arthur, she faced a tough time.

4

Shooting Star, 1907-1917

Returning to Madras married to Clara, Galletti was now at a critical point in his career development. Simla events had embarrassed the Government of Madras deeply, but senior officials blamed Government of India counterparts more than their *enfant terrible*. Galletti was still considered a future leader—his pro-Boer position retreat suggested he was fundamentally sensible, his senior level connections were growing, important people found him witty, bright and good company, Clara was a distinct asset.

For the next few years Galletti's domestic arrangements were odd. Between 1907 and 1911, according to the *Asylum Press Almanack*, Arthur lived successively at the Prince of Wales Hotel in Royapettah, the beachfront Marine Hotel and the D'Angelis Hotel in Mount Road. As a Secretariat man he moved from Madras to Ootacamund during the hot season, so obviously calculated that hotel living was less expensive than supporting a house and associated service personnel. That was difficult for Clara, though, because the children came quickly: Arthur Junior in 1907, Robert in 1908 and Beatrice in 1909. Emma was born in Porto San Giorgio in 1911 while the Gallettis were on leave, and Isabella back in India in 1914. As was common among British official families the children went off at very early ages to Ootacamund, the boys to Breeks School and the girls to a Catholic church school. Even so, not having a regular house made Clara's life unsettled.

Despite this growing family, Galletti remained intent on reform. As Indian nationalist organization and sentiment built during the early 20th century, particularly in Bengal where the Raj encountered what it termed 'terrorist outrages', an apprehensive Government of India sought tighter control over dissidents. Newspaper criticism especially worried Delhi officials so the Prevention of Sedition Bill emerged to control publishing and curb free speech. In August 1907 the Government of India, alarmed that Indian soldiers were corrupted by current newspapers, sent provincial governments a full draft Bill. The Bengal insurrection was a major catalyst, discontent over the proposed provincial partition into East and West linking up with nationalist activity spearheaded by Bipin Chandra Pal, a Bengali radical now active in Madras. The Government of Madras responded to the letter quickly. R.H. Bradley, a liberal Acting Chief Secretary to Galletti's mind, informed New Delhi that Madras supported the proposal unreservedly.[1]

The imminent repression outraged Galletti's libertarian sense and he challenged it from inside the Government of Madras, a dangerous ploy. He asked his uncle Jack Collier to pass a spirited letter to Sir John Morley, Secretary of State for India in London and a Collier friend. Collier did not forward the letter, thinking it so critical of Galletti's Madras and New Delhi superiors as to be career-threatening. He did, however, convey the key points to Morley without naming Galletti but referencing a young, experienced and 'very intelligent' ICS man.[2] This young officer, said Collier, was 'much exercised' by the repressive measures emerging in India. Lord Kitchener, the military commander driving the measures was far too influential-provincial Governors feared him, his views on Indian politics were untrustworthy. Kitchener most certainly should not become the next Viceroy as was being mooted. Far from calming agitation, the informant continued, the Bill escalated agitation by encouraging governments like Madras to prohibit meetings, confiscate printing presses, summarily suppress

---

1   Government of Madras, GO 638, 8 August 1907, P/7695, IOR.
2   Lord Monkswell to Morley, 2 October 1907, Morley Papers, MS Eng. d 3566, Special Collections, Bodleian Library, Oxford.

political activity, and call out military forces to help the police quell demonstrations. Even moderate Indian opinion was now alienated. This disgraceful legislation should be scrapped.

Galletti's memoir version of this episode is instructive. It has Acting Chief Secretary Jack Smith (Arthur Galletti) opening a Government of India 'Secret' letter containing Kitchener's proposal for 'very drastic' press control legislation. Normally, the Chief Secretary conveyed these letters to the Governor who then discussed them with his Council members. The Governor, Sir Arthur Lawley being absent Galletti himself consulted Council members Sir Gabriel Stokes and Sir George Forbes. Stokes was a legendary ICS man having been Chief Secretary before joining the Council, and came from a long family line of Madras civil servants. Forbes, a Scot who arrived in 1872, established a reputation handling the late 19th century Rampa rebellion in the north of the Presidency, then transferred to the Political Department at All-India level. He returned to Madras in 1890 and joined the Secretariat.

According to the memoir, Galletti advised the pair the proposed Act was unnecessary and contravened British free speech principles. How could soldiers be undermined by newspaper articles written in English? They did not understand the language! Stokes agreed with Kitchener, suggesting Indians misinterpreted 'toleration' and needed firm, direct control. Forbes supported stronger control, but disliked the legislation. Lawley later agreed with Stokes, Galletti ordered to inform Delhi that Madras 'heartily supported' the measure.

The memoir version plays up Galletti's role in Madras deliberations, but distances him from the official decision. The sequencing is imperfect, however. Galletti's official service record reveals he was Acting Chief Secretary between 30 November and 2 December 1906, and official Government documents confirm that.[3] The legislation did not appear until

---

3   Government of Madras, Public, GO 12 (Press NP), 3 January 1907, P. 7694, IOR.

1907, so Galletti could not have acted as he suggests even if, as Under Secretary, he certainly undermined the legislation. Interestingly, the Government of Madras demanded later in 1907 that all officers observe the conduct manual and not attend, let alone chair political meetings.[4] That suggests Galletti was not alone in being upset by the legislation, because other officers also encouraged public protest.

The memoir version continues with an outraged Galletti writing several subsequent letters to his uncle who, without his nephew's knowledge, passed them to Morley. Galletti realised Morley had seen the letters, however, while reading a newspaper report of a Morley speech opposing repressive legislation driven by Raj officials who considered their Indian subjects misunderstood 'toleration'. That was the Stokes sentiment Galletti reported earlier to his uncle. Galletti's annotated copy of Morley's collected speeches highlights the key words in that speech delivered in Arbroath in Scotland. Even though just a Madras junior Under-Secretary, then, Galletti believed he helped the Secretary of State override conservative forces in New Delhi and Madras.

Morley sought more 'inside' information on matters Indian, according to the memoir, so Galletti reported the 1907 Godavari district disturbances known as the Cocanada Club riots, on which he took another contrary position. Galletti knew Cocanada, it was his first posting and he disliked the attitudes of many "society" members there. Because Godavari was politically active, Bipin Chandra Pal made it the first of his 1907 Presidency tour stops. Rajahmundry was the centre of his activities where, for several weeks, up to 20 prominent local students and other young men went around shouting *Vande Mataram!* (my sweet mother [country]), B.C. Pal's exhortation to nationalist activity. Holidaying students from Rajahmundry College, where Pal spoke principally, established a *Vande Mataram* Protection League

---

4   Government of Madras, GO 500, 26 June 1907, P. 7694, IOR.

to promote nationalist feelings in Cocanada.[5] The Executive Engineer on the big Dowlaiswaram Irrigation Project nearby informed the Inspector-General of Police there was:

No doubt that Chandra Pal's speeches have had a most wonderful effect in stirring up the place: people say that there is some big native society in Rajahmundry which is the cause of all the trouble, and that they are waiting orders from Calcutta to have a bigger shindy.[6]

When 'respectable' Europeans and Indians rode through Cocanada in carriages or on bicycles, these activist young men followed shouting nationalist slogans and generally embarrassing loyalists.[7] Student supporters surrounded anyone who remonstrated. Demonstrators targeted the local Municipal Chairman, 'an excellent type of the native' who opposed the nationalist campaign in the Godavari Collector's view. The boys stepped up their activities, supported by local lawyers and landholders angered by the Chairman's refusal to grant tax concessions.[8] The atmosphere smouldered for several days, then flared.

Captain David Claude Kemp, Indian Medical Service, was an 'on call' man in the Presidency, not the *resident* local medical officer as Galletti claimed later. Officially, Kemp was District Medical Officer in Cuddapah district but was in Cocanada briefly on vaccination duty.[9] Kemp was returning to town in a truck when three young men shouted nationalist slogans at him. As he recounted:

---

5   P. Sivasankara Reddy, *Civil Disobedience Movement in Andhra* (New Delhi, Classical, 2001), pp.15-16.

6   Executive Engineer Dowlaiswaram to Inspector-General of Police, 31 May 1907, CID Reports vol I, May-November 1907, APA.

7   *Madras mail,* 1 June 1907.

8   J.A. Cumming, Report, 30 May 1907, L/PJ/6/814/1821, IOR.

9   He joined the IMS after graduating from University College London in 1896 and was promoted Captain in 1902. He returned to London and completed a Diploma in Tropical Medicine in 1912, served throughout World War I, was promoted Lieutenant-Colonel in 1918 and retired in 1921.

They all called out *Vande Mataram* in an insulting manner... I might not have taken such serious notice of a boy's impertinence had not my patience been exhausted by the repeated insults I had already received during the previous weeks since Babu Chandra Pal's visit to the district.[10]

Overwhelmed by the tension of previous days he climbed down from the truck, caught then assaulted one boy. Spectacular consequences ensued.

Not content with hitting the boy, Kemp dragged him to the police station to lay a charge of insulting behaviour. [11] Several citizens witnessed this and a crowd gathered, incensed at the beating. Reaching several hundred in number and coming from everywhere, the crowd surrounded Kemp and the boy. Amidst the noise and commotion, the crowd demanded Kemp be arrested for assault. Police dispersed the crowd, but the agitated throng promptly reassembled outside the Police Sergeant's house, still demanding Kemp be punished. The Sergeant calmed the rioters momentarily, but they then marched *en masse* through nearby properties smashing pots and furniture. Learning Kemp had retreated to the Cocanada Club, founded in 1867 and the focus of European town life, the crowd rushed there shouting slogans and threatening violence. Fearing a major disturbance Collector J.A.Cumming, once briefly Galletti's superior, called for police reinforcements from nearby Rajahmundry and led an armed squad to the Club.

Kemp was bailed up on the top floor with three others: Reverend A.E. Stanley from St. Thomas' Church; W.J.M. Inkster, Secretary of the Club and of the Cocanada Chamber of Commerce as well as Manager of the Cocanada Trading Company; and E.O.

---

10 Captain Kemp to Personal Assistant to the Surgeon-General, 7 June 1907, Public Confidential 824, 31 October 1907, APA.

11 The following description is drawn mainly from the Cumming to Chief Secretary, 1 June 1907, L/PJ/6/814/1821, and *Madras mail,* 7 June 1907.

May, an assistant in the Cocanada branch of Simpson Brothers, the Presidency's principal transport firm. The crowd surrounded the Club then smashed through its lower level, almost demolishing the building. Cumming ordered his squad to charge the rioters, then thought better of it and attempted to reason with protest leaders.[12] He was immediately struck on the head by a flying soda water siphon and bled profusely. That stopped the riot. Seeing the Collector hurt, the protesters disappeared. Newspaper reports had Kemp's group playing bridge but Cumming found them locked in a windowless room, listening to events. Comically, the Collector put Kemp on a bicycle, ordering him to the railway station and a ticket for Madras. More than 50 people were charged with offences related to the disturbance over following weeks.

Sir Arthur Lawley and his senior advisors were incensed, convinced the riot stemmed from political unrest. It was sedition, pure and simple. Wanting B.C. Pal deported from the Presidency, the Governor wrote a 'wrong-headed' letter demanding action from the Viceroy, Lord Minto. Lawley was deeply conservative, believing Whitehall and Delhi craved popularity when they should rule strongly and concede nothing to Indians.[13] Provocatively, Lawley imposed an expensive police tax on Cocanada's Indian population, to fund increased local surveillance.

Galletti, however, claimed to have unofficial reports from Cocanada Indian friends that contradicted official ones. He argued the riots were not political, but the product of a feud between local leading Indians and an "arrogant and vulgar European community'. It was a controversial contradiction of his superiors.

---

12 G.R.F. Tottenham would argue later that Cumming, his first Collector, was among the weaker officers in Madras, incapable of taking decisive action on anything—Sir Richard Tottenham memoir, CSAA.

13 M.N. Das, *India under Morley and Minto: politics behind revolution, repression and reforms* (London, Allen & Unwin, 1964, p.134.

Galletti argued that two incidents sparked the riots. First, Europeans slapped two Brahmin boys in public for passing allegedly disrespectful remarks. The social affront to high caste dignity was aggravated because one of the boys, aged 11, was being married so the whole caste was on hand for the sacred ceremony and witnessed his humiliation. The European actions, Galletti claimed, were inflammatory. Second, Galletti's account had another boy beaten viciously by the resident European doctor, an Indian Medical Service officer and former regimental boxing champion. This was the Kemp episode. The doctor objected to the boy shouting *Vande Mataram*. After he beat the boy, an angry crowd chased the doctor to the Club where he and other Europeans held them off by throwing chairs from an upstairs balcony until the District Magistrate and police arrived.

Galletti argued that the crowds protested the arrogant, insensitive actions of overbearing Cocanada Europeans. Even in the Kemp case, citizens were incensed more by his treatment of the boy than by his reaction to the nationalist slogans.

Lawley and Stokes overruled Galletti's view that the riots were non-political and cancelled Cocanada's standing as district headquarters, transferring all government functions to Rajahmundry. Galletti drafted that order but warned the Collector unofficially and agreed with a sensible Chief Secretary, Bradley, that such change could not occur immediately, even if at all. Galletti and Bradley canvassed opinion from all possible government agencies to assess the shift's impact and, naturally, that information took time to collect. When Stokes discovered the order unimplemented he sacked the Collector, but Galletti remained in the Secretariat and the order cancelled.

In the memoir, Galletti then suggests that Morley, upon reading the alternative account, ordered the Government of Madras to cancel its initial decision. Again, this account accords the Under-Secretary more influence than the Viceroy or Governor. Galletti explained this simply: he and Morley were

Liberals while Viceroy, Governor and senior executives were Tories. The Secretary of State would rather listen to a fellow liberal than to conservative opponents.

This detail is important because while Galletti saw a purely local cause behind the riot, all other sources linked events to Bipin Chandra Pal's political activity. The Municipal Chairman, for example, was shocked the government did not move against Pal earlier. Indian business leaders met in Cocanada a few days later and echoed that view. They regretted Cumming's injury and argued that while Kemp's intemperate action initiated the riot, local support for nationalist sentiment would increase if agitators went unchecked. European and non-official Presidency opinion sought swift, sweeping and stern action against Bipin Chandra Pal and his allies. As the *Madras Mail* commented:

> The impotence of the sedition-monger is no argument for the toleration of such outrageous speeches as were delivered by Mr. Pal and his disciples.[14]

Galletti alone thought the riot caused by the ignorant, prejudiced views of local Europeans. While he disliked most Cocanada Europeans, his interpretation drew more from his view on the anti-sedition legislation—he thought ignoring people like B.C. Pal more constructive than confronting them publicly. This was the first appearance of Galletti's theory that 'Soul Force' was more effective in India than legislative repression. For Galletti, Kemp's action reflected the gross ignorance and poor behaviour of Cocanada's European community to which aggrieved Indians naturally reacted. Given that, he argued, stationing extra police in Cocanada at cost to the local population was unfair and discriminatory-Europeans, too, should pay because they caused the riot.

Galletti's stand raised further doubt about his 'soundness' among his superiors. Given Simla, the sedition legislation and now this, he was clearly unreliable. Undaunted, Galletti claimed

---

14   *Madras mail*, 28 May 1907.

proudly to have again alerted Morley who intervened on the side of righteousness. The evidence on that is unclear. The Secretary of State certainly fielded a Parliamentary Question about the riot, but that followed inquiry from Kemp's father after London newspapers reported his son seriously injured. Morley declined to countermand Government of Madras actions once facts were clarified, especially concerning the additional tax. The assaults and agitation sprang not from Kemp's action, Morley advised the House of Commons, but from Bipin Chandra Pal's political stirring of students.[15] However, another question to the Secretary of State, from newly elected James O'Grady of the Labour party, might just have come from Galletti via Robert Collier and his political connections—it concentrated on the Cocanada punitive police tax and was obviously based on detailed local information.[16] Galletti might well have leaked further information to someone other than the Secretary of State.

Even by his own account, though, the episode scarred Galletti. He claimed to have shown drafts of the Morley letters to Sir George Forbes, his then Chief Secretary. Forbes thought if the Secretary of State wanted a junior man write to him then that should happen. Besides, Forbes saw nothing exceptionable in the letters. Forbes took leave, however, and his replacement thought differently, reporting another draft to the Governor. Lawley summonsed Galletti, accusing him of betraying Government confidence and releasing official secrets. Galletti would be sacked from the Secretariat. Galletti appealed to Stokes, even though the senior man supported the press repression. While considering Galletti rash, Stokes thought he should remain in the Secretariat. Lawley relented but did not forget. Neither did others in the Secretariat.

---

15   Draft version of Secretary of State reply, L/PJ/6/819/2405.

16   See the O'Grady question in L/PJ/6/819/2405, IOR. O'Grady later became Ambassador to the Soviet Union and Governor of Tasmania.

This distrust of Galletti coincided with increasing Madras ICS nervousness about the broader political future. Morley was worried that Bengal partition agitation and associated nationalist activity might erode confidence amongst Indian moderates. To counter that he and Lord Minto, the Viceroy, pushed through minimal but significant political concessions. Previously, carefully selected Indians were appointed to All-India and provincial legislative councils. Now they would be elected in small numbers. The numbers and electorates would be tightly controlled but the electoral principle established, a reform long sought by Indian Moderates. It was an important symbolic shift, and disliked intensively by the ICS mainstream. Senior Madras officials demanded that the 'official' majority on Councils be maintained for as long as possible.[17]

Galletti should have been delighted because the reform mirrored his support for moderate Indians sharing national governance, allowing his key Indian friends to contemplate increased political influence. Curiously, though, he ignored the change in his memoir, emphasising instead his 'influence' over Morley at the micro rather than macro level. It was the first sign his strategic-level thinking outstripped his tactical-level actions, and that weakness persisted throughout his career. He cannot have missed the importance of the reforms. His main concern, though, was to establish the importance and influence of sympathetic 'on the ground' administrators, like him, rather than recognise the rising popular support for political reform. For him the future still lay with enlightened and paternalistic administrators. Such people, he thought, would improve conditions far more for average Indians than would grand strategists and Congress politicians.

That was why his Cocanada riots account discounted the political angle—he rarely conceded that nationalist political

---

17 Acting Chief Secretary GOM to GOI, 26 January 1909, GO 63-64, 26 January 1909, p. 8253, IOR.

sentiment could move local people whose concerns, he thought, were more mundane. The available Cocanada evidence contradicts that view. The Morley Papers do contain the original Monkswell letter about sedition legislation, but no other Galletti letters. They may have been written of course, but Monkswell probably did not pass them on for fear of his nephew attaining even more infamy. Similarly, Government of Madras papers are silent on discussions Galletti claimed to have with the Governor and senior officials concerning the affair.

The memoir version's fundamentals are accurate, then, but the alterations overplay Galletti's role as a fearless reformer with a respectful audience at the highest levels, influencing high policy and triumphing locally over petty and reactionary opposition. That intoxicating self-view took him to dark places professionally, about which Sir James Thomson warned him.[18] Thomson recalled Galletti had ignored his advice during earlier 'escapades', and imagined Galletti would take his 'own way to the end of time'. Any government, Thomson argued, expected full support for its policies from those who voluntarily joined its service. Agreed, a man did not forfeit all civilian rights when joining the ICS, but he should either serve wholeheartedly or resign to fight the government openly from outside. With his 'short experience and peculiar temperament', Galletti was 'undertaking a very serious business' in writing to senior British figures questioning approved policies in India. Perceptively, Thomson identified Clara as a wise woman to whom Galletti should listen before undertaking further reckless action. Sir Murray Hammick offered similar advice. He suggested others joined Galletti in disliking repression, but writing 'violent private letters' to influential people in England was highly unwise.[19]

Thomson and Hammick knew Galletti would ignore them. The Government of Madras prosecuted Bipin Chandra Pal for sedition when he finally reached Madras. In his memoir Galletti claimed

---

18 Thomson to Galletti, 29 October 1908.
19 Hammick to Galletti, 13 April 1908.

to have opposed the prosecution, an arrest would simply create a martyr. Galletti was overruled but reprised his 'get a message to Morley' tactic, leading to Morley's intervention overturning the Government decision. As earlier, the available evidence does not support the claim, but Morley did consider action: the India Office drafted him a 'stay' order against the Government of Madras. That order was never issued, however, once further investigation confirmed the grounds on which the Government of Madras action was based.[20] Galletti probably did approach Morley directly or indirectly, then, at the very time senior and influential Madras officials advised against doing that.

Galletti claimed his direct access to and pervading influence over Morley and London administrators remained so strong that when Sir William Meyer returned to Madras as Chief Secretary in 1909, he considered government authority threatened so curbed Galletti's freedom. Meyer, Galletti's contentious Simla Telugu examiner, removed him to deal with the princely state of Pudukottai whose ruler was in trouble for, among other things, marrying an Australian woman. Galletti thought his deployment also caused by further newspaper articles he wrote about the sedition legislation. Whether or not that was so, by going over his superiors' heads Galletti placed himself well outside the 'Steel Frame' of acceptable behaviour.

Remarkably, amidst this drama Galletti revealed his excellent analytical and intellectual skills in two scholarly forms: his mastery of the Madras archival records; and his deep interest in the historical context of his new country.

The second skill was demonstrated quickly in his 1902 translation of Kandukuri Veeresalingam's *The Vinodha Tarangini*, or *Pleasure's Whirligig*. Veeresalingam was the great pioneer Telugu social reformer who reawakened interest in the language's literature and in Andhra history and culture. Galletti

---

20   Draft telegram 30 September 1907, L/PJ/6/830/3346, IOR.

discovered the works when he was first in Madras, considering them far more interesting than the texts prescribed under the ICS syllabus.[21] He approached Veeresalingam who approved a translation.

In his introduction to the text Galletti suggested he chose the work for its brevity, but there were deeper reasons. The central story concerns an older widower who remarries a much younger woman. She betrays him with a younger man while all around young widows enter illicit relationships, one falling pregnant. These issues become court cases but having taken a bribe, a local magistrate overlooks the 'crimes'. The story borders farce, but showcases Veeresalingam's campaign to allow widow remarriage, remove "social" issues from the legal code, and eliminate local administrative corruption.

Arthur Galletti had personal and professional interests in this. Relationships and social reform interested him deeply, as demonstrated in the preparation for and conduct of his own marriage. Galletti's copy of George Bernard Shaw's *The Irrational Knot*, for example, contains penciled comments on: 'the irrational knot of marriage'; whether 'upper class' women were *all* pure, innocent and frigid; and whether upper class social attitudes were superior to those of the working class.[22] Galletti considered sexual abstinence abnormal, so in his view widow remarriage would create more rewarding lives and reduce social problems.

Galletti's second interest was his strong preoccupation with the lives and rights of 'ordinary' people whom he called "real" Indians. Veeresalingam depicted an intricate, tough, corrupt village world Galletti believed his colleagues did not understand or even recognise. Some colleagues knew more than he allowed, of course, but Galletti always believed that the higher levels of politics on both sides, especially the nationalist one, meant

---

21 See the approved list in *The Indian civil service manual: Madras* (Madras, Government Press, 1941 edn), pp. 22-3.

22 Shaw, George Bernard, *The irrational knot* (London, Constable, 1905).

little to 'real' people who trusted the British to alleviate their village lot. His ambition was to get ICS men out of the Secretariat and into the *mofussil* where they would better serve the British mission. He dismissed nationalist activity as irrelevant to local life, putting him increasingly at odds with Secretariat thinking as the years passed.

That emphasis on 'the people' convinced Galletti the Telugu taught to ICS men was far removed from that spoken in streets and markets, and he wanted to master the idiomatic version. Because of that he compiled a Telugu dictionary emphasising the language's 'common' aspect in contrast to the mid 19th century literary lexicon created by the great C.P. Brown.[23] Galletti began his dictionary while translating Veeresalingam, but completed it only in the early 1930s.[24] The 'street Telugu' emphasis emerges strongly, along with the 'people's' willingness to defy Raj authority. For example, he has an official opening a cattle show speech with the word 'ryots' [peasants]. Galletti's translation decodes that as meaning: "From Madras the great Board Member having deigned to come here from a great distance and what he says is "ryots." That captured Galletti's view of the cloistered Secretariat men, people who belittled and denigrated 'real Indians'. Another phrase goes: "how dare you ridicule me after having gone through an outlandish English education?" *Carmabhumi* he translated as "Pious India, just as the Yankees call the United States God's own country". He translated one expression as: "what are the police doing leaving so many lunatics to wander about in public?" Yet another emerged as "will the superior authorities dismiss a man without any reason at all?" "in clear reference" to his own career. The dictionary reflected his interest in social conditions and relationships with

---

23   Brown: C.P. *English-Telugu dictionary* (Delhi, Oscar, 2007 edn) and *Essay on the language and literature of the Telugus* (Delhi, Asian Educational, 1991 edn).

24   Galletti, A. *Galletti's Telugu dictionary: a dictionary of current Telugu* (Oxford, OUP, 1935).

several references to dancing girls, courtesans, pimps, obscene songs and *nautch girl* processions. He translates one expression as "better to celebrate the old man's funeral than his wedding,' echoing Veeresalingam.

Throughout his career, Galletti continued that deep interest in Telugu along with its implications for social reform and cultural understanding, and published Telugu pamphlets on issues ranging from basic concepts of Christian festivals like Easter to the role of co-operative societies in improving life for the 'people'. In the latter, his attitudes were displayed wonderfully in the title: *Sahacarula Parapati Sanghamalu [Cooperative Credit Societies]: Written in current Telugu and not in the dialect of the pedants whose continued use in Literature is one of those harmful Mamuls* [habits] *that prevent the Telugus attaining their intellectual majority.*

Galletti's language studies led him directly to the history and customs of every district in which he worked. That took him into the old records held in Collectorate offices, and he constantly instructed government on precedent based in those records. That interest extended beyond Andhra and, indeed, his most ambitious work involved editing Dutch records on the Malabar district held in the Madras records office, forerunner of the Tamilnadu Archives.[25] Galletti used his German skills to work on those records alongside Dutch missionaries, translating a mass of important records concerning the Dutch presence in southwest India. On the strength of that work, Galletti became a corresponding member of the Jakarta-based Dutch East Indies Asia Society.

His mastery of the records and their underlying bureaucratic procedures led to his second major scholarly interest, creating important legislative guidelines. In part he wanted to show government he could do it, but he also thought that pushing

---

25 Galletti, A. Rev. A.J. van der Burg and Rev. P. Groot, *Selections from the records of the Madras Government Dutch records, No. 13* (Madras, Government Press, 1911).

government towards more rational procedures and policies would improve life for 'real' people, and make work easier for field officers. His first effort was *The Madras Lunacy Manual for Magistrates* (Madras, Government Press, 1906). He retrieved every relevant Order ever issued by government, codifying and streamlining them so local authorities could process specific cases quickly and humanely. Galletti displayed a marvellous ability to find, rationalize and sequence discrete orders and policies in ways that made sense. He repeated the process with the Madras ecclesiastical guide, and early in World War I made a strong contribution to the reordering of municipal government in the Presidency.

During this same period, however, Galletti saw some strong supporters move on, replaced by men who saw things differently. In mid-1910 two senior Members of the Board of Revenue and Council retired quickly and unexpectedly. Service gossip had Sir John Morley, the Secretary of State with whom Galletti was supposedly in contact, informing R.H. Bradley and Sir John Atkinson directly they should expect no further personal advancement under the new reforms. They were reputedly too conservative for Morley who was sending the recalcitrant Madras Government a message.[26] Meyer's arrival as Chief Secretary in 1909 escalated the change and Galletti was assigned more proscribed work, principally with Pudukottai but also with other Madras states controlled by *rajahs*, including tiny Banganapalle on which Galletti also did historical work.[27]

In mid-1910, Galletti took timely leave for almost two years–apart from the two months leave taken in 1906 to marry Clara he had spent no time outside India at all. He returned to Italy to see his ill father who died early in 1912. The estate was inordinately complicated and Galletti spent most of his time unraveling the

---

26 Gwynn J.T. letter, 16 June 1910, J.T. Gwynn Papers, CSAA.

27 Galletti, A. *Selections from the records of the Madras Government: papers relating to the history of the Banganapalle State* (Madras, Government of Madras, nd [c. 1912]).

mess. He arrived back in Madras early in 1912, was posted briefly to Bezwada then back to Madras where he worked on municipal reform legislation for two years until early 1916. As World War I loomed, Galletti's identity and allegiances swung back into view.

Galletti compounded perennial suspicions about his loyalty by trying to import a foreign servant. As usual, there was a twist. The Gallettis advertised in Europe for a servant to help Clara with her daily work, especially when the children were home from school. The most promising respondent was Emma Helena Bechtler, a predominantly German-speaking Swiss citizen born in Allahabad in the United Provinces of India. She wished to return to India so was perfect for their needs with her European background, language capability and Indian experience. An elaborate exchange unfolded between Madras, New Delhi, London and Geneva via Zurich. The complication was that although Ms Hechtler was 'British', being born in India, she was denied a British passport being now a Swiss resident. The Secretary of State had to gain permission for her entry to India from the government controlling the first port at which she arrived. That was Bombay.[28] Eventually Emma Hechtler gained permission but by then the Gallettis had changed their minds, so she never arrived. For anti-Galletti Secretariat forces this was further proof of his perversity, pro-European and anti-English attitudes. It was also an occasion when he was simply unlucky—government procedures made the appointment almost impossible, and he was seeking the best possible result for his family. His reputation and record rather than the matter itself caused the official indignation.

When World War I broke out Italy was technically a member of the Triple Alliance with Germany and the Austro-Hungarian Empire, so should have marched against Britain and the allies. Given Galletti's Italian status, he would then have become an alien. However, Italy sat out the opening phase of the war then in early 1915 joined the allies against Austria-

---

28   See L/PJ/6/1348/309, IOR, for some of this.

Hungary and further, in mid-1916, against Germany. Between 1915 and 1917 the Italians made little headway against Austria on the Italian Front, then suffered a major defeat at Caporetto in October-November 1917.

Shortly after the war began Galletti contributed an article on Italian viewpoints to a book published in the name of the Governor, Lord Pentland.[29] He wrote the piece in September 1914, around the time the German cruiser 'Emden' fired over 100 shells on Madras destroying 350,000 gallons of oil and inflicting a psychological blow on British India. Arguing there was "no such thing as a national mind', Galletti divided the Italian nation into three groups. Military and naval officers wanted to declare war on Austria immediately, he thought. The upper and middle classes supported that view. The working classes, however, opposed war strongly following bitter experiences supplying soldiers to die in Italy's imperialist North African adventures.

Significantly, Galletti wrote, the world thought the whole Italian nation supported those adventures, because the international press never reported unarticulated working class oppositionist views. Now, however, Italian life had changed greatly as all classes travelled throughout Europe seeking work, seeing new ways of governing. Italy was experiencing great democratic change unlike England, he continued, where the "old tyrannies of squire and parson and magistrate, the old quaint medievalisms and insularities subsist." Apart from his brother-in-law [Willy Salvadori], Galletti argued, no sensible Italian supported the Austrians against whom Italians fought during unification. Most Italians now supported war against Germany—Italians made no distinctions between Germans and Austrians, he said! However, the former Prime Minister and politically influential Giovanni Giolitti advocated neutrality, so Italy would not join the war immediately.

---

29 A. Galletti, "Italy and the war" in G.A. Natesan (ed.), *All about the war: the Indian review war book* (Madras, Natesan nd [1915]).

There were three important aspects to Galletti's article. First, it revealed great insight into Italian political conditions and related European war views. Second, it demonstrated an ability, even a willingness to set aside blind nationalist acceptance of the war, as well as normal 'national' ascriptions on whether countries were 'for' or 'against' the conflict. Third, Galletti assessed the issues clinically rather than patriotically. These points contrasted starkly with the piece written for the same book by his Council Member, Sir Alexander Cardew.[30] Cardew's Nietzche was a half-mad, bloodthirsty philosopher not worth the name who suffered from 'unreasonable egotism'. Nietzche's imagination of the Superman driven by blood and iron rather than human sentiment created the 'pernicious doctrines" now displayed by Germans at war, and underlay the philosophy and doctrines, the 'mental attitude', of 'Pan-Germanism' now pursued by the German state. Cardew thought it 'perfectly clear that the German people themselves entirely endorse the actions of their rulers". Hopefully, the 'impending punishment' of defeat would "help restore them to a saner attitude towards life'. Cardew's Germany, unlike Galletti's Italy, was a nation of non-dissenting people with but one thought, domination over all others whose welfare was immaterial. Galletti's article stood out, his comments on English 'democracy' angering Madras Europeans.

Soon after the editor, G.A. Natesan asked Galletti for a revised version to appear in the *Indian Review's* June 1915 edition. Natesan was the sort of person to whom Galletti warmed. A Brahmin still only in his mid-thirties, he was an aggressively productive entrepreneur who supported the Indian National Congress, thrived on vigorous debate and supported many local causes. Possessing 'a rough and brusque exterior', he was also the sort of man who bothered senior Madras officials.[31] Galletti quickly

---

30 Cardew, A.G. "Nietzche and the war", in Natesan (ed), pp. 289-90.

31 See the entry on Natesan in *Who's who In India* 1911, (Lucknow, Newul Kishore, 1911).

wrote "Why Italy Has Declared War?" declaring himself an ICS member and *Cavagliere Della Cornona D 'Ítalia,* the title awarded for his services to the Madras Italian community.[32] Again, British readers disliked his apparently divided loyalties. He revisited his earlier argument that Italian upper and middle classes supported Britain and the Allies while the 'mass' opposed war. In Italy, he continued (meaning, no doubt, unlike India) mass opinion was considered by political leaders. Why otherwise, he wondered, did the Italian controlling classes take nine months to join the Allies formally? Creating attitudinal change among the masses in 'so democratic a country' as Italy, he suggested, required time-consuming consultation. Italian support for Germany ebbed steadily, he continued, as Italy's influential classes watched German power spread across Europe, undisturbed and unchallenged by Britain. Galletti asserted Italian military forces were stronger than the British, able to raise up to two million men, however only 750, 000 would be required to detain the enemy along the mountain front that would be dominated by the *Alpini.* Two points should be remembered, he concluded: Italy declared its neutrality before England and France declared war; and Italy did not enter the war only when Britain and the Allies looked like being clear winners. Italy made a principled decision and entered when the outcome was highly uncertain in wake of Britain's Dardanelles fiasco.

His rational, even innocuous observations enraged the Madras commercial elite with T.E. Welby, the *Madras Times* editor, leading a delegation to the Secretariat to complain. Welby was extremely conservative, and shifted to Calcutta soon after as Secretary of the European Association that opposed all constitutional change. Welby's delegation argued that Galletti savaged British strategy by declaring the Dardenelles campaign a failure, and by criticising Giolitti who was highly

---

32 For Galletti's version of these events, see his memorial to the Governor [1930], Galletti Papers.

regarded in allied quarters. This antagonism towards Galletti was compounded by strong anti-German and even anti-Italian feelings as demonstrated in the forced repatriation from Madras of nationals from those countries: by September the number was almost 250.[33] German and Austrian citizens who remained were banned from travelling to sensitive areas like the Nilgiri Hills.[34] Well over 100 Italian firms were identified as passing into India inquiries from German companies seeking to beat trade bans.[35]

Galletti claimed he wrote factual, 'dispassionate history' while others pandered to over-passionate nationalism that ignored facts and was fuelled by hysterical fears. He was right, but Secretariat bosses like Alan Butterworth and Alexander Cardew, the Nietzche 'expert', yielded to Welby and forbade Galletti permanently from public writing. Galletti resented that bitterly. A year later, he wrote to C.G. Todhunter, the Chief Secretary, accusing him and the-then Chief Secretary Butterworth of not checking facts before bowing to the public pressure. Galletti could not resist a barb: "what price now Dardenelles expedition and the alleged Prussian victories of 1915?"[36] The following day he withdrew the comment, fearing it might be construed as a 'challenge'.

The Battle of Caporetto routed the Italians, and Galletti volunteered to go with British troops to the Italian front as a liaison officer between the two armies where he would, he said, serve opposite his brother who filled a similar role for Italy. He saw the Governor and the Private Secretary to the Viceroy to press his case, but was refused permission to leave India. Neither Madras nor Delhi wanted him anywhere near a war zone, and there were strong reasons for that.

---

33 GOM GO 2092 Judicial, 3 September 1915 in Madras Proceedings P/Conf/11, 1915, IOR.

34 GOM GO 1105 Judicial, 19 May 1915, Madras Proceedings P/Conf/11, 1915, IOR.

35 GOM GO 1321 Judicial, 14 June 1915, Madras Proceedings P/Conf/11, 1915, IOR.

36 Galletti to Chief Secretary, 16 November 1916, Galletti Papers.

In mid-1916, while serving in Chittoor District, Galletti informed the Chief Secretary that Italian authorities were demanding he pay the war tax imposed on all Italians exempted from military service.[37] Galletti wanted to clarify his position, seeking Secretariat assurance his leave and pension rights would continue if he was called up to the Italian army, unlikely though that was. This was simple enough but Galletti's attitude, record, approach, litigiousness and ability to alienate ensured that the 'nationality' affair, as it became known, stretched over five years and confirmed him as a difficult person.

He received no response for 10 months, because the Government of Madras referred the issue to the Government of India that referred it to London for a Secretary of State ruling. Acting Chief Secretary Lionel Davidson wrote to Delhi, urging no support for the renegade. Because Galletti insisted on retaining dual nationality, Davidson wrote, he could now be called to serve a 'foreign power'. That would be embarrassing because all ICS officers should serve in a British or British Indian military unit if required. Galletti should "be now required to renounce his Italian nationality so as to relieve himself from the liability to which he draws attention".[38]

The Governor and his senior advisors anticipated difficulty with Galletti and were determined he declare firm and unequivocal allegiance to Britain, remembering his recent war articles and earlier pro-Boer ones. The Government of India demurred initially. One official thought Madras 'very arbitrary' in pressing Galletti to renounce Italian citizenship. Italy was an ally, after all; insisting on renunciation would be 'particularly graceless'. Galletti was unlikely to be called up for Italy, so Government should await any Italian request before declaring

---

37 Galletti to Chief Secretary, GOM, 10 July 1916, Galletti Papers–also in Notes Political–A. October 1916, Nos 257-258, NAI.

38 Acting Chief Secretary GOM to Secretary, Home, GOI, 31 July 1916, Notes 257-258, October 1916, NAI–the following section drawn from this file.

a policy. The Government of India insisted, though, that it had two claims on Galletti: as a British subject, and as a Crown servant. The Secretary of State, Herbert Samuel, had just ruled that dual-nationals must renounce such status if they wanted to serve the British government. As the case reached more senior Government of India officers, sympathy for Galletti dwindled.

Alexander Muddiman was just a year older than Galletti, but after a stellar Bengal career transferred to the Government of India and became Secretary to the Legislative Department in 1915. He later served on the Viceroy's Council and was Governor of the United Provinces for a short while before his early death in 1928. When Muddiman saw the file, he commented acidly that Galletti seemed 'rather a hyphenated kind of Englishman'. As a British subject Galletti, like the Irish maverick Roger Casement, owed total allegiance to the Crown and if he transgressed should receive 'the usual reward for such an indiscretion'. Galletti might risk a treason trial in Italy, by refusing to pay the tax or report for service, but that was the fate of people choosing 'to keep a foot in both countries". It was, another senior officer considered, remarkable that the India Office had allowed such a man to enter the ICS in the first place.

The Government of India submitted Galletti's case to London for resolution, remarking that he "seems hardly to appreciate his position or to realize fully the obligations" incurred in becoming a government officer. Whatever the decision on Galletti, Delhi argued, no more dual nationals should enter the ICS. On 9 March 1917 the India Office, after consulting the Foreign Office about possible Italian reactions, instructed Delhi to direct Madras to direct Galletti to renounce his Italian citizenship.[39]

Galletti contested the decision immediately.[40] He would not proceed with the matter, he declared, and it now occurred to him he might not have to renounce. During his Oxford days

---

39 See GOI, Public, Notes-A. May 1918, Nos 535-543.

40 Galletti to Chief Secretary, 25 May 1917, and 12 June 1917, Galletti Papers.

he served in military volunteers corps, and was currently in the Indian National Defence Force. Further reading of the Italian Civil Code suggested he might have lost Italian citizenship already by serving in a 'foreign' military service. He provided further detail on how, first, he postponed his Italian service by paying a fee then, second, switching that service liability to his brother. Clemens Galletti did the training in *lieu* of Arthur during 1905-06 and was now serving with the Italian forces. Furthermore, Galletti himself was nearing 41, and after that age the Italians would not call him up-had Italian law on that changed, then the village Mayor would have informed Galletti who paid the man a pension as a former land steward on his properties!

Galletti lectured the Governments of Madras and India that it was unwise to provoke a diplomatic incident with the Italians at this delicate point in the war. Dual nationality and tax liability were tricky matters prone to taking 'an awkward turn'. Government was advised to leave well alone.

Galletti prefaced this with a private letter to Lionel Davidson that also reached Delhi.[41] He hoped the Italian authorities would not be bothered anymore. If he was called up the ruling could be challenged then, but challenging now would embarrass both Government and Galletti. He did not want to deprive his children, especially his sons, of the opportunity to gain dual nationality. He himself could have renounced earlier in life and would do so now if necessary—'I am not therefore taking up the attitude that to renounce one country for fear of having to fight for it is a thing which simply is not done, or anything of that sort'. In fact, he wrote, he defied his father in the 1890s by threatening to renounce Italian citizenship in order to take the Oxford scholarship rather than accept the Italian military commission engineered by his father and favoured by his mother. In writing to his father, Galletti had described "the glories of the British

---

41 Galletti to Davidson, 6 June 1917, GOM Public GO 1003 (Ms) 6 August 1917, TNA.

Empire in India and the career there on which he had set his heart'. His father threatened to remove him to Italy by force, but did not do so. He did cut off financial support, however, causing Galletti's reliance on Collier money and tutoring.

This response hardened Delhi attitudes further.[42] Muddiman believed Galletti was trying to evade the Secretary of State's orders. Galletti must obey the original order to renounce Italian citizenship, and the Government of Madras should ensure that happened. Galletti agreed to discuss the matter with the Italian Consul-General in Calcutta, but doubted he could renounce. During September 1917 Galletti met senior Madras government officials suggesting to the Governor's Private Secretary, T.E. 'Tommy' Moir, that the Galletti solution remained the best![43] By then Galletti had received further complicated advice from the Italian Consul-General who argued Galletti was still a Torre San Patrizio taxpayer liable to Italian laws. Galletti then met Madras Council member H.F.W. Gilman, Sir Alexander Cardew and the Governor but the meetings were inconclusive, Cardew having 'a bee in his bonnet' about Galletti's intransigence.[44]

Galletti now wrote a 24 page memorandum to the Secretariat, complaining that he 'felt like a spectator in the street watching persons dancing in a ground-floor room'.[45] He had not seen Government of Madras case files (which he should not have had access to anyway), he said, but they should confirm he had cleared the citizenship issue before joining the service. Repeating the arguments as to why he should not renounce Galletti invoked the name of F.E. Smith, now Lord Birkenhead, who was at Oxford with him and who had confirmed the original legal position. Government was now breaching his ICS contractual rights by instructing him to relinquish dual nationality, and the Secretary of State had no legal

---

42 See GOI, Home Public, Notes-A. May 1918, Nos. 535-543, NAI.

43 Galletti to PSG, GOM, September 1917, Galletti Papers.

44 Galletti to Gilman, 1 October 1917, Galletti Papers.

45 Galletti to Chief Secretary, 30 September 1917, Galletti Papers.

power to issue the order. Galletti would comply if directed–but would also turn out for the Italian army if ordered to do so! Galletti complained he was 'between the upper and the nether mill stone. I did not acquire a double nationality. I was born with it'. He sent those provocative views off to the Government of India.

S.R. Hignell, a senior Home Department officer about to join the Legislative Council, considered that submission 'prolix, self-contradictory and involved', alienating any sympathy Galletti might otherwise have attracted.[46] The matter probably looked 'big' to Galletti, Hignell continued, but given present circumstances it would be 'Gilbertian' to bother the Italian government. Muddiman was more scathing. Galletti had exploited his double nationality and 'insinuated' himself into the ICS so as to gain a lucrative appointment while avoiding Italian military service. Now there were disadvantages in dual citizenship, he continued, Galletti was complaining. Once Galletti retired, Muddiman predicted, he would "throw off the English nationality which has been a convenient ladder for his support throughout his adult life". The man was entitled to no sympathy whatsoever.

Muddiman exaggerated the position, even twisted it, but revealed just how much Galletti alienated influential people in Madras and India. The matter was referred back to London and Edwin Montagu, the new Secretary of State, advised Delhi to inform Galletti he must renounce Italian citizenship.[47] Galletti's position was 'quite anomalous' and must be resolved. The Government of Madras directed Galletti to visit Calcutta and resolve the matter personally with the Consul-General. Galletti, typically, advised the Consul-General he was coming, drawing the man's attention to "another peremptory order" issued by the Government of Madras. That remark reached Delhi where one officer thought Galletti guilty of "a very childish and insubordinate indiscretion... Megalomania seems to have fairly overcome Mr Galletti."

---

46   GOI Home Public, Notes May 1918, Nos 535-543, NAI.

47   This section from GOI Home Public, January 1920, Notes 313-322, NAI.

Now incapable of yielding ground, Galletti composed a Memorial of Protest to the King, forwarding it to the Government of Madras. He referred to the 'cold and unkind and incomprehensible order' to terminate his Italian status.[48] Galletti withdrew the submission soon after, because he was by now in even bigger trouble over his Horsleykonda actions. Unbeknown to him, Madras never forwarded the Memorial anyway, possibly by accident but probably because officials wished to avoid further embarrassment. As one last twist, when Galletti did finally renounce citizenship he incurred an Italian fee that he demanded the Government of India pay. That aggravated matters further, the government pursuing him relentlessly to ensure he comply fully which he did, finally in 1922!

While Galletti fought those battles further Indian political change was in prospect. Recognising the war afforded Indians a chance to press political concessions, Annie Besant created the Home Rule League during 1916 using Theosophical Society networks across India to establish branches and stage protests.[49] Directed from her headquarters near the Adayar Club, this embarrassed the Government of Madras severely. The movement mushroomed drawing in Indian moderates, many of whom were leading Madras Brahmins and former government supporters. Mid-war, the Government of India and its provincial administrations struggled to handle the outbreak. In June 1917 Madras authorities arrested Annie Besant and interned her at Ootacamund, causing even more protests across India. Under instructions from London and Delhi the Government of Madras released her in September 1917, the Secretary of State trying to assuage public opinion by announcing further constitutional reforms. That was the backdrop for Galletti's next drama.

---

48   Galletti to Chief Secretary, 17 February 1919, Galletti Papers.

49   Owen, Hugh "Towards nationwide agitation and organisation: the Home Rule Leagues, 1915-1918 in D.A. Low (ed.), *Soundings in modern South Asian history* (Canberra, ANU Press, 1968).

5

White Mutiny

Two aspects of the new Indian constitutional change proposals known as the Montagu-Chelmsford Reforms alarmed Madras ICS men. First, power over selected provincial policy areas would transfer from the ICS to elected Indian ministers. Conservative ICS officers anticipated this split authority (known as 'dyarchy'— the term coined by Galletti's Simla mentor and Madras menace Sir William Meyer) ending life in India as they knew it. Second, 'Indianisation' of the superior civil services would accelerate, especially for the ICS. Fewer Europeans would enter the service, those already serving would see their contractual conditions deteriorate. Fewer 'prestige' promotion positions would be available. Many officers, believing their careers wrecked, deplored the initial non-provision of compensation for those now seeking early retirement.[1] There was an additionally provocative twist to the Madras position. One reform proposal suggested Indians recruited in Europe be paid European rates. The Madras Board of Revenue protested, why should Indians get equivalent pay? Board Members believed European ICS members should now be guaranteed even higher pay than Indians.[2]

That apprehensive, defensive and belligerent approach made Madras civilians the most conservative within India's European community, resisting even modest reform change and

---

1   For the India-wide expression of this attitude, see Claude H. Van Tyne, *India in Ferment* (New York, Appleton, 1923, pp. 58-9.

2   Board of Revenue Proceedings, GOM, Mis 460, 5 April 1918, P. 10919, IOR.

compromise proposals.[3] Edwin Montagu, the Secretary of State for India visited Madras near the end of 1917 and considered the Government there 'an impossible institution'. Officials were 'obstructive, angry, sullen, effortless'. Lord Pentland, the Governor, opposed change vehemently, believing even the earlier and mild Morley-Minto changes disastrous because Indians would never be fit to govern themselves.[4] Montagu noted a 'simply appalling' change in Madras attitudes. All had been harmonious on his first visit five years earlier. Now British hated Indians who reciprocated, Hindus and Muslims bickered, government officials openly favoured non-Brahmins. In Madras, he believed, "officials administrate and do not govern."

Gilbert Slater, Professor of Indian Economics in the University of Madras and a government 'insider' at the time, later confirmed Montagu's frigid reception.[5] The Governor and ICS senior officials were convinced the reform proposals were premature, resented Montagu's intervention that released Annie Besant, and believed the Morley-Minto reforms had yet to be fully exploited. Outside government Galletti's friend C.P. Ramaswami Iyer was the only person to agree with Montagu's proposals, according to Slater. There was, however, a deeper and sharper edge against Montagu whose appointment as Secretary of State astonished Pentland and his Madras advisers.

Put as simply as possible, Indian mints had several years earlier been restricted in the amount of silver coins they could produce. As a result, a complex system arose through which India's sterling commitments were met in London by the sale of bills that entitled

---

3   For an outline of this, see Robb, Peter "The bureaucrat as reformer: two Indian civil servants and the Constitution of 1919" in Peter Robb and David Taylor (eds), *Rule, protest, identity: aspects of modern South Asia* (London, Curzon, 1978).

4   Venetia Montagu (ed.), Montagu, Edwin S. *An Indian diary* (London, Heinemann, 1930), pp. 109-138 outlines his experiences in Madras.

5   The following sections drawn from Gilbert Slater, *Southern India: it's political and economic problems* (London, Allen & Unwin, 1936), ch. xxv.

the purchaser to receive in India rupees with which more export goods might be purchased. Those rupees were made available in silver sanctioned by the Government of India. This system was influenced significantly by the climatic conditions in India that determined the quantity and quality of exports. In good monsoon years the demand for silver in India was high to meet the rupee demands, in poor years it was low. The Secretary of State, in effect, was the single greatest influence on the silver market.

A 1907 famine caused silver demand to decline. Following seasons were good but the then Secretary of State did not call the usual tenders for supply of the necessary silver. Dealers, banks and individuals speculated heavily in anticipation of demand and the silver price soared. Then, suddenly, the India Office announced that no further tenders would be called because the firm of Samuel Montagu and Co. had provided all necessary silver supplies in a secret deal. The price crashed, several other firms were bankrupted, a bank in Bombay fell, and innumerable European and Indian investors were ruined. Edwin Montagu was Under-Secretary of State for India at the time, his father the head of Samuel Montagu and Co.

Pentland and his advisers were astonished that, given such recent history, Edwin Montagu could now be placed directly in charge of Indian currency and trading conditions. His reformist zeal simply added to their concerns and, it must be said, his being Jewish helped add to their scorn. By the time Montagu arrived in Madras he stood little chance of changing their minds on constitutional matters.

More than ever, Galletti found himself in a system programmed to resist change, and at a time of other serious pressures: Mrs Besant's Home Rule agitation coincided with serious food shortages and grain riots. On one occasion, Galletti had to hurry out to the Chittoor markets and emphasise that government would not tolerate looting despite local rumours to the contrary. Within this tense, volatile atmosphere Madras ICS members created a formal Association, a union to represent and lobby for their interests during reform negotiations. This was unprecedented, confirming the depth and extent of opposition to the reforms. Other provinces produced similar bodies, but Madras was first and most outspoken. Sir Alexander Cardew and H.R. Pate were prime movers and Arthur Galletti's dealings with them, plus his reputation for being difficult, doomed the rest of his career.

Cardew was an old style India hand. Born to an English clergyman and Scots mother, he reached Madras late in 1882 after attending Somersetshire College in Bath and Queen's College, Oxford. After initial district service he became Secretary to the Malabar Lands Committee, beginning a long Secretariat career across the key judicial, legislative, and revenue departments. Colleagues thought him a literary man who drafted elegant minutes on all subjects but eschewed the sports and games preferred by many. Critics considered him a legally-minded bureaucrat with too little *mofussil* experience and too much Secretariat service.[6] Inspector-General of Prisons was his first command post, he served later as Collector of Madras and Chairman of the Harbour Trust Board. By 1904 he was Secretary to several departments and appointed to the Madras Legislative Council. In 1908 he became Secretary to the Revenue Department, was appointed Chief Secretary in 1912 and shortly later knighted for his work. From 1914 until his retirement he was on the Board of Revenue and the Governor's Executive Council. It was a conventional, conformist career.

The 'White Mutiny' affair came near the end of that career, and even by Madras standards Cardew was extremely conservative on political reform. In 1913, he was attacked vehemently by an Indian member of the Royal Commission on The Public Services in India who despised Cardew's insistent view that allowing Indians to undertake ICS entrance examinations in England

---

6   For one view, see Gwynn J.T. letters, 2 August 1907 and 8 April 1912, J.T. Gwynn Papers, CSAA.

would automatically reduce European cadre numbers.[7] Cardew preferred advancing India by administrative action rather than by the political advances of our time'. That is, the paternalist bureaucrat rather than the ballot box should determine India's future. He was an active paternalist, though, undertaking extensive prison reform work, especially after his retirement, and doing much to improve life for untouchables.

He 'inspired in no small degree' the conservative Government of Madras response to the Montagu-Chelmsford reforms.[8] Significantly for Galletti, Cardew became Acting Governor in March-April 1919 prior to his retirement, positioned perfectly to attack the 'People's Collector'. Lady Mary Cardew and Clara Galletti being good friends added complication. Their friendship dated back to Galletti's Secretariat days in Madras and Ooty. Whenever Clara was in either place, she called on the bird-and nature-loving Lady Cardew whose company she enjoyed and who regularly entertained the Galletti children while they were at school in Ootacamund.

Henry Reginald Pate, three years younger than Galletti, was educated at Clifton then King's College, Cambridge, arriving in Madras late in 1904. Appointed first into the important Tamil-speaking Tanjore district he spent considerable time in the field, much of it in Tinnevelly where he produced the District Gazetteer that appeared in 1917 when Galletti became Collector there. In 1916, early in his career, Pate became Secretary to the Revenue Department where he remained during the period of the White Mutiny. Seconded later to the Government of India as Deputy Secretary of the Army Department, he returned to Madras as a Collector before resuming as Secretary of the Revenue Department in 1928. From 1929 until his 1934 retirement he was Second Secretary to Government, a member of Galletti's despised 'Board'.

7   Report of the *royal Commission on the Public Services in India: Appendix Vol. II-Minutes of evidence taken in Madras* (London, HMSO, 1914), pp. 120-123.

8   *The times*, 14 January 1937.

Cardew and Pate were the most prominent Association leaders but powerful fellow committee members backed them. L.E. Buckley, the Chairman, was a Board of Revenue Member; T.E. (Tommy) Moir was Private Secretary to the Governor and would later become Chief Secretary and Member of the Board; Mr. Justice W.W. Phillips was a senior judge (who shared accommodation with R.A. Graham who also became Chief Secretary soon after); and G.T. Boag was an influential Secretariat man.

Hilton Brown's presence demonstrated the strength of opposition to the reforms. Brown was a novelist who, under the title "H.B.", wrote regularly for *Punch* throughout his Indian days and years later, after independence in 1947, returned to live in south India. He was said to 'imitate Kipling' with his 'delicate satire and irony' when writing about south Indian life.[9] Like Galletti he was instinctively liberal, inclined to challenge Board and Government, but on this issue held very different views from Galletti because of the perceived threat to service conditions. The importance of the Association was underlined a few years later in one of his novels with the hero, a member of the Association, despairing that it was all too late to make a difference and that Europeans would become a minority in the service. One character, a senior judge, suggests that ICS officers had experienced 20 years of growing Congress opposition matched by 20 years of absent support from provincial, national and 'Home' authorities.[10] That suggests the depth of anxiety and dissatisfaction then prevailing, and that Galletti challenged.

Other inaugural ICS Association members reflected this broad attitude and opposition. A.R. Knapp was still there, described by a junior colleague as a short, stout but able and hardheaded man, for which read traditionalist.[11] Lord Willingdon, the new Governor,

---

9   Singh, B. *A summary of Anglo-Indian fiction*, (Delhi, 1934).

10   Brown, Hilton *Dismiss!* (London, Methuen, 1923), pp. 112-168.

11   Gwynn J.T. letter, 8 April 1912, J.T. Gwynn Papers, CSAA.

thought Knapp's opposition to the reforms so strong he might not return after scheduled home leave.[12] Sir Frank Noyce was a Madras ICS officer with a distinguished All-India record, and a history of supporting Galletti. No diehard he was worried, however, by the reform proposals. M.E. Couchman was yet another Board member. J.C. Molony was well-known for his writings on Madras and its history—he worked closely with Galletti while seconded to the Rajah of Pudukottai shortly before the war.

Galletti, then, seemingly stood alone in defying Madras reforms opposition, with even his few usual supporters this time arrayed against him.

David Washbrook identifies another contemporary development isolating Galletti from the broad group.[13] Normally Government's traditional allies and supporters, the leading Madras Brahmins moved closer to Congress, Washbrook argues. Cardew headed a senior ICS group that responded by promoting non-Brahmins to reserved government posts, so placing them in powerful positions. Joining Cardew were Sir Lionel Davidson, Sir Murray Hammick (Galletti's early career sponsor) and H.F.W. Gillman, all senior ICS men and all ill-disposed towards the reforms, although Montagu considered Gillman slightly more open-minded—unfortunately, he died just towards the end of 1917 so his restraining influence was lost. Among Brahmin targets for this group were Galletti's important contacts C.P. Ramaswami Iyer, P.S. Sivaswami Iyer and his troublesome publisher G.A. Natesan. Those connections, however tenuous, put Galletti further offside with the Cardew group who actively encouraged public comments like those from 'A Christian' who suggested that Indianisation of the ICS would be, in fact, Brahminisation when everyone knew Brahmins had always failed when elevated to senior positions.[14]

---

12   Willingdon to Montagu, 20 May 1919, Eur D 523/19, IOR.

13   Washbrook, D. A. *The emergence of provincial politics: the Madras presidency, 1870-1920* (Cambridge, CUP, 1976), pp.

14   "A Christian" Letter to the Editor, *Madras Mail*, 3 January 1919.

The Cardew clique push was very effective: Sir Valentine Chirol, the influential London writer and diplomat reflected its views fully in his contemporary account of Madras.[15]

Galletti was challenging a powerful and closed network.[16] Moir lived at Government House, privy to the Governor's reform and service issue discussions. Hemingway, who leaked the Horsleykonda story, lived at the Madras Club as did Pate (a career—focussed bachelor until his sudden marriage to an army widow during his mid-1920s Delhi relocation). Galletti's foibles and activities were well known and discussed at the Club. Cardew lived in the senior executive enclave at Adayar as did Lionel Davidson, who became Chief Secretary, a renowned bureaucrat who dealt uneasily and poorly with Indians.[17] Davidson would retire at the introduction of the reforms because, as his then Governor indicated, he could not adapt to the new order.[18] A.Y.G. Campbell, one of Galletti's main *bêtes noir*, lived at Adayar but also represented another closed network. He was District Grand Master in the Masonic Order popular with many other ICS men in the group—Buckley was Campbell's immediate predecessor in that post and he himself was preceded by Hammick. Boag would later succeed Campbell as District Grand Master, while Molony was yet another high ranking Mason. In yet another strand Cardew's daughter, Janet, was married to C.E. later Sir Edgar Wood, Managing Director of Parry and Co. (Parry's, as it was long known), a major Madras commercial house. Wood was also a member of the Madras Legislative Council. The strongly conservative business community, earlier

---

15 Valentine Chirol, Sir *India old and new* (London, Macmillan, 1921), pp. 222-4.

16 The following details are conveniently seen in the successive annual editions of *The Asylum Press Almanack and directory of Madras and Southern India* (Madras, Asylum Press).

17 Gwynn J.T. letter, 8 April 1912, J.T. Gwynn Papers, CSAA.

18 Lord Willingdon to Lord Reading, 1 April 1922, Reading Papers, MSS Eur E 238, IOR.

upset by Galletti's war views and pro-German reputation, was well connected to conservative ICS elements so the People's Collector was surrounded. Sealing the Government/business community concern was rising industrial unrest, especially in the Madras mills, and postwar food shortages.[19] Both provided Congress with additional opportunities to criticise British rule, so Galletti's intervention was even less welcome.

Someone leaked the first ICS Association meeting minutes to *New India* journalists who immediately published them under the banner headline: 'An ICS Association Formed—Reforms Criticised'.[20] The leaked draft statement was an extensive, melodramatic lament for the imminent decline of the European officer in India. His social and political importance would evaporate when made subject to the whims of elected Indian politicians. Promotion prospects were gone given the reduced numbers of 'superior' posts available. His district social life would disappear, being the only European there apart from his wife for whom life would become unbearable. ICS prospects were 'depressing', and all this was created without reference to serving officers. There were just two ways forward in the Association's collective view: either there should be no change whatsoever and the reforms scrapped, or financial assistance made available to service members seeking escape.

With so many senior ICS officers involved, government could not ignore this now public challenge. Pate was asked to confirm the reported comments. Were they accurate and, if so, how had they appeared in *New India*? Was the draft submitted either to the Government of India or the Secretary of State? Pate replied that the published report was merely a rough draft, not the final letter circulated to ICS members. The matter was confidential, it's public appearance a mystery! The government took no further

19 GOM Proceedings, P/Conf/48 1919, IOR.
20 This may be seen at Official Memorandum (Public Dept. GOM) to H.R. Pate, 805-1, 1 January 1919) in GO 115, 6 March 1919, P 10677, IOR.

action on this clear public criticism of the proposed reforms, confirming that reform scepticism and criticism characterised the Madras ICS and its senior executive.

The Secretariat's attitudes and arcane ways dismayed Lord Willingdon when he arrived in Madras as the new Governor early in 1919, smarting from his non-appointment as Viceroy which post he received a few years later. Writing to his close friend Edwin Montagu, Willingdon declared:

> The whole ICS here seem a different breed of men to those I've seen elsewhere: stodgy, bucolic looking, and I should think very difficult to shift.[21]

Willingdon returned to the theme frequently: Chief Secretary Lionel Davidson was disgruntled and saw danger in every speech made by an Indian; Knapp was stirring up fellow ICS officers about the iniquities of the reforms; Campbell was 'slow and sticky'. There were deep divisions between 'Secretariat' men and those out in the districts, and Secretariat workings were 'appallingly meticulous'.[22]

The Secretary of State and the Government of India knew that already, though many Delhi officers shared the reform doubts articulated by their southern colleagues. In October 1918, for example, the Government of Madras informed Delhi officially that 'the Governor in Council' (for which read the Governor's senior ICS advisors) entertained 'very great doubts as to the success of the scheme [dyarchy]', and repeated that view well into 1919.[23] That produced an extraordinary interpretation within the Government of India. It suggested that many permanent British officials in India had no experience themselves of participating in democratic institutions, so were 'frankly skeptical of their

---

21 Willingdon to Montagu, 15 April 1919, Willingdon Papers MSS Eur D 523/19, IOR.

22 See his letters of 23 April 1919 and 20 May 1919, *ibid.*

23 GOM to GOI, 19 October 1918, L/PJ/9/3, IOR.

suitability to an Eastern country'. Such officers worked daily with and sought to safeguard the best interests of ordinary people who possessed no political aspirations.[24] This was highly paternalistic, and steered attention away from the serious issues at the core of the opposition.

It was into this atmosphere and context that Galletti pitched his public response to the ICS Association's position paper, and H.R. Pate bore his wrath.

Pate represented everything Galletti was not: his service record was impeccable and conventional, he fulfilled early promise, succeeded at the All-India level, gained senior command positions easily and as anticipated. As Secretary to the new Madras ICS Association he aroused in Galletti a mixture of envy, scorn and ridicule. Even so, few anticipated Galletti's ferocious, public onslaught when Pate invited all Madras ICS officers to join the association, and to consider a draft submission to the All-India constitutional reform commission.

Even by Galletti standards, the outburst was spectacularly misguided. He composed a three-page open letter to Pate.[25] A local Chittoor press typeset and printed the final version. Galletti copied that printed version to all members of the Madras Commission dealing with the reform process; all ICS members of the Governments of India, Bombay and Bengal; the Lieutenant-Governors of the United Provinces, Punjab, Bihar and Orissa; the Chief Commissioners of the Central Provinces and Assam; and all retired ICS members on the Secretary of State's Council. Galletti ensured that every senior Indian civilian knew his views. For good measure, he slipped copies to northern and western Indian newspaper editors knowing they would publish. (That undercut his later claim he sent the submission 'confidential' and had no idea how it reached the papers).

---

24 See the correspondence in L/PJ/9/3, IOR.

25 A. Galletti to H.R. Pate, 16 December 1918, copy in possession of the author.

He was vitriolic. "Your draft is just one long, dismal whine. It is full of political innuendo; it is peevish, not to say mutinous in tone." He even attacked the writing style: "I suppose the [poor] grammar is due to your being beside yourselves with indignation when you composed this exquisite phrase." Galletti, like Willingdon, divided Madras ICS officers between 'real' district officers and Madras 'bureaucrats': "We *Mufassal* moderates are not going to be rushed into a White Mutiny by a clique of headquarters extremists". He insulted Pate, insisting any submission be prepared by someone who inspired confidence, not a 'junior member of the service' (that is, Pate, only three years younger than Galletti and substantive Secretary to the leading government department that served what, in this same letter, Galletti termed 'the paltry Board of Revenue').

Sarcasm, personality politics, envy and spite overshadowed Galletti's important debating points. He wanted the reforms to stand a chance of success: "I am for a move forward and I am optimistic about the Montagu-Chelmsford scheme's effect on our position." As well as an opportunity to assign India more political responsibility, he saw a chance to lift ICS housing, allowances and travel conditions. He went too far in three particular respects:

First, he lectured Pate on how reforms should follow a European model, arguing for a French or Italian style Prefecture system. Collectors would become Prefects in direct touch with Ministers, living in appropriate style so they might "dispense oriental hospitality and frequently entertain the Indian public'. As 'the son of an Italian deputy', naturally, he would provide all necessary information about relations between prefects and deputies as well as the general workings of the system!

Second, he puffed his own importance far too much. He pointed out, loftily, that he ran a Prefecture system as Collector in Tinnevelly where a 'council head' dispensed routine orders to subordinates, Galletti himself "fully occupied with [more] important work."

Sir Christopher Masterman was that 'council head' and many years later confirmed these arrangements, but less positively than Galletti.[26] Masterman recalled Galletti as a 'notorious' service figure, it being 'something of a mystery how he ever got into the ICS," despite his 'exceptional intellectual ability'. The Tinnevelly Prefect system had the senior Indian Deputy Collector rather than Masterman in charge, because the former had superior experience and knowledge. Placing an Indian in charge at such a sensitive time politically pleased Galletti if not his superiors. If that officer and Masterman agreed on any given issue, they acted accordingly. If they disagreed, which was rare, Galletti would adjudicate. According to Masterman, the serious disadvantage was that eminent local figures, expecting to deal with the Collector, disliked appearing before junior men. The system ended when the Deputy Collector criticised an entry in the District Superintendant of Police's diary and Galletti forwarded that to Madras. The Inspector-General of Police sought an explanation and it transpired that Galletti, over whose name the criticism appeared, had never seen the diary.

Galletti's third over-extension was that while wanting to give the reforms a chance, he supported the Montagu-Chelmsford scheme much less than his own, the one he had "thought out so long ago as 1902" when *he* "started the Andhra movement."

This blatant self-promotion and dismissal of others confirmed many Madras officials in thinking Galletti arrogant, ambitious and addled.

His stand won Indian admirers, though. P. Sambasiva Rao, an Ellore lawyer, was pleased that at least one ICS man held progressive views, and hoped Galletti would not be punished for his stand.[27] K. Narasinga Rao, a lawyer from the highly politicised Guntur district, wrote as a 'Moderate' to appreciate an ICS man

---

26   Sir Christopher Masterman memoirs, copy with the author and copy now also in India Office records.

27   P. Sambasiva Rao to Galletti, 4 February 1919, Galletti Papers.

supporting the legitimate aspirations of the Indian people.[28] These and similar letters strengthened Galletti's long held self-image as the only ICS man with Indian interests truly at heart.

Galletti's ferocious attack dismayed his family, and supporters like H.D.C. Reilly, a judge in North Malabar district that was on the eve of the Moplah rebellion.[29] Henry D'Árcy Cornelius Reilly's reaction tested Galletti's logic. An architect's son educated at Merchant Taylor's College and Corpus Christi College, Oxford, Reilly arrived in Madras a year before Galletti. Early on he loathed India but came to love it deeply and, after the standard district work, specialised in law becoming a full district and sessions judge in 1916. He became a High Court of Madras judge in the mid-1920s and retired in 1934, but stayed in India until 1947 and served as Chief Justice in the High Court of Mysore. Significantly, when leaving Malabar he was thanked publicly, being 'well known for his sympathy with Indian aspirations'.[30] He was little if at all removed from Galletti's own liberal disposition.

Reilly suggested Galletti had breached confidence-circulated confidentially, the draft should have been discussed publicly only with Pate's permission. Any ICS member might disagree with the proposal, but disagreement must be with the argument rather than be rudely personal. Reilly emphasised that Galletti damaged only himself with such a petty, abrasive stance. After all, Reilly commented, he and others joined Galletti in welcoming the reforms scheme though it threatened to 'finish' the ICS and perhaps even their own careers. Like Galletti, they wanted the reforms to proceed, but he had damaged the cause. In adopting

---

28 K. Narasinga Rao to Galletti, 29 January 1919, Galletti Papers.

29 H.D.C. Reilly to A.M.A.C. Galletti, 27 December 1918, Galletti Papers. Ironically, Galletti's son Roberto would marry the daughter of the man who oversaw the hanging of hundreds of Moplahs.

30 See H.D.C. Reilly Papers, Ms Eng c 6956, Bodleian Library, Oxford, for his background, and Sir Patrick Reilly Papers, MS Eng c. 6916 for a memoir of his parents.

an aggressive, personalised position Galletti had undermined the progressive position to which many civilians were drawn and which Galletti himself espoused. It was a strong point.

It also demonstrated that views inside the ICS were more complex than Galletti's starkly depicted division between progressives and recidivist reactionaries. One officer from Central India, for example, also argued that the younger ICS generation was being ignored but would not accept the reactionary views of the older brigade. The younger men had an alternative proposal but were gagged by procedural rules.[31] Many Madras officers similarly struggled to balance the clear need for constitutional change, their own futures, and a gap between what they saw in policy and 'on the ground' requirements. They also balanced loyalty to their work and the service against that to the people over whom they ruled. During the controversy, for example, J.A. Thorne wrote a poem for the *Madras Mail* entitled, "The Services Thank Their Friends", including this verse:

A thousand thanks. Yet some of us recall
Such hackneyed words as duty, right, tradition;
Believe our India is built on these.
Shall we foreswear our heritage, and brawl Like hucksters
for the ear of a Commission,
Weighing our honour gravely in rupees?[32]

Galletti held these views and was intent on doing his best for the Indian people, but underestimated the extent of the same feelings held by many of his colleagues.

---

31 See "Letter From a Member of the Indian Civil Service" in Ernest Barker, *The future government of India and the Indian Civil Service* (London, Methuen, 1919).

32 See J.A.T. [John Anderson Thorne], *Verses* (Madras, privately circulated, nd) in the Lady Alice Stokes Papers, CSAA. Thorne served as Salt Commissioner during the Gandhi campaigns and later had a distinguished career at the All-India level, being knighted for his services.

Jack Collier castigated Galletti for similar reasons.[33] The painter wrote one of his longest and strongest ever letters to 'deplore the tone of your letter to Pate'. Seeing 'spiteful abuse' replacing reasoned discussion Collier, like Reilly, identified everything wrong with the letter: it was personalised, publicised, arrogant, flippant and dangerous for Galletti and his family:

> I am always in dread that you may go too far one day and do something that will be impossible for the authorities to overlook however much they may like you personally and appreciate your honesty and ability.

If that day arrived, Collier wondered, what would happen to Clara and the children, let alone Galletti himself?

Perceptively, Collier expressed what Galletti's superiors and colleagues must have thought often. His 'despised bureaucracy' was extremely generous in tolerating these outbursts over what was now a long period. The letter, 'in the worst possible taste', rendered Galletti professionally vulnerable at a time his experience, ability and understanding of India should help reconcile warring factions. "Really this makes me despair." It was made worse, Collier thought, by Galletti promoting his own scheme which "merely consists in the aggrandisement of yourself." That was another example of Galletti seeing how far he might provoke people without bringing on 'absolute disaster'. Collier concluded:

> It is a fascinating game like that of the children who run across the road in front of taxicabs but the excitement is hardly worth the risk.

That and subsequent Collier letters, according to Clara, had 'a salutary and chastening effect' on Galletti who was by then 'a little inflated' with his own importance.[34] It says much that

---

33 Sir John Collier to Arthur Galletti, 24 January 1919, Galletti Papers.

34 Clara to mother, 19 April 1919.

Galletti kept this deeply critical letter, and suggests he was well aware he had gone too far. It suggests, too, he was alive to the personality traits that tested colleagues and superiors.

Simultaneously, he was simply naïve. He was astonished and mystified when his letter to Pate appeared in full in the *Madras Mail*, New *India* and the *Madras Times* even though he had copied it to newspapers elsewhere in India. He protested to *Madras Times* editor, R.W. Brock, who in turn reported what Galletti should have known: Brock saw the letter in the *Bombay Chronicle*. Brock pointed out he could not ignore the letter once it became public, so he published. Interestingly, he had ignored an earlier ICS debate at Galletti's request, only to have the story appear in every newspaper but his own: "I decided to act the ostrich no longer."[35] The editor of Annie Besant's *New India* reprinted the letter from the same *Bombay Chronicle* source, so southern India was awash with copies of the Galletti diatribe.

Some newspapers decried Galletti's position. *The South of India Observer*, primarily the press outlet for tea and coffee planters, considered his proposed reform ideas far too 'roseate', and favoured the position held by those he attacked. His prefecture scheme was ridiculed as affording luxury to people like him with no efficiency increase. Ironically, Galletti himself was cast as a dinosaur.[36] The *Madras Mail* tried to ignore the row, arguing it was perfectly legitimate for ICS men to consider their position under the reforms because their employment terms would now change. This was not disloyalty, just reasonable self-protection.[37]

Galletti's public stand both embarrassed and infuriated Secretariat figures like Cardew and Pate, so they revisited his personnel file in search of retaliation opportunities. Consequently, Cardew wrote officially to inform Galletti that if he attended the ICS dinner preceding the Association meeting

35   R.W. Brock to A. Galletti, 26 January 1919, Galletti Papers.

36   South of India Observer, 8 February 1919.

37   *Madras mail*, 18 January 1919.

he must join the toast to the King's health. This was clear reference to Horsleykonda and a reminder that the Secretariat had the matter under review. Galletti replied he always did and would continue to observe such toasts, but he understood the letter's implications and began immediately rebuilding his position. On the last day of 1918 Clara recorded in her diary a "jolly little trip" to meet the Cardews at the railway station in Chandragiri, in Chittoor district. Lady Cardew was as "sweet as ever". Significantly, Clara wrote also:

> A [Arthur] fairly satisfied with result of visit and glad to have had his say with Sir Alexander Cardew about various official and political matters.

Galletti was seeking rapprochement with the Chief Secretary about to be Acting Governor. Early in January Galletti 'returned cheerful' from the Governor's garden party, feeling he had further retrieved his position. That was not certain, however, because public debate continued. Two weeks later Clara noted that "a letter in the [Madras] *Times* re A's circular somewhat disturbed my rest." By late January *Hindu* columnists were suggesting Galletti would be shifted to an "insalubrious" district as reprisal for his outburst. Galletti boasted his actions had "killed the Revolt of the ICS", Clara lamenting he was forever unhappy 'unless he gets into hot water'.[38] The Gallettis speculated the Government of Madras might not punish him precisely because that would look like agreement with the pro-nationalist *Hindu*— but they were worried.

Galletti gained some satisfaction during January 1919, because following the ICS dinner at which he did drink the King's health, the ICS Association agreed to debate his resolution that a reworded memorial on the reforms replace Pate's original version. The revised submission emphasised the likely

---

38   Clara to mother 29 January 1919, Galletti Papers.

changes in service conditions and their consequences. Galletti also proposed that a two-man inquiry travel the Presidency to assess all members' views, his nominees being L.E. Buckley, first Member of the Board of Revenue, and F.S. Monahan, a Senior Commissioner from Bengal, chosen because Galletti believed him a fellow progressive. The proposal was lost, but redrafting continued for several months so Galletti did have an impact.

He was soon in serious trouble, however. During February 1919 he received a curt official directive from Madras concerning the abiding nationality status argument. G.C. Todhunter, Acting Chief Secretary, informed Galletti that the Secretary of State himself was concerned that orders given to Galletti in 1917 were still unexecuted and believed Galletti "should be required to comply". Galletti was instructed to resolve the matter with the Italian Consul-General in Calcutta within a month.[39] Clara believed that Secretariat officials were considering all ammunition at their disposal.[40] If so, they had plenty and it increased daily as prominent Indian leaders publicly decried the ICS position and pointed to the man who had identified the 'White Mutiny'.[41]

Galletti responded typically to the nationality directive. While he believed he might easily relinquish then later reclaim Italian status, he did "not choose to submit without a protest to the unreasonable and bullying attitude of the British Government." Galletti replied on 17 February enclosing a copy of his letter to Calcutta—along with a protest Memorial, addressed to His Majesty the King.[42] Galletti was not completely preoccupied by this problem, however—he wrote yet another letter to the editor, this time revealing that a European (that is, himself) was

---

39 G.C. Todhunter to Galletti, 4 February 1919, Galletti Papers.

40 Clara to mother, 19 February 1919, Galletti Papers.

41 For example, the anti-ICS meeting reported in *Madras mail,* 15 February 1919.

42 Galletti to G.C. Todhunter 17 February 1919, Galletti Papers.

two years earlier considered for appointment as Chief Secretary in the princely state of Mysore. The matter did not then reach the newspapers [because it was confidential], but showed that the current controversy over such an appointment was misinformed.[43] Once more, Galletti's revelation confirmed his senior officers' views that he was an incorrigible troublemaker.

The Memorial to the King challenging the nationality traced Galletti's 'Englishness', stressed his Collier grandfather was a Privy Council member, and argued that the Royal Family was closely associated with successive Italian kings and notables such as his forebears. He declared the Government's approach high-handed and unfair. This was madness, as even Galletti soon realized. Early in April, he wrote to the Government of Madras: as he had 'some sense of proportion' and not wishing to bother the King with personal matters, he withdrew the Memorial.[44]

Galletti redoubled efforts to repair relations with Horsleykonda guests, guessing the matter would resurface. Clara was deeply concerned, and played a central role in Galletti's rescue campaign over the next three months. On 10 February she recorded a letter from F.R. Hemingway who had just stayed with them at Chittoor. A senior Madras ICS figure, Hemingway was also in Chittoor around Empire Day and was widely believed to have spread the story to official circles, having spoken first with Alfred Tampoe according to Galletti's memoir. Clara and Arthur considered Hemingway 'a Tory and Imperialist of the deepest dye" with whom they disagreed on everything.[45] Hemingway's view on Galletti's beliefs and behaviour mirrored those held in the Secretariat. The same day, Clara noted that a postcard from Mrs Fischer, prominent in the tent discussions, had 'good effect' and she insisted Arthur dictate an immediate

---

43 "Truth" to Editor, *Madras Mail*, 19 February 1919.

44 Galletti to Chief Secretary, 12 April 1919, Galletti Papers.

45 Clara to mother, 5 February 1919, Galletti Papers.

and accommodating reply. The Gallettis were contacting Horsleykonda witnesses, gauging how their views and possible evidence might appear under inquiry.

In early March Galletti was informed officially there would be a formal enquiry into his Horsleykonda behaviour, so he faced his most serious career crisis yet. Cardew had reviewed the files, spoken with several key figures, sought and gained an official account from Tampoe, and initiated formal action. Galletti was charged, as he put it, with 'lying' to Cardew about the toast and with 'conduct unbecoming'. These were most serious charges in the ICS context.

Clara's deep concern stemmed from her first hand account of events.[46] Her own political attitudes were clear when she noted that 24 May was Empire Day and added: '(whatever it may mean)'. She thought her husband's views even more radical. She had expected Arthur back early that day, but he missed the missionaries' high tea and arrived only in late afternoon. They then went to the Tampoe dinner that, while 'excellent', went on for far too long. That aside, it was 'a very pleasant evening.'

However, towards the end of the evening:

Mr Tampoe called upon Arthur to propose the King's health and monsieur flatly declined to do it!

At the time, then, Clara believed Galletti publicly refused to propose the King's health. If she thought that, then so would have all others present, challenging Galletti's argument that no-one saw him drink the toast quickly. According to Clara, the rest of the company drank a toast 'and no-one seemed to take offence' at her husband's action. Even if true of those there, it was not of those in Madras when the story spread—Galletti had transgressed a paramount Raj social rule. Clara thought her husband behaved badly, but not from a loyalty viewpoint:

---

46   Clara to Mother, 30 May 1918, Galletti Papers.

I don't think it was right, not because I see any sense in this absurd loyalty to "Georgie" [the King], but because I consider that his behaviour as a guest was not quite gentlemanly and tactful.

As the official investigation began, even Galletti's most loyal supporter believed he had neither proposed nor saluted the King's health.

Cardew and Pate engineered an exquisite revenge. In his letter to Pate, Galletti suggested an 'eminent person' preside over submissions from the moderate and extremist camps then produce a considered, balanced submission. His nominee was Sir William Ayling, elevated to the Madras High Court in 1912 and who became Chief Judge in 1921. The Government of Madras promptly appointed Ayling to investigate Galletti, proceedings to be conducted as a formal legal hearing. Galletti unsuccessfully sought a judicial rather than Secretariat hearing, believing the ICS prejudiced against him because of the White Mutiny affair. He even considered protesting the Ayling appointment because the judge was an ICS man rather than a standard civil judge.

Clara was now agitated because Galletti lightheartedly drafted several versions of a submission to Ayling, and seemed to dismiss the severity of the crisis. His main strategy, he suggested, would be to 'talk a lot'.[47] Similarly, he recorded that 'what I will actually say the Lord will put into my mouth', 'as near the truth' as possible.[48] His supporters were shaken—Galletti was in this position precisely because he could not keep his views to himself. His frank admission to Clara that it was 'perfectly true that I was showing resentment by flippancy or perverted humour' caused even more anxiety.[49] Galletti seemed not to recall one of Sir John

---

47   Arthur to Clara, 18 April 1919, Galletti Papers.

48   Arthur to Clara, 19 April 1919, Galletti Papers.

49   Ibid, Galletti Papers.

Collier's major points: a sense of humour must be restrained less it become a nuisance, even a danger in Galletti's case.[50]

Despite the lightheartedness, Galletti was stressed. He admitted to declaring strongly republican views and to belittling the King, even if arguing and believing he acknowledged the toast fleetingly. The weeks before the hearing saw him and Clara negotiating statements and support from as well as mending fences with Horsleykonda witnesses. Clara apart, Galletti's strongest support came from Alfred Tampoe, the man most embarrassed by Horsleykonda.

Alfred McGowan Coomaraswami Tampoe, an Anglo-Singhalese, was educated at the prestigious St Thomas' College in Colombo, Stevenage School in England then Clare College, Cambridge. People like him entered and prospered in the service only with great difficulty, but he had ability and determination. Four years younger than Galletti, he arrived in Madras late in 1905 to serve in several districts, becoming a Sub-Collector in 1913 and in which capacity he served Galletti. He wrote later to Galletti that "no superior officer has ever treated me with greater fairness, consideration or generosity than you."[51] That explains why the Gallettis resided with the Tampoes during the trial, why Tampoe rehearsed Galletti's defence and typed his submissions. The Tampoes helped the Gallettis prepare other witness statements, and coach those giving formal evidence. Tampoe himself gave evidence, so during the preparation phase he and Galletti made sure their stories tallied.

To Clara's joy, Tampoe's nephew wrote from Singapore declaring he had seen Galletti drink the toast. However, he could scarcely be brought all the way from Singapore to give evidence, and Ayling had already finalised witnesses and submissions. Galletti arranged to ask Tampoe a leading question on the matter, Tampoe would answer immediately before Ayling ruled the question inadmissible.

---

50   Sir John Collier to Galletti, 24 January 1919, Galletti Papers.

51   Tampoe to Galletti, 20 May 1919, Galletti Papers.

Throughout March and April the Gallettis interviewed and wrote to witnesses, rehearsed the defence, and remained nervous. Clara recorded that they discussed little else and that Arthur paced his room constantly, a sure sign he was apprehensive. J.C.H. Fowler, a district subordinate and legal expert, took Galletti through likely questions and emphasised the seriousness of the situation. At one formal function during this period, Galletti made an elaborate public show of drinking the King's health and ensured an account appeared in local newspapers.

Lady Cardew was ignoring Clara's letters, however, and in early April Cardew became Acting Governor. Clara wrote:

> We trust that Sir Alexander won't take advantage of his short term of Office to try and punish Arthur for his alleged crimes.[52]

In a letter written just before the hearing, Clara confirmed her anxiety: "I cannot feel very happy or easy in my mind."[53] Arthur could well be dismissed from the service. That was almost unprecedented in post-1857 India because, invariably, the ICS yarded its black sheep privately to avoid embarrassing publicity, especially during politically sensitive times. Galletti was still young and intelligent enough to begin again somewhere else, but Clara worried about their children. Tellingly, she commented that while Galletti anticipated a serious reprimand, 'he would mind being dismissed'.

Clara reached Madras before Galletti, primarily to speak with witnesses ahead of the inquiry to confirm their evidence would provide strong enough support. She was met at the railway station by the *Zamindar* of Singampatti, an old friend of Arthur's who would endure his own drama a few years later when his son shot dead the principal at his elite school. Singampatti delivered her to Saidapet where Alfred Tampoe was now Collector. Over

---

52   Clara to mother, 26 April 1919, Galletti Papers.

53   Clara to mother, 19 April 1919, Galletti Papers.

the next two days she road her bicycle around Madras in the strengthening sun, gathering support and preparing the case.

The hearing was conducted at Sir William Ayling's home, The Mansion, in Nungambakkam, then and now an elite residential suburb. It lasted a day, and began with Galletti's grilling of Tampoe. Several missionaries were called, including the MacFarlanes who protested they could not be expected to remember such distant events. Galletti claimed to prove wrong a missionary's evidence about the seating plan: if she could not remember to whom next she sat, how could she remember the events themselves accurately? Some witnesses remembered remarks being made to Galletti along the lines of "if you have republican views like that, how can you take the King's pay?" and "I will stand up for Georgy if you will not". Until half way through, it appeared that Ayling believed the worst, but by the end of the hearing Tampoe thought the judge had a more moderate view.

Clara's diary page for Saturday 17 May 1919 was headed "Red Letter Day", further indication of just how worried she had been. The post brought Ayling's report, effectively clearing Galletti of serious wrongdoing. Arthur was "pleased and relieved at it's being as good and satisfactory as possible". In fact, "A [Arthur] declared he could have written it himself".[54] He was lucky, his supporters knew. Tampoe, like others before and after, tried to convince Galletti he should not tempt fate again, because it placed great strain on Clara. Tampoe went on:

> I know you have some delight in the intellectual zest that comes of a skilful defence under heavy odds...[but] ... Perhaps, and all your friends wish for it, you will be able some day to do with a stroke of your pen what you are not able to effect now with the struggle of your whole body, and let us in patience wait for that time.[55]

---

54 Clara diary entry, 17 May 1919, Galletti Papers.
55 Tampoe to Galletti, 20 May 1919, Galletti Papers.

Tampoe pointed out that while this battle was won, its root cause was clear and victory not permanent—Horsleykonda was the excuse rather than cause for the Ayling inquiry. Galletti's real problems came from a widespread misunderstanding of his precise views throughout the service. Tampoe was "in full accord" with Galletti's views on Empire and loyalty, but not with his expression of those views. Tampoe believed several ICS officers either ignored or misinterpreted Galletti's views in their search to avenge the attack on Pate. Galletti was tried because his careless, reckless behaviour gave conservative ICS elements opportunity to repay the public humiliation suffered by the conservative cause. Tampoe warned that while people like Pate held powerful positions, Galletti was vulnerable. It was perceptive and prophetic advice.

Galletti's own reaction ignored the gravity of the situation, as demonstrated by the "true and authentic" long poem he sent his son after the Ayling report appeared.

> *In his tent on Horsleykonda*
> *Mr Tampoe gave a dinner,*
> *He invited over yonder*
> *Missionaries and a Sinner.*
>
> *Saints and Sinners sat together*
> *In the tent on Horsleykonda*
> *It was May and else wet weather;*
> *Oér these facts let us now ponder.*
>
> *It was May. The sun was burning*
> *The poor Sinner climbing Konda*
> *It was heat to rain-storm turning*
> *When the Sinner climbed up yonder.*

The poor Sinner got some sun-stroke
As he climbed up Horsleykonda
He bore ill a buckling sun-stroke
Which Mercy struck at him up yonder.

With a sun-stroke at the dinner
He was struck on Horsleykonda;
Pity 'twas that this poor Sinner
Did not take his time to ponder

Rumination upon the sun-stroke
Struck at him on Horsleykonda,
Brain affected by the sun-stroke
Made him angry over yonder.

N his right was Tampoe's lady,
Rev'rend Nicholson beside her,
Memory is rather shady
How others sat at Horsleykonda.

This version he remembers
Of that dinner on that Konda
Of some dinner party members
As he dined he got no fonder.

Ladies present at the dinner
On that night at Horsleykonda
Bit with venom that poor sinner
As from fang of Anaconda.

Sat on left of this poor sinner
One fair ven'mous Anaconda
Chaffed and heckled at the dinner
Another dame on Horsleykonda.

That dame's name was Mrs Fischer
Sat on left but over yonder
The poor Sinner would now wish her
Nér to have dined at Horsleykonda.

You must speak on King and Empire
Tampoe said on Horsleykonda,
Sinner was in such a temper
That his mind began to wander.

Would not speak on King and Empire
On that night at Horsleykonda
Such are awful 'fects of Temper
And not taking time to ponder.

Sat down quickly after drinking
The King's health at Horsleykonda,
Sat down quickly, never thinking
Ços his mind began to wander.

He was hauled 'fore Justice Ayling
For that scene on Horsleykonda,
There was sorrow, weeping, wailing
For that incident up yonder.

Understood quite well Judge Ayling
All that scene on Horsleykonda
Found 'twas but a moment's failing
Due to bite of Anaconda.[56]

This was amusing and revealing. The sunstroke defence was flimsy because all other accounts reported poor weather that day. Galletti avoids explaining the discussions that led to the

---

56   Galletti to Roberto Galletti, 2 June 1919, Galletti Papers.

friction. He portrays himself as victim rather than perpetrator, stipulating carefully that he had toasted the King's health—even Clara was now convinced of that despite her original account. The only sign of contrition comes in the concession that he had not considered the possible consequences of his action.

He later suggested that Lord Willingdon thought the only person emerging badly from the affair was Cardew who initiated a false claim in retaliation of the White Mutiny. Galletti considered himself a Willingdon favourite, the Governor recognising an exception to the normal Madras ICS stodginess. Going further, Galletti argued that the expressed views of people like Kipling and Cardew revealed elements of mental disease, because how could Indian aspirations be denied and how could the service think otherwise? For himself, he 'hated Imperialism' which he would forever resist.

The strain on the family was obvious. During the summer season Clara went to Ooty, reporting to Arthur she attended a Government House "At Home": "feeling no longer under the Horsleykonda cloud, I felt more at my ease than normal."[57] She noted that [Sir Charles] Todhunter was affable. A distinguished and accomplished man, Todhunter was now permanent Chief Secretary and was acting on the Governor's Executive Council. It was vital for Galletti's future he not be alienated.

While Galletti believed he changed ICS Association views because its members discussed his draft amendments, in reality he damaged the cause of those seeking more positive reactions, as Reilly suggested. Begrudgingly obeying a Government of India request, Madras established an ICS Commission to discuss the reforms. Its membership reflected a strongly conservative rearguard action against Galletti's outburst. The Commission's chairman was L.T. Harris, member of the Board of Revenue and prominent founder of the ICS Association. Within two years he and Galletti would clash directly. H.R. Pate was included as

---

57   Clara to Arthur, 7 June 1919, Galletti Papers.

was A.R. Loftus-Tottenham, a close friend of Pate's and himself extremely conservative on reform. J.G. Burn was a Highland Scot who arrived in Madras in 1894 and took the legal side, became a High Court judge in 1916 and was now approaching retirement. P.I. Painter joined only in 1914 and was now additional Professor of English in Presidency College. He left India early in 1925 following introduction of the reforms. R.H. Courtenay was early on in his career having arrived in 1910 and he, too, was now on the legal side as registrar to the High Court. This was a conservative group.

Galletti had one friend at court, Alfred Tampoe, but the Commission predictably followed the line run by the Secretariat throughout 1918 into 1919. The Commission reported the ICS to be seriously understaffed in Madras. Retaining the full list of 'prized' promotion posts for leading men was crucial to future recruitment. Harris and Tampoe argued that healthy compensation should go to officers wishing to leave because their conditions of service had changed so radically. Galletti could take comfort from just one recommendation—ICS officers should now have their tents paid for by Government rather than bearing the costs themselves.[58]

During all this, however, Galletti retained his *insouciance*. Early in 1919, the Madras Revenue Department asked all Collectors for reports on the state of revenue collection, especially concerning the forfeiture of property in lieu of paying tax. In Chittoor, Galletti reported, forfeiture had declined steeply compared with the preceding two years. That was the result of his excellent work rather than any improvement in seasonal conditions. He reported holding three general meetings with peasants every year, learning directly about their problems and devising ways to alleviate them. One meeting, mainly with

---

58 This discussion can be followed in Acting Chief Secretary GOM to Secretary Home Dept GOI, 2 September 1919 and 23 October 1919, P. 48, IOR.

the Reddi caste, discussed how to prevent the fragmentation of landholdings. The second investigated how to prevent disputes arising over grazing rights.

The third was a telling one, discussing the local management of irrigation rights. Galletti reported that:

> The conference was in favour of an autocrat, not of a Committee, and an autocrat has been appointed accordingly in two or three villages by way of an experiment.[59]

There were two important aspects here. First, Galletti did not discuss the appointment of an 'autocrat' with the Board, believing his own views to be correct and, of course, that his views on the Board's inadequacy were indisputable. Second, and more interestingly, here was the great believer in Indian rights plumping for an authoritarian solution to what was a significant local problem. That he did so in the midst of a massive crisis brought on by his republican and democratic views, and his stubbornness, makes the situation only the more remarkable.

Galletti had a strong following among Chittoor people, however. He left the district early in 1920, posted to Nellore. Later that year he returned for a ceremony in Narapayanavanam *taluk*, hosted by the President of the District Board.[60] Galletti's portrait was unveiled, and he was declared "The People's Collector" as well as "easily the most popular Collector we have had for some years." He was praised for closing local liquor shops and relocating them to the town outskirts. That was considered strong and necessary action—unfortunately, a shop owners' appeal against the order saw the Board of Revenue reverse Galletti's stand, another mark against it in his view. For local people, anything Galletti did not

---

59 All this may be seen in Board of Revenue, Proceedings 19, 4 February 1919, Board of Revenue Proceedings January-June 1919, P. 10684, IOR.

60 Testimonial from Hanuman Library Association, Naraparvanam, 3 October 1920, Galletti Papers.

achieve was the system's fault, not his. A "democrat in politics', 'in full sympathy with the aspirations of the Indians', he alone stood against the ICS White Mutiny.

Galletti then served in Nellore as Collector. Described by Valentine Chirol as a 'very sleepy hollow', this was the sort of place the government placed people who needed to be kept out of the limelight. While there was some political activity springing from Gandhi's renewed political activity, Galletti's main activity was dealing with Hindu-Muslim disturbances rumbling on after some serious disturbances in 1919-20.[61] Chirol visited Arthur and Clara Galletti there, and described the work as largely routine and boring, the Collector having to keep alert to the latest attempts by Hindus and Muslims to antagonize each other. That included driving processions down streets occupied by the major temples or mosques, and playing loud music or placing offensive food and drink outside the sacred sites or chasing away the latest celebrants dressed as lions or tigers. [62]

After a year of this, Galletti took leave to Australia while Clara returned to Europe. He returned to Madras late in 1921, and to a surprise.

---

61 Girija, S. *Freedom Movement in India* (Nellore District) (Delhi, Discovery, 1990).

62 Chirol, Sir Valentine *India old and new* (London, Macmillan, 1921), pp. 289-290.

6

Guntur

His career prospects now in the balance Galletti was posted as Collector to Guntur district, almost 200 miles north of Madras along the coast on the Bay of Bengal. It was an ICS 'prize' district but Galletti would spend only a very short time there, from 26 November 1921 until 7 February 1922. In those few short weeks his professional ambitions were ruined permanently, his health undermined, his self-confidence rattled, his views about India and its people challenged. It was *the* turning point in his life.

Late in 1920, at Mahatma Gandhi's request, the Indian National Congress launched a huge Non-Co-Operation campaign that put mass civil disobedience into villages, towns and cities across India, with citizens ignoring or defying all official government institutions, policies, procedures and practices. The goal was to have the British leave India. Gandhi determined that passive resistance would steer the campaign, his non-violent philosophy taking the high moral ground from Raj police and military forces. Non-Co-Operation swept north and west India more intensely than the south between 1920 and 1922, but strong protest centres did emerge in the Madras Presidency. In Telugu-speaking Guntur district, particularly, local Congress leaders linked a no-tax payment campaign with Gandhi's mission, making the district *the* Presidency's 'hot spot' as well as one of the leading national sites. Peasants refused to pay land and water taxes, local grievances dovetailing perfectly with national aspirations.

Guntur lay in the heartland of the Telugu-speaking Andhra region Arthur Galletti promoted so keenly. A wealthy district, the Krishna river on its northern boundary brought fertile alluvial soil making agriculture extremely profitable. The massive mid-19th century government-funded Krishna-Godavari rivers irrigation scheme boosted that natural productivity, and connected the region directly to the Madras markets via the Buckingham Canal. Guntur landowning families grew even wealthier by growing grain and cash crops like tobacco, and were highly attuned politically. Those families dominated local political associations from the mid-19th century onwards, and after 1885 also controlled local branches of the Indian National Congress. Simultaneously, however, they maintained close connections with the local British administration.

A long tradition of protecting and promoting local interests underpinned those trends. From the late-18th into the mid-19th centuries the Guntur political and financial elite resisted Madras central authority, creating a complex social network within local government agencies and political groups. Madras thought it controlled Guntur, but the district really ran to a local pulse.[1] As early as 1854, the Guntur Collector reported that the Madras Natives Association was canvassing funds from wealthy landed families to promote political agitation against the government.[2] That pattern continued through the later 19th century and into the 20th as Congress politics broadened.

Local village administrators were central to this, the British relying on them to maintain order and collect revenue. Late in the 19th century the Government of Madras proposed increasing revenue by raising Guntur land and water taxes, arguing that increased prosperity meant increased capacity to

---

1   Robert Eric Frykenberg., *Guntur district 1788-1848: a History of Local Influence and Central Authoity in South India* (Oxford, Clarendon, 1965).

2   Collector Guntur to Commissioner of the Northern Circars, 8 March 1854, *Proceedings of the Northern circars,* March 1854, TNA.

pay. The local population objected, and a string of new political organizations emerged to contest the proposals. Village officers were pressured to assist political activists and many local secret deals undercut government authority even further. Krishna-Godavari district landholding populations led the opposition, but Guntur was close behind and activity there simmered into the 20th century. Anti-tax leaders aligned themselves increasingly with Congress, many taking senior positions in local, district and provincial Congress bodies, as well as in the strengthening Andhra Movement.

Financial, cultural and political sensitivities coalesced powerfully so that when Non-Co-Operation arrived in 1920, Guntur immediately produced major demonstrations and became the most difficult district in the Presidency. The Inspector-General of Police toured the region, reporting to Madras that conditions were 'so inflamed' they were 'highly likely to cause disorder'. A "more vigorous" policy was needed to control the situation.[3] Significant south Indian Congress leaders and Gandhi supporters like Konda Venkatapayya and Duggirala Gopalakrishnayya came from Guntur, basing their campaigns there to exploit the conditions identified by the Inspector-General. Throughout 1921 there were mass action campaigns in the forest lands, government authority was paralysed in localities like Palnad and Peddinandapad, Raj officials were boycotted throughout the entire district.

By late 1921 the Government of Madras was deeply troubled by Guntur developments and, upon his return from European leave, appointed Arthur Galletti there to counter Congress campaigns. It was an extraordinary decision, to say the least. Galletti had a long record of disagreeing with most major new

---

3   See Davidson, Board of Revenue, to Marjoribanks, Chief Secretary, 20 August 1921—this is contained in a mass of material entitled "Material for the History of the Freedom Struggle in Andhra [MFHSA] compiled and available in the State Archives of Andhra Pradesh.

government policies, and was generally considered pro-Indian. However, his memoir version of the appointment has Lord Willingdon, the Governor, appointing him personally as the only man possessing the necessary 'strength of character'. There is no evidence other than Galletti's to support this claim—but it could be correct, because it is unlikely his Secretariat foes would have supported the posting. That is, Willingdon would have had to overrule them in order to appoint Galletti.

The principal difficulty in accepting the memoir explanation lies with the clear evidence that Willingdon wanted tough and direct action in Guntur and more widely—he was at this point so irate with Government of India inaction that he travelled to New Delhi determined to resign if immediate and harsh action was not sanctioned.[4] If he wanted tough action though, why choose Galletti whose track record supported Indian aspirations and opposed direct intervention?

Willingdon wrote to the Secretary of State in January 1922 identifying Guntur as a major trouble spot because of the no-tax campaign. He foreshadowed a countermove: if peasants refused tax payments he would requisition their land in lieu of payment. That would frighten them, Willingdon argued, because Indians prized land above all else.[5] Despite that threat the no-tax campaign proceeded, led vigorously by Venkatapayya and his colleagues, and within two weeks Willingdon informed Montagu that Madras was struggling with the movement: "it is a d...l of a job."[6]

By early February, Willingdon was alarmed. The agitation had taken hold, exacerbated by Government of India inaction. The Government of Madras faced a financial crisis as a consequence. It had an Rs 65 *lakh* revenue shortfall already, mainly caused

---

4 Willingdon to Montagu, 28 February 1922, Eur D 523/20, IOR.

5 *Ibid.*, 25 January 1922.

6 *Ibid.*, 5 February 1922.

by the campaign against tax payment. Government kept that sensational information confidential because, officially, Gandhi's campaign was portrayed simply as an irritant when, in fact, it threatened Government authority. If that financial shortfall continued, Madras would have to raise a loan from the Government of India. That would force re-imposition of a tax to fund employment of the all-important village officers. That tax was abolished earlier because it was extremely unpopular, so re-imposition would intensify already serious political agitation.[7]

Willingdon, then, needed a Collector who might restore control in Guntur. Could he have identified Galletti as that man given the latter's criticisms of the constitutional reforms, his belligerent actions against fellow ICS officers, his long record of claiming to be 'for the Indians', and his professed views on negotiation and patience as the means to improve the situation in India? It seems unlikely, because Willingdon now had no appetite for patience let alone toleration. If Willingdon did not impose Galletti on Guntur, then, how did 'The People's Collector' land there?

It is just possible that Secretariat officials calculated the posting could break Galletti for good. After all, the hardline policies he would have to impose contradicted his declared political instincts, so he might just refuse the appointment. He would then be at government's mercy, and several senior figures were still after blood following the 'White Mutiny' affair. One piece of intriguing evidence supports this possibility. The prevailing ICS conduct manual forbade officers from participating in, supporting, organizing or condoning political meetings and activities. When Non-Co-Operation erupted, that rule prevented officers from raising effective counter-propaganda so, in mid-1921, the Government of India changed the rules, carefully. As the Government of Madras subsequently directed, officers would no longer remain silent while facing 'revolutionary

---

7   *Ibid.*, 11 February 1922.

activity'. They must oppose openly any demonstrations, and contradict misinformation brooked about by agitators. They could not personally organize anti-Congress meetings but must attend and speak freely at meetings staged by Raj loyalists.[8]

The order read as if government had Galletti personally in mind. He was renowned for ignoring rules against being at or addressing 'political' meetings and for flouting the official line. Now circumstances were changed, government prescribing precisely the activity ICS officers must undertake. It was masterly. Men like Galletti could not themselves organize anti-Congress activity but must participate in pro-government activity mobilised by others, counter radical political suggestions, and openly oppose misstatements about British policy as well as radical Congress political agendas. Given that Galletti was considered pro-Indian and therefore pro-Congress, a republican democrat and critic of the British position in India, this new policy trapped him. If the plan was to corral Galletti, it worked brilliantly.

According to Clara the previous Collector, Henry Sopwith Shield (in his late 30s with an above average career record) was considered by government as too weak to deal with Guntur. That concerned Galletti, because if government wanted a tough and direct prosecutor he was not the man. He wanted to promote negotiation, tolerance, understanding and sympathy. Yet toughness was precisely what Willingdon and his senior officers demanded. Even so, Clara reported she and Arthur hoped to "make a success of our stay in Guntur however hostile the atmosphere may be."[9] That created a tension: Galletti needed success to reinstate his stocks with government, but was already suggesting he might disregard government policy. At this crucial time, any such defiance would be crushed by senior officials.

---

8   GOM (Public), GO 265, 2 May 1921, IOR.

9   Clara to her mother, 17 November 1921, Galletti Papers.

One Guntur journalist rejected the government's view of Shield.[10] The outgoing Collector, though junior, displayed strength and initiative in dealing with and subduing Non-Co-Operation. He was shrewd, knew when to apply pressure and when to let matters run their course. Shield confronted and dealt with serious no-tax activity in the forest lands but did not martyr major leaders, sapping the movement's momentum. The significance of his transfer, according to the writer, lay with government's "mysterious" administrative approach. Guntur had seen eight different Collectors in just three years, according to the informant, and that destabilised the troublesome district. Local loyalists, the writer concluded, hoped Galletti would be as 'equally good and sympathetic' as Shield.

Galletti later outlined his methods for dealing with movements like Non-Co-Operation, confirming the iniquitous position in which he now found himself:

> Agitations in India should be met with infinite patience and the avoidance of even an appearance of provocation.[11]

Congress must be allowed to agitate all it wanted because, ultimately, broad public support would dwindle. If government prosecuted agitators sparingly and reluctantly, the public would respond positively. Indians appreciated insightful understanding, he suggested, but despised any government that either feared or was contemptuous of the public. When the Government of Madras released Mrs. Besant early following her 1917 Home Rule agitation, he argued, Indians were grateful—that interpretation overlooked the fact that government was ordered by Delhi to release her, and that substantial demonstrations accompanied the release. The same was true when Gandhi was released just two years into a six-year term, Galletti suggested. Reverting to

---

10   "A correspondent", *Madras mail*, 10 November 1921.

11   Draft, Galletti to Secretary of State, nd, Galletti Papers.

his earlier Morley theme Galletti argued that Indians understood, respected and responded to toleration. The ICS, concomitantly, fomented misunderstanding because it was:

> Still full of racial feeling and the belief in the superiority of the white race.

ICS officers resented political change for India, he argued, because that threatened their individual power base, sources of livelihood and self-importance. Their now precarious position aggravated the fears, as demonstrated by the fierce Madras ICS resistance to Montagu-Chelmsford service conditions and political-constitutional shifts. If the ICS was excluded from the political machinery, Galletti argued, with the Viceroy and sympathetic governors like Galletti dealing directly with popularly elected Indians, moderate India would be satisfied and agitation subside.

Galletti conceded that Gandhi and his lieutenants, who made 'a religion of their patriotism', would not be persuaded—Gandhi, though a Galletti friend, would not hear reason. However, those people would subside in importance because most Indians would support a tolerant, sympathetic government rid of the arrogant ICS.

The argument reveals how much Galletti was isolated from his service colleagues by this point. Most of those colleagues now considered Congress as a serious, rising political force while government policies became reactive rather than innovative, obtuse rather than insightful.[12] Had his extreme views been known in the Secretariat or Government House, Galletti could not possibly have been appointed to Guntur. Appointed he was, though, and he shifted in to take charge on 26 November 1921, Clara following a few days later.

In its official account of the period compiled in 1925, the Government of Madras revealed just how serious a situation

---

12   See Hilton Brown's novel, *Dismiss!* (London, Methuen, 1923), p. 111.

Galletti encountered.[13] By December 1921 mass resignation by village officers disrupted government activities, and the Non-Co-Operators were widely influential. There was, it appeared, 'a state of affairs bordering on anarchy', a big admission from the authorities.

Nonetheless, the early signs were hopeful for Galletti. Gandhi added the abolition of untouchability to his campaign agenda, dismaying his socially conservative principal Guntur campaign supporters.[14] It was widely thought that local non-Brahmin merchants had only joined the Brahmin Congress leaders in the belief that Swaraj (freedom from the British) would eliminate all taxes, a powerful incentive transcending traditional inter-caste suspicions.[15] Gandhi's proposed abolition of untouchability was a reform too many, however, and several socially conservative upper caste merchants withdrew, some even burning Swadeshi cloth in public to reject symbolically both Gandhi and Congress.[16] Exploiting that division, Galletti attended anti-Non-Co-Operation meetings in the restive Palnad taluk, his activities reported in the local newspapers. It was 'not beyond his condescension' to do so, ran the report curiously—the correspondent was still unsure of Galletti's approach and commitment to dealing with the agitation. A month later, though, the same writer credited Galletti with "high intellect and mature experience" in taking up the no-tax issue with "all seriousness[17]

After the promising start, though, things went very wrong, very quickly. By early January Clara reported that Arthur was deeply depressed, almost non-responsive in face of the intense

---

13 *The Non Co-Operation and Khilafat Movements in the Madras Presidency*, Home Poll 185/1925, GOI, NAI.

14 *Madras mail*, 14 December 1921.

15 That view was confirmed by Sidney Wadsworth stationed in the area at the time: Sir Sidney Wadsworth papers, CSAA.

16 *Hindu*, 24 January 1922.

17 *Madras mail*, 19 January 1922.

pressure. There were desperate family discussions, Clara writing to her mother that "we must not hastily take any step that might prove unnecessary."[18] Galletti was threatening to resign from the ICS in protest at government policy. Clara was alarmed that would ruin her family's prospects. The debate dominated the following weeks during which Galletti struggled to cope with events.

Galletti went on tour, camping out in areas of rampant no-tax activity.[19] He returned to district headquarters only to arrest, try and imprison identified ringleaders but he did not order mass arrests, contrary to Madras expectations. While on tour he discussed the political situation with village officers and their families, reflecting back to the Board of Revenue their views on the campaign's origins. He attempted to discuss the situation with Congress leaders, too, but given Non-Co-Operation principles they would not meet him. By early January 1922 he reported Guntur "in revolt".[20] In one *firka*, he said, officers had resigned in 17 of 18 villages so the tax non-payment was significant. A later Government of Madras report noted that in Guntur throughout January only Rs 3.5 *lakhs* of the required 14.75 were collected—'passive obstruction' was 'everywhere'.[21] Guntur was in revolt, the government thoroughly alarmed, and Galletti close to despair.

Sadly, this period turned the Gallettis' inherent belief in and support for the Indian people. By resigning *en masse*, in their view, Guntur district village officers abrogated solemn contractual duties to support what Arthur and Clara considered radical and unnecessary Congress demands that would

---

18 Clara to Mother, 12 January 1922, Galletti Papers.

19 Copies of several of Galletti's daily reports to the Board may be seen in the MFHSA collection.

20 Galletti to Board, 8 January 1922, MFHSA.

21 The *Non Co-Operation and Khilafat Movements in the Madras Presidency, Confl*, GOI Home Political 185/1925, NAI.

break the true order of things. Galletti sympathised with the officers' cause, considering them British India's backbone. He believed government policy towards them wrong-headed, causing inordinate discontent unrecognised by government and unremarked by the media. However, he despised their direct action, thinking they had sold out to Congress radicals and rejected sensible political progress. People he had long considered supporters were now the enemy, no matter how much he sympathised with their grievances. According to Clara, they both thought India now in a mess with no obvious solution.

Reflecting the high anxiety stalking official circles, Clara recorded her conversation with a military officer accompanying the Prince of Wales during his Madras trip. The Prince's Indian tour was arranged as a morale booster but coincided with the height of Non-Co-Operation. He was greeted everywhere with demonstrations, riots, uproar and confusion including Madras where the official line was that 'mob members ran like rabbits to their burrows' while the authorities acted with restraint.[22] Clara's informant reported the Madras riots as much worse than acknowledged publicly by government and that the Prince was close to a nervous breakdown, so distressed was he by what he had seen.[23] Arthur Galletti suffered a similar breakdown, overwhelmed by and unhappy with his instructions from government, particularly following a visit from a Board of Revenue Member.

Leonard Tatham Harris, in Madras since 1893, became the Fourth Member of Galletti's despised Board in 1919 and shared his colleagues' doubts about their Guntur Collector's reliability. Harris toured Guntur early in January 1922 to assess conditions

---

22   Claude H. Van Tyne., *India in ferment* New York, Appleton, 1923), pp. 126-8.

23   Clara to Mother, 19 January 1922. Galletti Papers G.R.F. Tottenham, Private Secretary to Lord Willingdon at the time, considered the visit went off well despite disturbances in which at least one demonstrator died. He did confirm, however, that the visit worried Willingdon who considered it "ill-timed" and unfair to the Prince. Sir Richard Tottenham Papers, CSAA.

first hand, he and Galletti disagreeing on almost everything. Harris' account of a regional Collectors' meeting depicts Galletti as contrary on almost everything.[24] Galletti considered the situation extremely serious and Harris accepted that, but his solution was directly opposite to that recommended by Galletti. Harris called for armoured cars and armed troops, so 150 soldiers arrived in Guntur in mid-January.[25]

When he first heard this, Galletti telegraphed both the Secretariat and regional military command suggesting a 'mischief-maker' was dispatching orders deploying troops. This was clearly a joke, Galletti suggested. He personally had matters fully under control, and troops were not required.[26] Those troops arrived, nevertheless, and the Secretariat had yet more evidence of Galletti's idiosyncratic response to orders. Some of the troops were *en route* to Lahore following deployment in Malabar where they fought the Moplahs, so their presence further inflamed local nationalist sentiments. The army staged demonstration visits to what government considered the most disaffected villages. Galletti still sought reconciliation, however, believing villagers revered him. He hated what was happening, said so, and word reached Madras he was failing. Chief Secretary R.A. Graham wrote immediately to encourage Galletti: all in the Secretariat, he said, 'fully realize the difficulties' and offered their 'full support' because they were "glad to see you are tackling it with determination."[27] Graham and his colleagues had by now received Harris' formal and informal reports on Guntur, and were worried.

---

24 "Notes of Collectors'Meeting Held at Bezwada", 13 January 1922, Galletti Papers. MFHSA.

25 Madras to Delhi telegram, 149, 17 January 1922, Home Poitical F 529/1922 M.CDO/Guntur, NAI—the troops were to 'co operate' with the District Magistrate [Galletti].

26 Galletti to Chief Secretary, 17 January 1922, MFHSA.

27 Chief Secretary to Galletti, 17 January 1922, MFHSA.

Galletti and Harris differed totally on what was happening and what was required.[28] Galletti argued village officers were resigning because "Government are ignoring the resolutions of their conferences, diminishing the menial establishment without consulting them and [considering] the resolution of the National Congress."[29] His obvious support for that Congress resolution and for the village officers alienated Galletti from his superiors, and from his colleagues confronting Non-Co-Operation around the Presidency. Galletti claimed most influential resigning officers were wealthy men driven not by "political reasons" but by frustration with government's ignoring their grievances, most especially about the reduction of their supporting work force. Bluntly, Galletti suggested further mass resignations would follow if government did not restore the workforce. Similarly, he sought to stay government's intentions to strip village officers of their hereditary rights.

Harris saw it differently. He recognised the village officer complaints, but identified district and local Congress organizations as the prime agitational cause. Those bodies staged meetings all over Guntur and adjoining districts, advocating tax non-payment. In mid-January 1922, Harris declared that if Congress went unchecked for another two weeks government would lose control entirely, at incalculable political and economic cost. "The first necessity is an immediate show of force in the worst affected district, i.e. in Guntur," he suggested. Guntur was at the centre of the trouble, Non-Co-Operation flourished there and loyalists received no support. This latter point was important because, at that point, Gandhi gave local

---

28 See the reproduced Government of Madras documents, Venkatarangaiya, M. (ed), *The freedom struggle in Andhra Pradesh (Andhra): Vol. iii* (1921-1931) Hyderabad, Andhra Pradesh State Committee, 1965, pp. 261-278, 296-302.

29 For an example of the government's response, GOM, Revenue Department, GO 1958, 14 August 1920, TNA—the government admitted to a huge number of petitions, but responded positively to almost none.

Congress bodies the power to determine their own actions, and many local moderate Congressmen wanted the campaign suspended. The leaders, however, argued the movement was strong and should continue.[30]

Harris thought Galletti was not exploiting this Congress internal division efficiently or sufficiently enough. The 'agitator' was not being curbed and should be, either by applying a stronger legal regime or by marching in the troops and, in Harris' view, the latter would cause less longer term resentment. He clearly disagreed with Galletti on this point, and on another—unlike Galletti, Harris wanted the hereditary rights bill strengthened and implemented immediately. If a village officer was dismissed for disloyalty then his family should lose rights permanently, not temporarily as proposed in the draft bill. Harris noted Galletti thought the situation grave, and Collectors in adjoining districts feared increased difficulties if Guntur went unchecked. Those Collectors were clearly voicing to Harris their anxiety about Galletti's approach and performance.

That is reflected in an elliptical but telling point Harris aimed directly at Galletti. He referred to the administrative histories of the districts concerned: Guntur, Krishna and Godavari. Guntur has seen six Collectors over the previous three years (differing from the newspaper reports), Krishna three and Godavari two. The present trouble, Harris observed, was "in the inverse order of the number of changes and *the personality of those named*" [emphasis added]. There is no question that he saw H.H.F.M. Tyler in Krishna (who joined the Board of Revenue four years later) and G.T.H. Bracken (who had just left Godavari and later became Chief Secretary) as far more reliable than Galletti with whom he had serious disagreements, as revealed in Clara's letters.

---

30   Venkatarangaiya, pp. 210-14.

Gilbert Slater, now seconded from his Professor of Indian Economics position to be Acting Director of Publicity for the Government of Madras, confirmed Galletti's interpretation but added a twist that revealed some ICS senior views.[31] Like Galletti, Slater put the trouble down to the *karnams* and the *munsifs*, but for very different reasons. According to Slater the *karnams* were invariably Brahmin but the *munsifs* were non-Brahmin. The latter successfully mobilised the Justice Party vote in the Legislative Council elections and the former, resenting their lost influence, turned towards the Congress Non-Co-Operation campaign and made it highly effective. In Slater's view, significantly, the situation in Guntur and elsewhere was saved only by Gandhi's calling off the campaign when violence appeared. If this view was held widely in Madras, which it probably was given the promotion of non-Brahmin interests, then Galletti's sympathy for the *karnams* would have been interpreted as support for the Brahmins, so he would have been even further at odds with the official policy position.

Most observers, too, reported the troop march as highly effective, supporting Harris' analysis over Galletti's.[32] Everybody including, Non-Co-Operators turned out to watch the troops and all were entertained, said the reports. Konda Venkatapayya thought 700 troops were needed to arrest him then control the ensuing rebellion. Following the march some resigned village officers returned to work, again strengthening the Harris view. Local Congressmen quietly dropped the untouchability issue, but the merchants withdrew from Non-Co-Operation. If only the government would now send the leaders to jail, argued the observer, all would be well.

---

31 Gilbert Slater. *Southern India: it's political and economic problems* (London, Allen & Unwin, 1936), ch. xxix.

32 *Madras mail,* 19 January 1922.

Government decided Galletti needed help so drafted in as Additional District Magistrate the well-regarded and tough New Zealander T.G. Rutherford, a former Collector in Krishna. He was sent to deal directly with the most troublesome localities. While there was some Secretariat discussion about similar appointments being necessary elsewhere, concern about Galletti's activities directly inspired the appointment. Rutherford's reports revealed revenue collection and penalty tax gathering as almost non-existent, so crucial were the now resigned village officers. Congress filled the vacuum caused by the government's paralysis, Rutherford suggested. Despite the difficulty, Rutherford did not "have the wind up—indeed personally I am rather enjoying it."[33]

Government was delighted to hear that because Galletti clearly was not enjoying the experience—he was almost inactive, reacting violently to small issues and acting erratically. One newspaper report had a woman Non Co-Operator raped by troops and Galletti vehemently denied it: "I cannot deal with all lies."[34] He was right, because the newspaper withdrew the allegation, but his response caused consternation in Madras. Galletti decided to prosecute the newspaper proprietors, filing the charge under a criminal code section Secretariat lawyers believed could not possibly return a conviction. Flurried exchanges rattled between Guntur and Madras with argument and counter-argument debating legal nicety, Congress demonstrations continuing all the while.[35]

Madras lost patience with and confidence in Galletti. Alongside his flawed newspaper prosecution, he changed position dramatically on other crucial matters. Having not wanted troops in the first place, he now protested vigorously

---

33 Rutherford to Chief Secretary, 26 January 1922 in Venkatarangaiya, vol. III, pp. 275-7.

34 Galletti to Chief Secretary, 19 January 1922 in Venkatarangaiya, vol. III, p. 298.

35 See the materials in MFHSA.

at their possible withdrawal. He was facing 'open rebellion', he said, and could not function without the troops and, indeed, an augmented police force should be transported in now. A 'big stick' was needed to deal with this insurrection.[36] The Chief Secretary recorded it was now impossible to understand what Galletti was thinking from one moment to the next. First he did not want the troops, and accepted them only for 'demonstration' purposes. Now he did not want them to leave and suggested he might actually use them. If Galletti required additional police he should have asked much earlier, because they would have to be fetched from elsewhere in the Presidency.[37]

Somewhere in the week beginning Monday 23 January 1922 Chief Secretary R.A. Graham and his senior colleagues decided Galletti must leave Guntur, and began negotiating with H.A.B. Vernon to be his replacement. By 4 February Vernon was discussing accommodation options and motor vehicle purchase with the Secretariat. Government was already briefing him on the Guntur situation and he was consulting background files. Galletti knew nothing of this, obliviously remaining in the field where he faced a growing problem. The local military commander reported that civil disobedience and the non-payment of taxes were 'in active operation in the whole district'.[38] Shortly afterwards, the Government of Madras reported to Delhi: "Collector regards situation serious and has apparently not succeeded in collecting appreciable amount yet."[39] The *Madras* mail ran a banner headline: "Serious Situation at Guntur: Non-Payment of Taxes."[40] Madras reported further to Delhi that the no-tax movement was not only embarrassing but threatened Government's economic lifeline with a severe budget

---

36 Galletti to Chief Secretary, 22 January 1922, MFHSA.

37 R.A. Graham note, 23 January 1922, MFHSA.

38 Col. Dawes to District HQ, 20 January 1922, GOI Home Political F 529/1922 M. CDO/Guntur, NAI.

39 Madras to Delhi telegram, 24 January 1922, *ibid.*

40 *Ibid.*, 21 January 1922.

crisis about to be revealed publicly. No village officers threatening resignation would be allowed to do so. They would be sacked and forfeit their traditional family rights to office. Galletti had lost that argument. Collectors were to move immediately against non-payers, revised legislation expediting the seizure of goods and the selling of land to meet obligations. The Peddinandapad *firka* in Bapatla *taluk* was identified as the most troublesome spot and extra police were assigned there immediately, costs borne by the citizens under the very legislative provision Galletti fought against in 1907. He had also lost his toleration argument.

The situation was extremely serious with Galletti amidst one of India's most severe rebellions, as 'Zenda' of Guntur suggested.[41] For three weeks there was widespread non-payment of tax. Galletti and his fellow officers had their supply lines blocked while travelling the district. In some areas officers could not get their clothes washed, their hair cut, buy food, find accommodation when away from home, or receive service in post offices. Large crowds of Non-Co-Operation volunteers, often numbering in the thousands, harassed them wherever they went. Protest flags, songs and chants everywhere greeted Galletti and other officials, and posters supporting Non-Co-Operation stared out at them all over the district. Cars were stoned in several villages, government officers were physically at risk if they showed themselves anywhere in several areas of Guntur. The Guntur municipal council rejected government educational funding grants and raised public money to run its schools independently. The council also resolved to reduce house taxes. Resignation of public office was rife. Government loyalists received no support and Non-Co-Operators ran supreme.

Many loyalists believed punitive action was delayed too long, allowing agitators too much leeway. 'An Indian' from Tenali, another seriously disturbed town, confirmed these views.[42] The writer suggested threats and intimidation confronted loyalists

---

41   *Ibid.*, 28 January 1922.

42   *Ibid.*, 3 February 1922.

everywhere, with village officers cultivating both sides in case Congress triumphed. Senior officials connived with agitators, government ignorant of and uninterested in developments. Loyalists went unsupported. None of this reflected well on Arthur Galletti—his successor later suggested 'a state of affairs bordering on anarchy" existed. Even the government admitted that it was facing an agitational force that for the first time spread beyond the educated intelligentsia.[43]

This was among the most difficult situations any ICS officer faced anywhere in India, and Galletti's informal accounts likely informed the literary description of Non-Co-Operation created by Hilton Brown. Brown shared Galletti's liberal views, but was also concerned about his future in India and that propelled him into the ICS Association Galletti attacked earlier. Over the years, however, they kept in touch. In 1923 Brown published *Dismiss!* the story of how an ICS man recruited to Madras before WWI was forced out to become a tea planter because Government in Madras, run by the Government of India, could not back up men in the field.[44] The hero's final decision to leave is determined by a riot in which many locals and at least one European die because of the 'final disastrous surrender to the extremist'. Clearly, Brown thought Galletti badly treated and poorly served and Galletti, in turn, used that description to frame his own memoir version of events.

Throughout the last week of January 1922 Madras officials issued Galletti with detailed and specific instructions on how to conduct affairs, because they had difficulty following his decision-making. He was no longer independent. Senior officers suggested Galletti had not informed them of his actions. In reality he was doing nothing, so overwhelmed was he by events. Government now, effectively, instructed him on what to do. That did not occur in

---

43   The general picture is conveyed in The Non-Co-Operation and Khilafat Movements in the Madras Presidency, GOI Home Political 185/1925, NAI.

44   Brown, Hilton *Dismiss!* (London, Methuen, 1923), pp. 191-228.

other districts where Collectors were regarded as more in control. Having the most difficult district controlled by a renegade, now stricken Collector worried Madras. If Guntur became lawless, as looked distinctly possible, martial law might be the only recourse and that would be a public relations catastrophe.

By early February 1922 the government admitted that less than five per cent of due taxes had been collected, but declared things were improving.[45] More village officers were returning to duty, Konda Venkatapayya himself had paid tax to avoid forfeiting his land. All tax was due by 10 February, government was confident it would arrive with the peasantry paying despite reprisal fears. The Additional District Magistrate, Rutherford, was improving matters considerably. Legislation for the speedier collection of dues had a difficult time in the Legislative Council, but was passed then effected immediately.

It was all too late for Galletti. He was removed from Guntur summarily and without notice on 7 February 1922. In fact, he was on his way to establish camp and conduct negotiations at Narasaraopet, another particularly difficult village, when he received the transfer orders.[46] He was removed to Chingleput district adjoining Madras, exchanging positions with H.A.B. Vernon who, according to a former superior, was "a man who did everything in some original way of his own".[47] Vernon determined to make his mark with immediate and tough action, some of which was disapproved of by his service colleagues. J.C. Molony, Galletti's old friend, took a dim view of Vernon surrounding a Guntur village with soldiers, then collecting tax at bayonet point.[48]

---

45   Madras to Delhi telegram., 4 February 1922, GOI Hom Political F/529/1922 M. CDO/Guntur.

46   Rutherford to Chief Secretary, 7 February 1922, MFHSA.

47   Horne, W.O. p. 186.

48   Menon, K.P.S. "My life and work in the I.C.S." in K.L. Panjabi (ed), *The civil servant in India* (Bombay, Bharatiya Vidya Bhavan, 1965).

Clara did not know whether to be pleased or alarmed because her husband now believed he would face charges, even dismissal for having failed in Guntur. He was destroyed: "Everything seems to him insurmountably difficult."[49] His fears were justified. When the government later collected Non-Co-Operation reports from Collectors, Galletti's was suppressed. He took a very different line, in action and reporting, from that desired by government and as exemplified in H.H.F.M. Tyler's report from Krishna.[50] Galletti was unhappy with the troop presence, or at least with their specific use, and was intent on dealing directly with Congress leaders whom he claimed to know and understand. He considered himself well known and well liked by those directly involved, those who had to pay tax, and was confident he could keep them in line. All that failed. As his plans and beliefs crumbled so did his resolve and will. The government did think he failed, as confirmed by A.Y.G. Campbell almost a decade later.[51]

This was his lowest career point, and quite probably the lowest in his life. He was deemed to have failed, a staggering blow to his sense of self, intellect, work and character. Not surprisingly, then, Galletti attempted to set the record straight several times later, and in some senses even to rewrite history.

His revisionist efforts began during 1929 as Gandhi prepared for his next major passive resistance campaign and when the Viceroy, Lord Irwin, toured Tinnevelly where Galletti was by then Collector. Given Congress preparations, Irwin naturally asked Galletti what he thought the new Civil Disobedience campaign might bring. Galletti recounted his Guntur experiences, following

---

49 Clara to mother, 8 February 1922, Galletti Papers.

50 H.H.F.M. Tyler to Chief Secretary, 9 February 1923, J.P.L. Gwynn Papers, CSAA.

51 A.Y.G. Campbell note, 16 January 1931, GOM Public (Special) GO 270 Confl. 17 March 1931, TNA.

up with a written account sent privately to the Viceroy.[52] That account provided the basis for several articles Galletti sought unsuccessfully to publish through the late 1930s and after World War II.

While his post-event versions all contained variations, the central themes remained constant. Galletti argued that the ICS comprised two sorts of people: the 'Sole Force' (law and order men, as he termed them), and 'Soul Force'. The latter, men like him, were in a distinct minority but in 1922 included Lord Willingdon. This was a questionable claim, given Willingdon's actions and recorded views. For example, it is highly likely he was passed over for Viceroy in 1918 because of his opposition to the Montagu-Chelmsford reforms.[53] Soul Force men believed in and trusted the good sense of the people they ruled, according to Galletti. They tolerated all opinions, but opposed legislative repression including Press Acts that restricted information and free speech. The Sole Force, alternatively, feared the people, repressed divergent opinion at every opportunity, and believed in the lock and key: "The ICS has always believed in resolute governance and coercion."[54] The Sole Force, in Galletti's view, dominated the Madras administration. Moreover, the Madras repressive forces were advantaged during Non-Co-Operation because the Viceroy, Lord Reading, removed restraints imposed on them in 1908 by John Morley following Galletti's actions over the Bipin Chandra Pal affair. This, too, was a challengeable claim in several respects, but reveals how Galletti saw his life as a liberal administrator unfolding, and places the Guntur episode in context. It also helps explain his view of his subsequent demise.

---

52 "Lord Willingdon and the Guntur No-Tax Campaign of 1922", Galletti Papers.

53 Peter Robb, "The Bureaucrat as reformer: two Indian civil servants and the Constitution of 1919" in Peter Robb and David Taylor (eds), *Rule, protest, identity: aspects of modern South Asia* (London, Curzon, 1978).

54 Galletti to Signore Podesta, 14 July 1936, Galletti Papers.

In one revisionist version, Galletti wrote that Willingdon selected for Guntur an officer well-known for his sympathy with Indian:

> aspirations and for his popularity with the educated classes in the Andhra country, among whom he had many devoted personal friends.

Recognising a fellow Soul Force man, then, Willingdon chose Galletti as the man to deal with the uprising. Galletti accepted the assignment, but on the stipulation that he would not employ force to the point of bloodshed as apparently demanded by New Delhi. Willingdon agreed, saying he did not want bloodshed either. The two agreed that troops might show force but not use physical violence. This point might have been made to underline the fact that soon after Galletti left Guntur, Vernon led a police firing that left some demonstrators dead.

Willingdon's detailed instructions, according to this Galletti version, required direct contact and negotiation with local Congress leaders like Venkatapayya and Gopalakrishnayya. Galletti did so immediately as he always did in any new district, knowing such interaction would shock the Secretariat Sole Force. That does not match the official record because the leaders refused to meet him. That aside, Galletti's views on his beloved Andhras were simplistic, even on their leaders who were highly intelligent and well-educated. They were prosperous, educated, cultured, proud and curiously enthusiastic, he thought, but had no patience so their political movements always flared and expired rapidly. Again, this was at odds with the growing government view about the serious threats now posed by Congress, especially in the Telugu country.

This pinpoints an abiding Galletti strategic blind spot, because all the evidence suggests that someone like Duggirala Gopalakrishnayya should have been someone with whom Galletti might work closely. Twelve years younger than Galletti, Gopalakrishnayya was born in 1889 to an orthodox Brahmin family based in 0where his father was a school teacher. The father, however, was really a Guntur man where his family were small scale landholders and landlords.[55] Brought up in Guntur by his uncle and grandmother, Gopalakrishnayya was married at 14, and matriculated at 17. After a few years he and a few friends sailed from Guntur to Edinburgh where he spent the next six years studying, graduating with a Masters degree in economics. He returned to Guntur in 1917 as Mrs Besant's Home Rule activity grew, working as a teacher while becoming politically active. In 1919 he became a full time political worker, and a key leader in Guntur politics and especially the actions that Galletti confronted. In fact, Gopalakrishnayya was jailed for a year for his political actions, and was released just as Galletti arrived in the district.

Here was an obviously intelligent and cultured man, the sort of Indian with whom a liberal like Galletti might fashion a compromise. There were three main reasons why that did not happen. First, by the time Galletti arrived Gopalakrishnayya was past the point of accepting moderate reform, his experiences suggesting that British policy would never devolve enough power quickly enough. Second, Galletti's own view of Congress leaders was by now a blanket one, they were all unworthy of consideration. That revealed his inability to sense the unfolding political shifts, and to work them into his own liberal views of an Indian future. Third, Gopalakrishnayya's landholdings, in Galletti's view, placed him outside those 'real' Indians for whom the Collector sought a future. Had those barriers been removed, it is tempting to think that things might have turned out very differently. Sadly, Duggirala Gopalakrishnayya died from tuberculosis a few years later at just 39 years of age.

---

55 Verma B.R. and Unniakrishnan K. (eds), *Encyclopaedic bibliography of Indian freedom fighters (Delhi, Commonwealth, 2004), vol. 1.*

Galletti claimed that the 1922 no-tax campaign was typically mercurial, opening on 10 January 1922 and all but over by the time he left Guntur a month later. Willingdon's sagacity and Galletti's unique skills combined to suppress the uprising 'with great rapidity and little public notice'. By 1 April 1922, he claimed, the entire annual tax was with government, not just the instalment refused by the agitators, with the total sum collected an all-time record for any Presidency district. Gandhi's campaign was 'entirely discredited', the Mahatma later telling Galletti it was 'the most decisive check he ever received'.[56] Galletti believed that result arose because he travelled the district freely, respected everywhere for his efforts and good intentions, while other officers were assailed on all sides, refused supplies, threatened, even assaulted. According to him, he saw through the cynical and misleading actions of people like Venkatapayya who kept the whole truth from the Mahatma. Venkatapayya, for example, paid tax through a third party while advocating non-payment by others; pursued a tenant through the courts to seek delayed tax payments; had family members treated in government hospitals while publicly advocating Non-Co-Operation. Galletti revealed all this to local people who, he claimed, recognised the campaign's superficiality and its threats to their futures.

Galletti's fuller analysis of the rebellion's underlying causes demonstrates the depth of his local knowledge, the extent of his disagreement with Harris and, perhaps, his inability to recognise the changing political environment. It must be remembered, Galletti said, that tax non-payment was a favourite Andhra tactic, evident since the early 19th century. Over time village officers, especially the *karnams* became extremely wealthy, but lost the respect of other peasants who themselves derived prosperity and influence from the British irrigation schemes. Village officers felt they lost respect from the British, too, as symbolised by their low wage and government's attempts to

---

56   Galletti to Signore Podesta, 14 July 1936, Galletti Papers.

reduce their support. In 1918 the officers formed an association to represent their grievances to government, establishing a newspaper to promote their concerns. They did not need the demanded wage increases, Galletti argued, because other income sources made them wealthy, but they needed the higher wages to regain respect. This was complicated, Galletti continued, because village officers were almost exclusively Brahmin and so became targets of the rising anti-Brahmin movement because of their importance to British control in the localities. Given that, anti-Brahmin forces joined Congress to swell Non-Co-Operation ranks. In the background here, of course, was the apparent anti-Brahmin policy inside the Secretariat to which Harris was privy.

According to Galletti the moneylenders were drawn into this unusual alliance, sensing British control might collapse and wanting to keep their options open for working with whoever might become locally powerful. Moneylenders were vital in the 1922 campaign because tax instalments were always paid with borrowed funds, tiding peasants over until grain was sold later in the year. In fact, as recognised years earlier in government manuals and gazetteers, in 146areas moneylenders were frequently grain traders as well, so close was the bond between the two activities.[57] On top of these coalescing forces, Galletti suggested, Madras bureaucrats ordered immediate reductions in the numbers of staff supporting the village officers, with 142 sacked in the politically sensitive Bapatla *taluk* alone. The village officers immediately met in Peddanandipad *taluk*, agreed to resign and that area drove the no-tax campaign.

Galletti agreed with Harris that the constant turnover of Collectors was a contributing figure, but naturally did not share the Member's views on the characters of those Collectors! In Galletti's view a young, energetic and able Collector like Rutherford should be placed in districts like Guntur for at least

---

57   *Godavari district Gazetteer* (Madras, GOM, 1907), p. 112.

five years to learn local ways, understand the local influence networks, and work out how to counter bodies like Congress and its opportunistic leaders.

This point was discussed increasingly inside the Secretariat and the service. In earlier times Collectors spent several years in the one post with transport difficulties making constant relocation almost impossible. As roads improved and cars replaced horses, as communication intensified and government became more centralized, posting rotations sped up. That meant Collectors spent less time in the one place, and many old hands thought that meant local intelligence networks weakened. By World War I and immediately after, as the Guntur case shows, many districts had a string of Collectors going through a revolving door, and that did little to stabilize local administration.

Galletti, then, attributed the campaign to local grievances taken up and exploited by Congress. Neither Congress itself nor even Gandhi was the major cause. In Galletti's mind he broke the campaign easily because he knew those local issues and, for example, without reference to Madras cancelled orders sacking support staff to mollify village officers who really did not want to resign.

Following his return to Madras the Chief Secretary, Robert Graham, informed Galletti he was transferred because government thought his nerve had failed. Clara agreed.[58] Galletti's depression lasted for months, his changed physical appearance startled all who knew him. India had changed for him and Clara. The Chauri Chaura incident in north India, where 22 policemen were burned to death by a Congress crowd, shocked them both. Members of the Indian Club in Guntur, where the Gallettis were regular visitors, shocked Clara by refusing to condemn Congress over the incident. She wrote that her contempt for Indians was

---

58   Clara to mother, 18 February 1922, Galletti Papers.

growing every day.[59] It took months for Galletti to declare he would stay in India for his full term appointment, and Clara described him looking like an ill man or even a 'loony'.[60]

Galletti's memoir version of the Guntur story is fascinating, because it is really an allegory for the effective end of his Indian career. Written separately from his contemporary then revisionist accounts, the memoir has Jack Smith (Arthur Galletti) called to Madras for a private meeting with a Governor's Council member, Sir Lionel Davidson, who advises that S[hield] wants to leave Guntur because the task is too difficult for him. Europeans were in danger, village officers resigning *en masse*, Shield was denied supplies while in camp, taxes were withheld, the whole region was in open revolt. The local Congress chief and member of the All-India Congress Committee, Konda Venkatapayya, was at large and the district out of control, in the government's view. Davidson declares that government considers Smith/Galletti the only man up to the job. Davidson reports, too, that Delhi has authorised the use of troops to quell disturbances, suggesting 'a little judicious bloodletting' will calm things.

Discussions then ensue between Davidson, Willingdon and Galletti during which the latter makes a fine distinction between 'force' and 'violence'. He will accept a show of force, but troops must not enter villages and there will be no firing—except at ducks on local ponds to amuse the natives. Galletti will employ 'Soul Force', like the Mahatma, but assisted by economic force. He will seize property in lieu of unpaid taxes, and threaten resigning village officers with permanent and irrevocable loss of hereditary right to office. At the conversation's end, Galletti asks if he will be transferred should his methods fail. Willingdon replies he can give no assurances.

---

59 Clara to mother, 8 February 1922, Galletti Papers.
60 Clara to mother, 18 February 1922, Galletti Papers.

Galletti goes to Guntur to implement his plan, knowing he has only Willingdon's confidential support and that conservative Secretariat antagonists will replace him with a 'law and order' man at first opportunity. He approaches Konda Venkatapayya who, predictably, is unavailable but who, according to this version, pays his taxes via his brother and has the women in his family treated in a government hospital, all the while running the Non-Co-Operation Campaign. Galletti has this information published in the *Hindu* newspaper and Venkatapayya loses face. Galletti then sees the Provincial and District Congress Secretaries indicating they can stage whatever meetings they want, say what they want, publish what they want and not be suppressed (all this was in Telugu, according to the memoir, Galletti happy to join 'the boycott of English' that was part of the campaign). He would punish non-payment of tax, however, because tax was the government's lifeblood and the source of progress for the 'real' Indian people.

Three Congress members then advocate the non-payment of tax and are arrested. Galletti provides them an opportunity to recant, they reject it and are jailed for one year. The seizure of property in lieu of tax begins. In this version, though, it is all very amicable. A herd of cattle is rounded up and taken away from Adoni village but the people run after the officials, pay the tax, then stage a play about the adventures of the cattle!

Galletti joins Guntur's 'educated native' club, alternating between that and the European one. He offends the Presidency's Inspector-General of Forests by ordering him back to Madras because he cannot guarantee his safety. Galletti himself is safe because he is respected, even loved by all. Local people know him as a man of peace who favours freedom for India. He dutifully attends a regional Collectors meeting convened by a Member of the Board of Revenue [Harris] but resolutely goes his own, correct way. It is purely a local matter, he says. The *karnams* are striking for better conditions, not resigning, and village officers cannot collect tax without the *karnams'* accounts. One rich peasant says if he does not pay tax, the funds will buy more jewels for his wife rather than go to Gandhi.

Galletti hires hordes of clerks to assist his campaign without seeking Madras approval. Tax collection begins, all signs suggesting success. He then goes to the disaffected town of Tenali where he is assassinated by agitators who know their movement is doomed if he is not stopped. Smith/Galletti is killed because his goodness and popularity are defeating political extremism. He had to be stopped because he threatened the future of Congress.

It is likely that this version was also based on Hilton Brown's literary account of the campaign that itself directly reflected Galletti's Guntur experiences. The twist is that while Brown's ICS man leaves the service for another career, Galletti's character perishes. This is a telling difference because whereas Brown saw a future, Galletti really saw no way out because India had taken a turn of which he disapproved.

While the memoir version has a solid factual basis in fact, key events and actions are modified to suit the case being made. The allegory, though, is clear. Smith, or Galletti, is the only man who could save the British from themselves, but was stopped because vested interests within the Secretariat wanted to prevent rather than advance change. His "assassination" was, in reality, his rapid transfer out of the district. Smith/Galletti argued that while the taxes had only started to come in when he was transferred they would have come in fully, justifying his campaign. All the while, his Madras enemies were out to get him at the first opportunity. His fraternising with the locals and his general popularity signified his being in tune with the aspirations of the people, and against the reactionary Madras forces. The reactionary forces won.

The interest lies, first, in the version of events then, second, in the ending. If the memoir version is close to correct, and evidence suggests it is, then Galletti clearly believed in the correctness of his own approach irrespective of Guntur ground conditions. He was firmly convinced of his own power to deal with the locals and to 'win'. The ending shows that in Galletti's mind, Guntur marked the psychological highpoint and endpoint of his career.

That is surprising because Galletti clearly collapsed in face of the campaign with the work done largely by his deputies, especially Rutherford whom he regarded as an excellent officer. For years later, though, Galletti recalled Guntur as the height of his success and *the* way to deal with India and Congress. In his 1935 Telugu dictionary there are at least two references to Guntur. In one, he referenced *"asprusyudu"* (untouchable) by recollecting that Gandhi's Non-Co-Operation campaign collapsed once untouchability became an agenda item, and he repeated the story of the *khaddar* burning. In the second reference Galletti demonstrates the use of *cutra* (plot) by having a village headman, one of those allegedly resigning, say *'idi Brahmana cutra"*, "this is a Brahman plot'. Galletti continued to believe, against all evidence, that Congress had weak support within the general population, and that Indians everywhere believed sympathetic men like him guaranteed the future.

Years later, significantly, Galletti received a response from Lord Willingdon to whom he sent yet another version of the Guntur episode. On that response, Galletti made a series of annotations for 'HB' (Hilton Brown) to whom he sent a copy of the memoir. It was, he told Brown, "all fact except for the murder from which Willingdon saved me by transferring me. Otherwise I would have been like Ashe" [Ashe was a Collector murdered in Tinnevelly in 1911].[61] In other words, Galleti was not transferred from Guntur because he had failed, but because his life was endangered and Willingdon wanted to save his Soul Force man.

---

61 See Willingdon to Galletti, 7 May 1936.

7

Falling Star, 1922-1930

Compounding his professional pressures, Galletti's personal life by now resembled *A Passage to India*. Throughout their marriage, Arthur and Clara held divergent attitudes towards sex and love. Clara considered herself a passionate, devoted and enthusiastic person who needed to focus on one person in her life, her husband. For her, sex was an essential element in her love for Arthur. Continuing his pre-marriage arguments, however, Arthur viewed sex as a purely functional matter between two people who, matched by character, chose to spend their lives together. Sex enabled them to have as many children as possible. That was healthy, but unrelated to love.

Clara tried constantly to understand his views, but found them frustrating and unconvincing. Her diaries show that from about 1917-1918 until the mid-1920s she was generally unhappy with their sexual relationship, mainly because Arthur considered that it satisfied a physical appetite more than expressing affection. She moved into her 40s during that period, and the onset of the menopause concerned her deeply because Arthur wanted still more children, as he told her, and she was desperate to produce them. Combined with what she regarded as his unfeeling approach to sex, her failure to conceive added frustration. She was deeply unhappy personally, extremely worried by Arthur's reckless approach to his career, concerned by what would happen to their children if he was sacked, and saddened by the growing loss of family members back in Italy— her beloved sister Margot (Margherita) died in 1924, her sister Laura in 1928.

Clara was evidently deeply depressed. Her attention to household duties was obsessive, forever cleaning and mending and making lists of things for cleaning and mending. That suited Arthur. As well as keeping her occupied, these activities meant Clara kept immaculate household accounts, informing him exactly how much he could spend on planned future world trips. That financial rashness caused Clara more concern. She was continuously ill, but willed herself to incessant physical activity: walking, playing tennis, cycling everywhere she could. That helped match Arthur's equally frenetic physical activity, but also helped prove she could carry on. A startling change in her appearance resulted. In Tinnevelly towards the end of World War I, Christopher Masterman considered her the thinnest woman he had ever seen. That description jars with vibrant photographs of young Clara but matches the graying, saddened images from this period.

She felt neglected by Arthur and that inspired violent mood swings, no doubt compounded by the menopause. Playing tennis, snooker, cards or any other vaguely competitive activity Arthur mercilessly, publicly berated what he considered her poor play. She would tolerate attack for a while then explode, burst into tears and leave the venue, usually one of the local clubs where members became accustomed to spectacular Galletti domestic disputes. This talented and beautiful woman was nearing collapse.

While in Chittoor, however, she met C. Deveraja Mudaliar. He was an Indian lawyer, a public prosecutor appearing before Arthur in court. Routinely, for a respectable Indian professional man, he married early and led a conformist family life. A reflective man, he had cultural interests beyond his work and read widely, thought deeply and discussed willingly. He was a good tennis player. Unlike most young Indian lawyers of the time, Deveraja Mudaliar eschewed Congress politics, was satisfied with his career and prospects, and enjoyed district station life where he had standing and respect. Because Arthur and Clara attended both the European and Indian clubs, they met him frequently. While Arthur was away on camp or otherwise absent from Chittoor, Clara usually attended the clubs alone. That provided opportunity for her and Deveraja Mudaliar to meet, play tennis and discuss their own ideas on literature, art, culture, music and politics.

The inevitable happened: the lonely, worried, depressed Clara found in the Indian lawyer someone who listened, considered and respected her views, and sympathised with her concerns. She found someone who cared about her. As she put it wonderfully, however, 'they stumbled but did not fall'. They kissed a lot, no more than that, and Clara announced to Arthur she was in love with Deveraja Mudaliar. She remained faithful to Arthur who was her husband whom she loved even if she did not feel loved back, she said, but another man was now in her life.

She suggested that had Arthur understood the interplay between desire and emotion then, first, he would have avoided Nancy in Simla and, second, not driven Clara towards another man.[1] She craved affection, she said, because Arthur forever belittled, dismissed and criticised her views. That drove her towards "D", as she identified him, 'not entirely...but in very great measure'. Arthur might separate desire from emotion, but she could not. Moreover, she did not want to separate those emotions, because freeing herself from emotion would remove her desire and she definitely did not want that. Sadly, she wrote, even at her most loving and even lustful moments she never experienced with Arthur what one novelist described as that 'delicious all-overish feeling'. She knew she was capable of reaching and needed that feeling.

This situation was potentially toxic. As E.M. Forster and others noted, British India was deeply prejudiced about interracial fraternisation. In larger cities, particularly, clubs were organized strictly along racial lines with unstated but powerful social

---

1   See her letters to Arthur, 30 January 1924, 5 January 1927 and 30 January 1927, Galletti Papers.

rules governing who might mix with whom and when. Strong enough normally, the code was overwhelming when gender became involved. It was unthinkable that a European woman, even a strongly independent and intelligent Anglo-Italian one, would contemplate a relationship with an Indian man no matter how light-skinned and intelligent. That was demonstrated, for example, by the contempt for mixed race children. A 'touch of the tar brush' or 'country' invoked social death, contempt for the 'Chi Chi' being deeply seated and felt. In a gossipy small town like Chittoor, there was enormous potential for scandal.

Galletti initially feigned flippancy at Clara's announcement: 'how funny!' was his immediate response. Things then turned bizarre. Personally he was neither concerned nor cared, he claimed, but he must protect Clara's reputation. Galletti had deep concern for his own reputation, too. He was already in trouble professionally, so any revelations about Clara's even innocent relationship with an Indian would harm him further in Madras. So, he constructed 'ground rules' for Clara and her new friend: every kiss must be reported to him, the pair's voluminous correspondence submitted to him for approval, and he would sanction every aspect of the relationship.[2] Surprisingly, Clara and 'D' agreed, perhaps because they had little option.

The relationship proceeded that way for almost two years before Arthur sent Clara back to Europe on leave, and during her absence felt no need to vet the correspondence: Clara and Deveraja Mudaliar were physically apart, although she thought constantly about the lawyer while in England. In one letter to Arthur she wondered why her relationship with 'the Thambi' [younger brother], as she now called Deveraja Mudaliar, had developed: he recognised she was 'an ugly old woman', she

---

2   Clara also wrote many letters to Devaraja Mudaliar that were never sent. He destroyed them in the 1960s after receiving them from a Galletti family member.

recognized his physical slightness.[3] However, 'D' touched Clara's emotional needs and, as she argued, for her that underlay desire. The leave helped cool Clara's feelings, though, because when away from Arthur for long spells she missed him and, paradoxically, felt closer to him because of their inveterate letter writing. They wrote prodigiously when apart in India for even a day or so, but during long term separations the letters assumed deeper character and Clara felt that, in them, Arthur revealed far more about his feelings for her than he could in person.

She returned to India, the relationship with 'D' became more an older sister/younger brother one (they addressed one another as such from then on), and was tempered by a further long leave when Arthur and Clara went back to Europe during late-1923. During that trip one family story has Arthur turning up in Florence, where the girls were in school, dressed in colourful gypsy clothes and with his hair extremely long, perhaps a temporary escape from the social rigidity of south India. Clara's friendship with the Indian lawyer remained deep, though. When Deveraja Mudaliar's wife died young in 1923, for example, he wrote wrenchingly to Clara as the only friend in whom he could confide. Clara and Deveraja Mudaliar corresponded right up until her death in 1939, and over 20 years after that he recalled how much they had 'loved' each other.

As that alternative relationship steadied, however, Arthur Galletti escalated another deeply personal issue dividing him and Clara.

Clara long suspected Arthur had experienced other women before their marriage, but she never knew for sure. Arthur chose this difficult period to regale her with full details of the Nancy affair, praising the latter's sexual enthusiasm and performance. He also announced that Nancy was not the only one. He showed Clara the letters Nancy wrote to him, letters that remained in the house. According to Galletti's memoir, he lost his virginity

---

3   Clara to Arthur, 29 April 1920.

to a French woman met and paid on London's Edgeware Road. As Clara's diaries reveal, Arthur's later revelations included description of an Indian prostitute's 'black bush' and 'small bubs'. Clara was devastated. The 'Nancy affair' plagued her increasingly, aggravating her health problems. 'Nancy' dominated Clara's life thereafter and throughout the 1920s she was seriously depressed, largely the result of this new knowledge. She mixed jealousy with rage. Galletti sometimes referred to his time with Nancy as a 'temporary marriage', depressing Clara even more. Emerging from her own happy experience with Deveraja having not 'fallen', and dealing with her husband's almost messianic commitment to jeopardizing his career, she came extremely close to a serious breakdown and, indeed, may well have had one.

Clara considered herself seriously misled. She endured the long engagement, trusted Arthur, and tried to cope with his very different views on sex and love. She turned her own potential love affair into a friendship, dealt with everything Arthur inflicted on the family through his professional bravado, and fought through the serious social difficulties caused by those trials. She separated herself from her children to support Arthur, and ran a difficult household through innumerable shifts all over the Presidency. Having done all that she discovered herself, to her mind, betrayed.

Many years later, however, Arthur Galletti declared to his granddaughter Elizabeth Skinner that he and Clara both entered their marriage as virgins, and that he never touched another woman until after Clara's death. The second part of that statement is almost certainly true, but the first part is debatable. There is no doubt that he told Clara he had pre-marital experience, because the issue was the subject of discussion in many of their letters over many years. He also records the Nancy affair in considerable detail in the semi-fictional memoir. Then, Clara recorded in her diary that Arthur told her the details of the Indian prostitute. There is the possibility that he made up these stories in order to provoke her, or even to reflect upon opportunities passed up. On balance, however, it seems likely that he did not go virgin to the marriage, and that his later revelations were part of his campaign to separate sex from love.

Whatever the case, Nancy so dominated Clara's mind that Galletti determined the matter required resolution, and in the mid-1920s lit upon an extraordinary scheme by which to do so. He demanded they both write fictionalised 'love story' accounts of his affair and Clara's episode with Deveraja Mudaliar. The stories were submitted to four 'independent' referees for assessment of 'rights and wrongs'. Leading questions directed the exercise: should Arthur have succumbed to Nancy (remembering his version of the affair); was he callous in taking advantage of Nancy; should he have infomed Clara before their marriage? What those questions further suggest, of course, is that if he made up the Nancy story then it was an elaborate one, to say the least.

The four so-called 'independents' favoured Arthur far more than Clara who had little to say in their selection. The first was Galletti's mother, Margaret Collier. His uncle, Sir John Collier, was by now extremely experienced in dealing with Galletti's escapades. The third was Hilton Brown, fellow ICS man, published novelist, and member of the ICS Association committee lambasted by Arthur in 1918-1919. That left Margaret Cousins. The wife of J.H. Cousins, a minor Anglo-Irish poets' group member, Margaret was an accomplished concert pianist and social activist with a strong interest in women's rights. The Cousins' were Theosophists who shifted to Adayar in 1917 to work closely with Annie Besant. Clara met Margaret Cousins, liked her, and the two became good friends.

Margaret Collier's view was that 99 men out of 100 would have accepted Nancy's offer but, really, the girl was shameless! Sex was for the creation of children, not for animal pleasure (echoing some of Arthur's own views). Arthur probably should not have succumbed but he was just a man, after all.

Jack Collier was predictable. The affair was healthy for both Arthur and Nancy and, after all, she seduced him. It did no good having two virgins coming to a marriage so Galletti had solved that problem [he may have solved it earlier, of course]. Were Arthur to change anything he should not have told Clara at all, let alone before the marriage.

Hilton Brown's first reaction was hilarious. No publisher would support this as a credible plot for a novel, he opined. The "hero" [Arthur] was a cold, uncaring, unsympathetic even cruel person who needed far more rounding to become attractive. It was unsustainable to depict a European woman in a relationship with an Indian man, it was simply not the done thing. No publisher could accept that. Then, who would possibly believe a storyline where a husband dictated all letters between his wife and her "lover", interrogating then approving all interactions between the couple? Who would believe that? Who would agree to that?

Pressed for direct answers, Brown echoed Sir John Collier—the girl "was asking for it". Galletti acted as any normal man would. Galletti recorded in his "love story" that at the same time in Simla a fellow Madras ICS man [it was Hopetoun Stokes] received a similar offer from a "grass widow". Rather than taking her up, Stokes fled to the Club to protect his virtue. Hilton Brown thought him an ass. Stokes married much later in life, after he met Lady Alice Lawrence, grand-daughter of Sir John Lawrence the British hero of Lucknow in 1857.

Margaret Cousins alone lashed Galletti. His behaviour was disgusting. The woman was an aggressor, set on trapping the man in marriage and using sex as bait. He [Galletti] should have recognised and denied that. Perceptively, Margaret Cousins suggested the story's male character was simply ignorant of female psychology. That stood demonstrated, she argued, in any suggestion he had sex with Nancy to be kind to her. Really, he used her cynically, even cruelly, satisfying his needs. That captured Galletti's general approach to Clara, as was now obvious.

Galletti was delighted, gratified that three of the four assessors thought his behaviour predictable and, to his mind, defendable. He forecast Margaret Cousins' view, coming as it did from a founder and leader of the Women's Indian Association, an organization in which Clara was prominent by the early 1920s. The cost of 'victory' was immense, though. Clara was affronted, betrayed by all responses except Margaret Cousins', and wrote to Jack Collier attacking his views.[4] She felt abandoned, her diaries revealing increased insecurity, deepening sadness and pained determination to quell her fears.

Remarkably, having read Nancy's letters Clara developed a strong sympathy for as well as jealousy of her. Arthur betrayed both women, Clara concluded, because he whetted their sexual appetites, encouraged and exploited them with no intention of ever creating a genuine long-term emotional relationship. Nancy was treated badly, and Clara wondered if her own darkness might lift if she discovered that Nancy had not 'come to grief' because of the affair with Arthur.[5]

As late as 1929, Clara wrote to Arthur from Italy that she endured a 'paucity of endearments' from him throughout their marriage. Why could he not tolerate her views on the links between passion and desire? After all, they felt the same way about each other when they actually made love, so why could they not accept each other's philosophical foibles? "Would it not be more unselfish to think sometimes of what I like?"[6] Underlining the point, she observed that she wrote the letter at the very *Cassace* table on which she recorded the same arguments during the long engagement years.

---

4 Clara Diary, 24 December 1926, Galletti Papers.

5 Clara to Arthur, 30 January 1924, Galletti Papers.

6 Clara to Arthur, 9 September 1929—she was on leave in Europe while Arthur visited Australia, Galletti Papers.

Clara's next few years were dark, Margaret with Cousins one of the few people in whom she confided. While in Chingleput, Clara initiated and directed a local branch of the Women's Indian Association, the organization in which Margaret Cousins was so influential. In mid-1923, Margaret Cousins wrote "in black and white" to tell Clara just "how much of a help and a comrade in the work for women and in my own life you have been all this past year. ... I have so much admired your utter absence of pride of place, your energy and self-giving and your sincere sisterliness."[7] Margaret Cousins wished there were more Western women like Clara in India, women with ability and an organizational gift. Significantly, she urged Clara to remember her own abilities, achievements and skills at those moments of 'depression' that hit everybody who doubted they could reach their ideal goals. She enclosed for Clara a copy of her new book, inscribed "With love and best wishes to my good comrade in the cause of women, Mrs Galletti."[8] Margaret Cousins might have been the only person to recognise Clara's fragility, and how damaged she was by the professional and personal trials wrought by Arthur whom Cousins respected as an enlightened administrator if not as a man.

Clara responded to Margaret Cousins and later in 1923, for example, turned to her when she received what she considered a dreadful and insensitive letter from Arthur. She described the letter to her friend but did not share it directly. Margaret Cousins responded that she could well imagine the contents, and advised Clara to burn it then proceed with her life as if the incident had not occurred.[9]

The overwhelming point here is that Arthur Galletti was now challenged on all sides. He professed indifference to difficulties and claimed a thick skin. Throughout the 1920s, however, he

---

7   Margaret Cousins to Clara, 6 May 1923, Galletti Papers.

8   Cousins, Margaret *The awakening of Asian womanhood* (Madras, Ganesh, 1922).

9   Margaret Cousins to Clara, Christmas Eve 1923, Galletti Papers.

was drained by self-inflicted professional damage caused by his intemperate actions, and by a brittle home life where his intelligent, able and attractive wife was devoured by demons he visited upon her. His Guntur collapse becomes far more explicable in that context and so, too, do his coming adventures.

Additionally, Galletti now encountered his own health problems. Clara's diary entry for 8 May 1925 commented on a large swelling on his neck, a swelling that came and went periodically and worried her considerably. This was the first mention of the thyroid problem that Galletti developed but left largely undiagnosed until near the end of his career after which it was operated on in Auckland, New Zealand immediately following his retirement. Throughout Clara's diaries, too, there was constant mention that his eyes were 'not right' to the point where he must lie in a darkened room to escape glare and the accompanying pain. Most photographs from the period show him wearing darkened glasses. He was now 48 years old, and had clearly suffered a serious mental depression during his short spell in Guntur. That experience and the ongoing medical condition help explain much of what happened in the last third of his Indian service when he became renowned as a constant litigant and troublemaker, as even he recognised in one of his poems:

The Black Sheep of the I.C.S.

He is, alas, we must confess,
A member of the I.C.S.;
The blighted brute is more or less
An I.C.S.

But stauncher members must deplore
A fact he won't let us ignore;
He's cursed with rather less than more
Esprit de corps.

He pulls the legs of B. and G.*
And with illustrious ones makes free,
We cannot even make him see
the error of his ways.

When I.C.S. of white descent
Black men's equality resent
And very humbly represent
It's time we went,

The treacherous fool will not agree
But has the vile audacity
To call our mild and humble plea
White mutiny.

He is a man of strangest whim:
A Tin God by the Hooghly brim
A little tin god is to him
and it is nothing more.

He survived Horsleykonda but the 'White Mutiny' lived on in government folklore, and his perceived Guntur failure barred him from reaching positions above Collector. Indeed, there were constant questions about his continuing tenure even in that position, his increasingly combative behaviour raising constant possibility of his being sacked.

Following the Non-Co-Operation terrors Galletti was switched from Guntur to Chingleput trading places with H.A.B. Vernon, known in Madras as an Oxford rugby blue, brother-in-law of Madeleine Slade who became known as Mirabehn in service of Mahatma Gandhi, and 'the rudest man in the Service.'[10]

---

*   Board and Government

10   Vernon is not recorded as a 'blue', however–A.C.M. Croome, *Fifty years of sport at Oxford, Cambridge and the great public schools* (London, Southwood, 1913), vols. 1 and 2.

Galletti's most daring Chingleput achievement was having Margaret Cousins appointed as British India's first woman magistrate. The Gallettis had known the Cousins for some time, Margaret being the closest thing Clara had to a European friend during her time in India.[11] The Cousins were leading Theosophists and close to Annie Besant who, after her Home Rule Campaign, was disliked intensely by Secretariat seniors even if she was still invited to Government House. Around this time, an aide-de-camp who married the Governor's daughter reported Mrs. Besant the only Madras woman who still curtsied to the Governor. She deplored "the modern generation"! Melville Portal also reported that garden parties were perennially awful—1200 people attended one-and he, too, thought top hats unsuitable in India.[12] The Gallettis, then, flouted standard Madras 'society' conventions by mixing with the Cousins and Annie Besant, visits made easier because the Chingleput Collector's headquarters were physically near the Theosophists' Adayar base.

Margaret Cousins recalled her appointment clearly.[13] "Our friends the Gallettis" came for dinner and suddenly Arthur, in his 'incisive' voice, asked: "Mrs Cousins, would you like to be a magistrate?" Strikingly, even though they were close friends, it was always 'Mrs Cousins' and 'Mrs Galletti', another marker of the rigid social barriers prevailing in white civilian south India. Margaret Cousins had no formal claim on a magisterial position, apart from her strong interests in women's rights. This was no thought-out proposal, Galletti declaring: "It has occurred to me only now," confirming both his impulsive manner and

11 Catherine Candy "Relating Feminisms, Nationalisms and Imperialisms: Ireland, India and Margaret Cousins' Sexual Politics"In Women's history review, 3, 4 (December 1994).

12 Melville Portal to his parents, 21 January 1926, Portal Papers Eur F 472/5, IOR.

13 Cousins James H. and Cousins, Margaret E. We two together, (Madras, Ganesh, 1950), pp. 406-7.

his immediate conviction about being right. Margaret Cousins agreed to the proposal, Galletti put it to the Government of Madras.

Astonishingly, within a month the government agreed to appoint as a judge a Theosophist nominated by the ICS' blackest sheep. The most likely explanation for this appears in the Cousins' autobiography.[14] Several months earlier, while running her school in Chittoor, Margaret Cousins was invited by R.N. Ellis, the Collector, to attend a dinner in honour of the Governor, Lord Willingdon. Margaret Cousins put this invitation down to the Collector being a fellow Irishman. At the dinner she played piano, and was seated close to Willingdon who engaged her in lively conversation. The pair got on well despite their obvious political and social reform differences. When her nomination arrived, then, Willingdon had his own knowledge of Margaret Cousins and was not solely reliant on advice from his senior executives whom he distrusted anyway. Had he relied on their advice they undoubtedly would have opposed the appointment simply because it came from Galletti.

The appointment caused widespread interest across India and Galletti, who considered a woman's viewpoint was especially important in cases involving women, achieved an important first.[15] The supreme irony, of course, is that Margaret Cousins deplored Galletti's treatment of his wife, essentially because he hindered rather than enhanced her own interests in emancipation and advancement. Margaret Cousins later turned increasingly towards nationalist politics, was on the Madras beach for the 1928 Simon Commission protest meeting that ended in several deaths, then went to prison for supporting Gandi during Civil Disobedience in the early 1930s. The continuing friendship would not have improved Galletti's standing with official circles in Madras.

---

14   *Ibid.*, pp. 375-6.

15   See *Civil and Military Gazette*, 23 February 1923.

While in Chingleput, Galletti also took great interest in the 'Depressed Classes' (the untouchables in Indian caste society), for whom another of his initiatives used Government funds to open a home and training centre. Named Gallettipettai, the centre caused considerable local interest. His reported opening day speech attracted adverse Secretariat comment, because he declared that Mahatma Gandhi was "the real benefactor of the Depressed Classes in Chingleput and his name was a household name in all the *cheries* [slums]."[16] In the aftermath of Non-Co-Operation and the context of heading off Gandhi and Congress, those comments incensed senior Madras figures.

Late in 1923, after 18 months in Chingleput Galletti took leave for several months and on return was transferred to Cuddapah, recognized within the Madras ICS as a prime 'punishment' posting. There was no one cause for the shift, but it indicated that Galletti was seriously estranged from senior Secretariat officials. Within six months he took further leave and there was again family talk of him quitting the service. Financial pressure made that impossible, because the sons were at Cheltenham and plans were afoot to have the girls educated at a church school in Florence. At the end of 1924 things took a turn for the better and he was posted to Ganjam, the northernmost Madras district and one he and Clara both came to love.

Ganjam was huge, over 8,000 square miles but 'one of the most beautiful' Presidency districts.[17] The district had two distinct regions. The plains lay below the Eastern Ghats while the *maliahs,* the hill country, was populated almost totally by the Khond and Savara tribal groups. The hill country was known as the Agency, the Collector overseeing affairs as an agent for the Governor because no tax was collected directly from the people there. The district had several estates and *zamindari* holdings.

---

16   *Hindu,* 28 March 1923.

17   T.J. Maltby. *The Ganjam district manual,* (Madras, Lawrence Asylum Press, 1882), p.1. This section is drawn from the Manual.

Climatically, Ganjam was more pleasant than most districts with the hot season reasonably short and the rest of the year pleasant, apart from high humidity near the coast during the rainy months from June to November. District headquarters were at Chatrapur, a small but beautiful town distinctive for nothing else but being home to the Collector. The town stood above the sea, the ancient *banian* trees in the Collector's compound considered a tourist attraction. Chatrapur was 'relaxing', Clara thought. It lay 12 miles from the main town of Berhampore and within striking distance of Russellkonda, another beautiful hill station where bear and other wildlife flourished.

Traditionally, ICS men loved Ganjam because game hunting there was among the Presidency's best, and many hunting stories came from the district. One of Galletti's 19th century predecessors was Gordon Sullivan Forbes who joined the Madras service in 1838 and went on to become Secretary to the Board of Revenue around the time of the 1857 uprising. His lasting mark on India was his hunting book that typified Ganjam's reputation.[18]

Galletti loved the hill country, especially, and Clara thought him never happier than in those days. He was, she said, the "King of Kondhistan", lord of all he surveyed and architect of many grand schemes for road and bridge improvement, many of which he considered necessary for military purposes. His argument was that the hill country experienced many tribal uprisings so the military needed the quick access provided by better roads. In his view, he did more in three years to develop Ganjam than his predecessors had achieved in 30. He spent much time on tour, planning new development schemes. Galletti wanted to stay in Ganjam and become what he called the Perpetual Collector. It was well recognised, he argued, that districts like Ganjam and

---

18   Gordon Sullivan Forbes. *Wild life in Canara and Ganjam* (London, Swan Sonnenschein, 1885).

adjoining Vizagapatam needed long term appointees because they were large, difficult, complex and demanding. It took special men like him to make a difference.[19]

Clara found Ganjam life fulfilling, too, developing her own interests and exploring the region with Arthur while he was on tour. She befriended an elderly Canadian missionary whom she thought young in spirit. An excellent Telugu speaker, Miss Archibald had lived in the area a long time, and asked Clara if she would like to meet some Indian women: "I jumped at the suggestion."[20] Soon Clara was an active member of the Durbar Association, as the local Indian women's group was named because of its 1911 creation, the year of the Durbar. Clara spent considerable time with these women, emphasising how important it was that the advancement of women be used to drive the nation's development. She felt useful and appreciated.

Inevitably, the Gallettis also met alternative thinkers frowned on by government. One was Dr. Ernest Forrester Paton, a medical missionary Scot and renowned advocate for political change in India. After an early stint as missionaries, he and his wife left India because they were so appalled by British official attitudes towards Indians. They returned in 1920 to establish a North Arcot district ashram where Paton remained until his death in. Paton became a controversial figure in 1930 when he joined Gandhi's Civil Disobedience campaign and received a beating during a Madras demonstration. The Patons visited Ganjam frequently to assist Clara's other missionary friends, so senior Madras officials again saw Galletti mixing with known anti-government figures.

---

19   Galletti to Chief Secretary, 30 June 1926, Galletti Papers, and Galletti to Sir C.P. Ramaswami Ayyar, 12 October 1926, Galletti Papers.

20   Clara to Mother, 27 April 1925, Galletti Papers.

Content though he was, Galletti still sought promotion opportunities. He proposed that the Government of Madras keep him long-term in Ganjam but appoint him to Board of Revenue Member rank 'on paper', for which read pay scale. Alternatively, Madras might create a special and substantial pay loading for a Ganjam posting that he would then gladly accept.[21] Neither option was adopted by the Secretariat.

The suggestion was self-serving but demonstrated, first, how much he wanted to stay in Ganjam and how much he enjoyed being there and, second, that he had a deep-seated sense that his worth was unappreciated. He spent long spells on tour at great family expense, because "the Collector" still paid many camping costs despite the Montagu-Chelmsford reforms. Galletti, in fact, petitioned government to change tentage allowance rules. He claimed to tour more than any other officer, and he was probably right. Galletti loved walking and climbing, fishing and shooting, fording rivers on horseback and creating new tracks, dealing with tribals and solving local problems. Like many ICS men he was a keen hunter, if not a good one—Clara was thankful that he was a poor shot because she hated the number of animals killed in British India. He preferred the horses and cycles, but travelled in cars and trucks and learned to drive, badly. Madras and the Secretariat were a long way off, he could play the role to which he always aspired, "The Collector" of what was really a small kingdom. He professed himself happy and content to stay in Ganjam for the rest of his career but because his ICS status fell short of his ambition and pride, conflict soon loomed again.

In the second half of 1926, Galletti learned he was passed over for temporary appointment to the Board of Revenue. The post was only for two months but two things annoyed him. First, he considered himself the senior and appropriate man. He did not want the post but principle and, indeed, the rules demanded he be offered the opportunity. The second reason was more

---

21   Galletti to Chief Secretary, 30 June 1926, Galletti Papers.

personal, and possibly the dominant one, because the post went to H.H.F.M. Tyler, the Secretariat's star Kistna Collector when Galletti was dispatched from Guntur. Tyler had a low opinion of Galletti then, and said so to L.T. Harris and colleagues.

Henry Hewey Francis Macdonald-Tyler was the sort of person Galletti both envied and despised. The son of an Irish churchman and educated first at St Columba's in Dublin, he attended Rossall then Selwyn College, Cambridge. He was in the Irish XX at Bisley in 1898 and shot for Cambridge in the University matches of 1898-99. Hunting and fishing were his great passions. Just six weeks older than Galletti he arrived in Madras a year later and was soon sent off to manage Vizianagaram, among the largest of Presidency *zamindari* estates. By 1912 he was permanent Secretary to the important Department overseeing salt and other taxes. Unlike Galletti, Tyler went to the front during the war, serving with the Gurkhas before becoming a political officer in Mesopotamia, the same appointment Galletti yearned for on the Italian front. Tyler returned from the war to be awarded a CIE, made a success of Kistna, was appointed as Commissioner of Labour in 1926 and thwarted Galletti at least once more before his knighthood in 1930 and retirement in 1931. Macdonald-Tyler, as he was now known, returned to Ireland to become High Sheriff then Deputy Lieutenant of Londonderry.

Galletti immediately went into letter-writing mode, protesting the decision in yet another Memorial. Forwarding the Memorial to the Governor's Private Secretary, Galletti suggested that being overlooked like this was poor reward for 25 years of hard work and dedicated service.[22] He protested that his past was being held against him, unfairly. He repeated his claim that in 1907-08 his uncle had passed on letters to the Secretary of State and that the then Governor, Sir Arthur Lawley, became antagonistic as a result. Galletti recalled his published

---

22 Galletti to Private Secretary to the Governor, 6 August 1926, Galletti Papers, enclosing Memorial.

war articles and the subsequent ban on his public writing. He declared Horsleykonda an attempt to brand him a revolutionary when he was, in fact, a monarchist, and to punish him for his Montagu-Chelmsford reforms stand. As for Guntur, he triumphed without resorting to the use of violence or troops. In all these matters, he declared, his colleagues ran their case, lost, and held him no grudge. There was no reason for his being passed over now.

His interpretation of key facts was revealing. Where he believed and asserted he was successful in Guntur, most if not all others in the service saw it very differently. R.A. Graham said as much upon Galletti's return to Madras, and Clara herself recorded the depths of his despair in the period immediately after the transfer. Then, his Horsleykonda actions put him at odds with his colleagues and superiors, and he was lucky to escape serious censure. Similarly, his behaviour during the Montagu-Chelmsford reforms outraged those colleagues and superiors and he was lucky to escape dismissal. Believing that his colleagues ran their case, lost, then bore him no ill-will was optimistic verging on delusional.

Galletti was serious in pursuing the Tyler appointment. His campaign, however, involved more than writing directly to government and that led him into further serious difficulty. He wrote formally to all members of the Executive Council informing them of the Memorial, indicating he had:

An uncomfortable...feeling that my opinions or incidents in the past, which are mere reflections or eruptive symptoms of those opinions, are counted against me.[23]

The ICS men on the Council were Norman Marjoribanks and Tommy Moir, the latter having been on the original ICS Association in 1919 and himself elevated to Council over several others. They were well aware of Galletti's reputation and activities and were among those who disliked his 'eruptive symptoms'.

---

23   Galletti to Executive Council Members, 18 October 1926, Galletti Papers.

The other two members were Sir C.P. Ramaswami Iyer and Sir Muhammad Usman, both old Galletti friends. Ramaswami Iyer was a leader of the famed "Mylapore" clique that had been so powerful in city and Presidency politics since the later 19th century, with several of his close relatives being court officials while he was a wealthy lawyer. He was closely aligned with moderate Muslim groups and individuals like Sir Muhammad Usman, while his 'factional' boss Sir P.S. Sivaswami Iyer was the Minister for Local Self-Government between 1912 and 1916 when Galletti was handling reforms of that area in the Secretariat. These affiliations did Galletti little good by this point. The Mylaporeans had supported Mrs. Besant's Home Rule campaign, reacting against the Cardew-led official support for the promotion of non-Brahmins that was aimed specifically at undermining people like Sir P.S. Sivaswami Iyer. Perhaps without his knowing it, Galletti was in the middle of a power play involving his senior officers and leading local political activists. Sir C.P. had become a Minister under the Montagu-Chelmsford reforms, and was not well liked by senior ICS men.

Galletti, however, seeing him as a potential strong ally, now wrote privately to Sir C.P. complaining there was no valid reason for his non-appointment, and that this was just the latest punishment for his being pro-Indian, liberal and democratic.[24] He followed with an even more pointed letter to Sir C.P. from whom he sought protection against ICS vindictiveness. He was aggrieved, he wrote, but "my complaint is against my Caste, which treats me as a rebel." Moir and Marjoribanks were personal friends, he thought, but they held very different views from his own. Moir, for example, "thinks my opinions eccentric and dangerous or my conduct in Guntur weak—a wrong opinion held in good faith." Moir would have advised the Governor to by-pass Galletti, therefore, just as Galletti would have advised the Governor to by-pass Moir for Council membership because 'he is a reactionary'.[25]

---

24   Galletti to Sir C.P. Ramaswami Ayyar, 12 October 1926, Galletti Papers.

25   Galletti to Sir C.P. Ramaswami Ayyar, 17 October 1926.

Galletti considered his letters to Sir C.P. to be written 'privately', but they inevitably reached the Governor and other Council members who, rightly, thought Galletti was using the pretext of a private communication to influence official business. Moir was undoubtedly upset at being branded a reactionary even if he was conservative. He was Galletti's superior officer, after all. The letters were too much for the Governor, Lord Goschen, who believed his authority undermined because his appointment decisions were questioned. Galletti was summonsed to interview. This was serious but Clara believed Arthur 'had a good case', and that his 'pro-Indian views' caused his non-appointment.[26]

Galletti himself was worried, though, approaching the Governor's Private Secretary to indicate he would without question accept any reprimand from the Governor. Being Galletti, though, he added a poem:

> *Mr Galletti wrote from Ganjam*
> *Do you know who I am, I am, I am?*
> *The Governor replied from Madras*
> *Yes, you are an ass, an Ass, AN ASS!*

That impertinence ensured the reprimand meeting would occur. According to Galletti, the session went very well, starting with 'Donner und Blitzen' but ending in smiles and handshakes. The Governor considered Galletti's letters and Memorial a personal affront to his decisions. The letters to Sir C.P. particularly breached protocol because no ICS person could approach a Council individual directly, any approach must be to Council as a whole (as Galletti well knew). Galletti apologised for causing unintended anxiety, thanking Goschen for gifting him Ganjam.

Following that meeting, Galletti somehow came to believe that no senior officials wanted to bar him promotion because of his liberal views.[27] He was spectacularly misguided. His old

---

26 Clara to Mother, 25 October 1926, Galletti Papers.

27 *Ibid.*, 23 November 1926.

nemesis, A.Y.G. Campbell, became Chief Secretary in 1925 and remained so until 1930 when he moved to the Board. Campbell was perennially skeptical about Galletti's ability to hold high office, even that of Collector. In mid-1926, during Galletti's latest skirmish, Campbell outlined his ideal ICS officer:

> Something more is needed besides high educational qualifications to make a good administrator. Powers of leadership, a sense of discipline, driving power, tact, consideration for others, ability to co-operate and 'get on' with others.[28]

He probably considered Galletti the anti-model. Galletti could and would never reach senior positions while Campbell or any of his colleagues held power.

Providing yet more ammunition for his detractors, Galletti wrote for *Young India*, Mahatma Gandhi's main press outlet. On European leave during 1923 Galletti gathered considerable information on farming methods and practices there, especially in Italy, then applied the key principles to India. He argued that Italian irrigation practices essentially created paddy field conditions, so should be adopted in India to improve productivity. A crop rotation system, he argued, would improve pasture. That would improve cattle quality and so better protect the peasant's main capital investment. At present, he argued, Indian cattle were of very poor quality and remarkably unproductive.[29]

His criticism of Indian cattle health was cited by Mahatma Gandhi in *Young India*, then picked up by another notorious person. Katherine Mayo, an American writer, visited India to assess social conditions and the British establishment subsequently castigated her subsequent book, *Mother India*, for

---

28 Campbell note, 26 June 1926, GOM Public 831 Letter Confl 16 September 1926, TNA.

29 A. Galletti, *Paddy and Pasture* (Madras, Addison, 1926) reprinted from *The Statesman*, 20 September 1925.

casting British rule in poor light. The Madras Governor, Lord Goschen, entertained Mayo to dinner early in 1926 while she was researching her book, describing her as 'very pertinacious' in gathering information. That was his very English way of suggesting she was pushy and over-bearing, someone not to be trusted.[30] Mayo was especially concerned with the effects of child marriage, which she described in graphic detail, but she strayed into areas such as India's cattle health. She quoted long sections from Galletti's writings as proof that India sorely needed reform.[31] She described Galletti wrongly as "an Italian-trained specialist, domiciled in India", but her argument that he "has shown us in the cow's hunger one of the evil effects of British rule" would have confirmed for many Madras senior officials that their man had deserted the Raj. Galletti was not responsible for Mayo's writings and had no control over them, but he enjoyed the renegade role and did nothing to dispel possible Secretariat views on his beliefs.

Clara, meanwhile, was alarmed by the prospering of Italian Fascism. Some relatives like her uncle Mario were strongly pro-Mussolini but Clara herself was, as she said, "anti-revolutionary" and by definition anti-Fascist because Mussolini clearly proposed to rule by force, she believed. The family was strongly divided. Cynthia, for example, took Rabindranath Tagore to task for views attributed to him. Clara agreed with the poet, because he was also anti-revolutionary. Clara's mother was anti-Fascist and concerned to know her daughter was not going over to Mussolini like others in the family.[32] Even at this early point, Clara could say: "I fear and tremble for my country," convinced the Fascist phase would end in violence.[33]

---

30   Goschen Diary entry, 28 March 1926, Mss Eur C/429/4, IOR.

31   Mayo, Katherine *Mother India* (London, Butler & Tanner, 1927), pp. 207-10.

32   For example, Clara to Mother, 25 November 1926, Galletti Papers.

33   Clara to Mother, 30 November 1926, Galletti Papers.

Clara hit extremely low points personally during 1927, as revealed in her diary. In mid-January she was so depressed she hit Arthur physically. In response, he recalled his experiences with the Indian prostitute with whose performance he compared Clara's poorly. The day after, she wrote to another Indian friend and Arthur insisted she enclose copies of the 'love stories' he had them each construct for panel assessment. The ensuing row spilled onto the tennis court where his continuing criticism sparked what she termed one of her worst ever 'paroxysms'. That carried on to the house where Arthur poured a bowl of water over her, his attempt to calm her. A few days later he jokingly raised the incident with one of Clara's Chatrapur friends, Mrs. Carrick, who became extremely upset. There was yet another fierce argument and Clara fled.

Even her friends thought she was over-reacting. The Cousins' agreed with her views on the Nancy affair but thought she needed to understand others, including Arthur, might think differently. They were right, but she was unplacated. During March she wondered if she really might go 'mad', not helped by Arthur speculating on what woman he might find to produce the additional nine children Clara had not given him.

News of Galletti family tensions spread. Early in April a senior Secretariat member, C.W.E. Cotton, visited them in Ganjam and at dinner Arthur remarked that Clara was 'cross' and frustrated. Already depressed, Clara "exploded" and later tried to explain her 'madness' to the guest. Charles William Egerton Cotton, Madras representative in Travancore for much of the 1920s, was a cultivated if conservative man who at one time was Joint Secretary of the Indian Society of Oriental Art and closely associated with the Tagore family. From a wealthy Welsh landed family, Cotton was educated at Eton (he wore his old Etonian tie regularly) then University College, Oxford before joining the service. A small, dapper, monocle-wearing man he was a member of both the MCC and the prestigious White's club in London and had recently married the daughter of Sir Philip Mainwaring, the fourth baronet. Cotton's twin brother, a military officer decorated in both the Boer War and World War I, now managed an Argentine cattle ranch. Clara initially considered Cotton an understanding person to whom she might turn, but his seniority meant Galletti household atmospherics became well-known in Madras.

Arthur's only strategy to deal with Clara's state of mind was to continually and publicly criticise her 'depression'. Her constant reply was that she lived in 'Nancy's shadow'. There were moments of truce, even tenderness, but the mood was predominantly corrosive. Early in June Clara became so miserable that she turned 'frantically hysterical', then hurt her hands by banging them hard on the table while screaming, unable to control herself. Arthur began discussing a separation.

After seeing Clara in Madras C. Deveraja Mudaliar said he never imagined to find her so unhappy, distressed and depressed. He was shocked both by her state and by the cause—Galletti's views on relationships were 'barbarous and inhumane', a result of the Collector trying to be a Superman in all matters.[34] She became extremely ill, and Galletti wrote in passing to government that Clara was operated on twice.[35]

They then went on leave through the second half of 1927, to see Galletti's mother who by now was frail and elderly. Shortly before leaving, while reading a Sinclair Lewis novel, Arthur remarked of Nancy that one did not spend "three or four hours" in bed with a woman without having some conversation. As always, Clara recorded that such comments made her 'violent and abusive', and it seems either Galletti had no thought about the effect of his words, or that he deliberately provoked his wife.

While in Europe they spent a little time apart, and a highlight for Clara was hearing gi, though she did not enjoy the particular opera. She discussed her problems with her mother but gained little reassurance, because her mother observed that while she

---

34 C. Deveraja Mudalia to Clara, 27 March 1927.

35 Galletti to Campbell, 25 May 1927.

disapproved of sexual irregularities it was understood they were 'recognised and accepted' facts of life. Clara felt alone. The volatility continued on the way back to India, passion and pain intermixed, and en route through the Red Sea there was a huge row following which 'poor little Beat[rice] tried to comfort' Clara. On landing in Bombay Arthur berated her in public throughout disembarkation, mainly because he had difficulty getting some wine through customs.

They now learned Arthur was being transferred from their beloved Ganjam to Tinnevelly, a Tamil-speaking district he neither wanted nor liked. Clara was 'too upset to eat'. Galletti protested unsuccessfully, so was already back on stage as a serial litigant. He extended his reputation by infringing the Madras Club rules, reprimanded for taking Beatrice in with him. By December 1927, Clara was asking Arthur if he thought they would ever understand each other, and she was in the 'same old cycle of unhappiness and depression' as they set off for Tinnevelly.

By this time in the late-1920s, British India faced yet another set of possible constitutional reforms following the Montagu-Chelmsford ones that so worried the ICS and brought Galletti into such disrepute. During 1927 it was announced the Indian Statutory Commission chaired by Sir John Simon would tour India, gathering opinion about what developments should now occur politically and constitutionally. The Commission arrived, greeted by Congress protests all over India along with strikes and demonstrations and a fierce publicity campaign. There were serious demonstrations in major centres, including Madras where during February 1928 police lost control of the streets and fired on the crowds, causing at least two deaths.[36]

Events were quieter outside Madras, Galletti patrolling Tinnevelly but encountering no serious disturbances during the initial stages, although there were later newspaper accounts

---

36   Brian Stoddart. "The unwanted commission: national agitation and local politics in Madras city", *South Asia*, 5 (December 1975).

of some demonstrations in the port of Tuticorin.[37] The Simon Commission stayed in India for several months, and agitation continued throughout the first half of 1928. By then, the Legislative Council in New Delhi announced it would appoint a national committee to liaise with and advise the main Simon contingent.

Galletti printed up a version of the Presidency component from his 'federated India' scheme to emphasise that the Tamil, Telugu and Canarese regions should become immediately self-governing under any new reforms. British India would retain Madras and the Nilgiri to protect the planting industry. The ICS would be disbanded apart from ten sympathetic men retained as political secretaries to work with the provincial governor.[38] Galletti also contacted former Madras colleagues like Sir Joseph Bhore, now at the All-India level and closely involved in the Commission.[39] He should be called before the Commission, Galletti wrote, because he was the natural 'representative of the federal order of things" that had popular if unarticulated support. At national level Galletti envisaged a three-part system. 'British India' would remain totally controlled by the British and include all port cities, plantation regions, frontiers, agencies (as in Ganjam) and hill stations. That would create a small, prosperous and influential entity. The 'Free States' would include clearly language-based regions like Andhra, the Tamil country, the Canarese, the Oriya, and the Bengali areas. There, sensitive and intelligent British officers like Galletti would help Governors work with locally elected administrations. The 'Princely States' would remain as at present. This was all entirely acceptable to Indian moderates, he claimed.

The important point here is that if his scheme looked radical before World War I, it now looked far less so to rapidly growing numbers of Congress leaders, and even to progressive Secretariat thinkers. Galletti clung to long-term tutelage that might prepare

---

37 Clara Galletti Diary, 3 February and 22 July 1928, Galletti Papers.

38 Galletti to Secretary, Indian Statutory Commission, 3 July 1928, Galletti Papers.

39 Galletti to Bhore, 17 January 1929, Galletti Papers.

moderate Indians for self-rule but through the 1920s, even in Madras, there was a pronounced shift from accepting limited power transfer towards demanding fuller delegation of authority. Galletti's main Madras moderate contacts like C.P. Ramaswami Iyer and P.S. Sivaswami Iyer were losing their support bases, and even Congress leaders like S. Satyamurthi who advocated acceptance of limited power in the early 1920s were now more ambitious. Galletti's 'British India' segment meant retaining an economic and civil sway now unacceptable to Indian opinion and government seniors who foresaw logistic difficulty.

On 29 September 1928, however, Galletti received a letter from another old Madras moderate friend, Sir C. Sankaran Nair who announced he would chair the new Legislative Assembly committee established to support the Simon Commission. Sankaran Nair wanted Galletti as his Committee Secretary because there was no-one better equipped in experience, outlook or temperament.[40] There would be considerable work touring India to gather opinion, then a later stint in England to liaise with the British Government and Simon himself. Clara recorded that both she and Arthur were 'excited at the thought of Secretaryship'.[41] After all this time and torment, Galletti would get the stage he desired, an opportunity to broadcast his views and influence national policy as he thought he had done earlier in his career.

The dream dissolved instantly, because the next day Arthur and Clara learned from the newspaper that H.H.F.M. Tyler would be Secretary to Nair's committee. Tyler, the favoured Krishna Collector during Non-Co-Operation and then preferred over Galletti for the 1926 temporary Second Member's position, had again usurped what Galletti believed rightfully his. Clara and Arthur were devastated. In the time that Nair's letter took to arrive from Delhi the Government of India had canvassed a suitable

---

40 Sir C. Sankaran Nair to Galletti, 22 September 1928, Galletti Papers.

41 Clara Galletti Diary, 29 September 1928, Galletti Papers.

Madras name, because Sankaran Nair lived there, and produced Tyler. Galletti's name was mentioned, but rejected immediately. Galletti wrote to Sankaran Nair, declaring bitterly that 'Tyler is a reactionary', and presuming that was why the government of Madras engineered the appointment, because Tyler would maintain its arch-conservative stand. Galletti had hoped 'his good time and the good time for India was near' but, now that it was not, advised Nair to sack Tyler who would simply block initiatives. Tellingly, Galletti also reported he was in conflict with government over another matter, sedition charges were being laid against some Tinnevelly people 'in spite of my protests.'[42]

Even though it claimed no influence over the choice of Secretary, the Government of Madras could not have allowed Galletti's appointment given his views were so far removed from its own.[43] Another Nair letter arrived a few days later, declaring that 'too many Madras friends' in Delhi had dissuaded the Viceroy from appointing Galletti.[44] A few days later Sankaran Nair told Tyler himself that the Viceroy had been given two names but that the other man (Galletti) lacked sufficient tact to serve well in the post.[45] Tyler, in fact, had just arrived back reluctantly from European leave to learn Galletti was in the running for the post "to which I daresay he aspired. I should have been well enough content had he got it."[46]

Galletti responded to the disappointment with one of his finest letters.[47] He offered Sankaran Nair "heartfelt thanks for the greatest compliment ever paid" to him with the offer. It replaced his earlier highpoint when informed by Sir Mohamad Habibullah

---

42 Galletti to Nair, 30 September 1928, Galletti Papers.

43 C. Deveraja Mudaliar to Clara, 28 October 1929, Galletti Papers.

44 Sir C. Sankaran Nair to Galletti, nd, Galletti Papers.

45 Diary entry for 21 October 1928, *Sir Henry MacDonald Tyler Papers*, Public Record Office for Northern Ireland. I owe this reference to Sandi Stoddart.

46 *Ibid.*, 19 October 1928.

47 Galletti to Sir C. Sankaran Nair, 4 October 1928, Galletti Papers.

and Sir P.S. Sivaswami Iyer that he was as good as any Indian! From the beginning of his career, Galletti wrote, he realised he would not get on by displaying openly his true sentiments and feelings, but he did so consistently to serve the 'people of his adopted country'. His satisfaction came from quelling religious differences in Nellore, political ones in Guntur, tribal ones in Ganjam, and from improving life for Indians through his reform of the local self-government system and his contributions to knowledge through his work on the Dutch records. Throughout the years he struggled for what was right, but he suffered because government was still "treating popularity with the educated classes in India as a disqualification for higher office'. Similarly, government was still "treating sympathy with the aspirations of the people of India as disloyalty to England." Furthermore, the British administrations in India were:

> Yielding to the political prejudices of men who in 30 years of domination (only partially relaxed by the late reforms) over a subject people have shed those liberal and democratic principles that are the glory of England.

Those ICS men were now 'more embittered by the precariousness of their superiority'.

It was a powerful précis of his professional life, an anthem to what he believed should happen in India and, just possibly, a flash of self-realisation rarely present elsewhere in his writings, words or actions.

This was really the first direct and tangible evidence Galletti received that his career was stymied. After the White Mutiny affair he thought Secretariat types would allow him 'nothing' in future, but he did so on the basis of supposition mixed with gossip passed on by his remaining European friends and supported by his Indian friends forever saying that government blocked his way. He had believed his intellect, experience, outlook and ideas would prevail. Here, though, was a clear and unequivocal instance where he was the candidate preferred by a notable and influential politician (and one from Madras, to boot), yet denied because of his reputation.

Galletti half-heartedly protested with yet another Memorial, perhaps realising now his career had definitely, irrevocably and permanently stalled. It was all 'very mysterious', he complained to Board Member Hopetoun Stokes, because he was 'a better man than Tyler'. Galletti had no expectation of the decision being reversed even while pressing the Memorial. "I must not err through an excess of modesty this time," he wrote, arguing he had too meekly accepted earlier career rebuffs.[48] It was all too late now.

It was a dreadful time for the family. Clara was still seriously depressed. Throughout 1928 year Arthur told her repeatedly he thought her 'a bad woman' for succumbing to mental pressure, and she suffered periodic crises of confidence. Arthur provoked her constantly. During February she wondered in her diary "if he could only understand how much pain" he gave her. A few months later, in August, she noted that Arthur's "theories trotted out after dinner (God only knows how and why—except that they are always there to trot out)." Around the same time she attended church with the sermon delivered by the Bishop of Madras whose words made her "think too much of all that troubles me and has destroyed my faith in humanity."

Then, her children caused Clara further anxiety. Their daughter Beatrice, having been in a convent school for so long, now announced she wanted to become a nun. Arthur and Clara were shocked. It was not that they dismissed religion, far from it, but neither thought the world would be a better place if their daughter shut herself away. It was to them a waste of her talent. By mid-1928 Clara was anguished by the issue, writing several letters to Beatrice that were criticised roundly by Arthur and their son Robert. Beatrice arrived home for further discussions in October

---

48   Galletti to Stokes, 1 October 1928, Galletti Papers.

with Clara writing chillingly in her diary: "I feel towards her as I would towards an amputated limb." She spoke 'violently' to Beatrice and several fierce arguments erupted. Berto, meanwhile, took his father's side on several issues including the Nancy one on which, inexplicably, Clara had consulted the children. Clara feared Berto was becoming like his father, noting a tennis evening when Berto broke his racquet in rage and 'swore like a trooper'.

On 17 October 1928, Clara learned her mother had died in Italy, the latest of several family losses and by far the most devastating. Since arriving in India Clara had written to her mother every week, remaining part of her family there and maintaining strong relationships. The two did not agree on everything, but conducted strong debate and remained close despite the long physical separation. It was more the relationship of long-term friends than of mother and daughter, and it was the single most important bond with Italy for Clara, sustaining her long residence in a doubly 'foreign' place. Yet now here she was, on a boat to Colombo en route to Italy without having had the chance to say good bye to her beloved mother.

Following her return from Italy her relationship with Arthur, now in a savagely post-Simon Committee frame of mind, declined further. Early in December 1928 while dining with J.C. Stodart, the Tinnevelly District Judge, Arthur relentlessly harangued Clara about her tastes in light literature, her constant need for sleep, her appalling bridge tactics, and the weakness of her 'favourite poetess'. She kicked him hard but he did not stop, and 'the evening ended very badly'.

At the end of 1928 Galletti received yet another rebuff. As Collector of Tinnevelly he dealt regularly with the princely states of Travancore and Cochin. During his early Secretariat days Galletti enjoyed working with these states, seeing excellent opportunities for progressive men like him to join with enlightened princes to create rapid social and political progress. Galletti also dealt with several *zamindaris* held by wealthy landholders rather than princes but offering similar if lower level opportunities.

Galletti now thought transfer to a Government of India department might solve his career problem so early in 1928 wrote to Sir Denys Bray, Secretary to the Political Department, seeking transfer to the Political cadre pending appointment as the next political agent for the Madras States.[49] As Galletti pointed out, he handled Pudukottai and Banganapalle during his Secretariat days, was now familiar with Travancore, Cochin and Sandur and had written historical articles on them for the Imperial Gazetteer. He wanted, he said, to help develop 'very progressive' states like Travancore and Cochin. Properly, he forwarded his request through the Government of Madras but soon learned that, first, a new appointee was already identified and, second, the Government of India would not transfer him to the Political Department.[50]

Around the time of the rebuff he visited Travancore officially, and was told by a senior court officer that the position of Diwan (effectively Chief Minister) would soon fall vacant and that the ruler wanted to appoint Galletti. Following the Simon Commission and Political Department disappointments this was a glittering prospect He would run his own ship, answer to the Government of India rather than Madras where his enemies were numerous, be extremely well paid and, above all, direct the affairs of an entire State at a time of significant national political change.

Had he played his cards like the skilled bridge master he was he might have pulled it off. The Government of Madras had tolerated years of 'Galletti trouble' so, as yet another period of political tension approached, senior Secretariat officials might

---

49 Galletti to Secretary, Political, GOI, 5 March 1928, Galletti Papers.

50 Private Secretary to the Governor to Galletti, 8 March 1928; Chief Secretary to Galletti, 25 May 1928, Galletti Papers.

have thought having Galletti in Travancore a better prospect than his continuing as Collector where he might have to be demoted or sacked. In short, he would be less of a public relations problem in Travancore. Sadly, Galletti overplayed his hand.

He wrote immediately to Sir Denys Bray, informing him confidentially of negotiations and pontificating on how Travancore would develop under Galletti leadership.[51] His Travancore informants considered that 'a strong man is required', so naturally approached him. However, Delhi and Madras opinion must be considered, Galletti wrote, because the Diwan's post went traditionally to an Indian though there was an 1810 European appointment precedent. He needed senior opinion, he continued, before continuing negotiations with Travancore and receiving a formal offer. However, he noted, if the ruler discovered the terms under which Galletti would accept the post then a formal offer might disappear. Galletti would demand that the ruler immediately begin decentralizing state authority, and developing responsible government with democratic principles including a popular vote. In other words, Galletti would ask the ruler of Travancore to relinquish total power, a clear indication of what Galletti wanted for British India. It was a defiant declaration. Galletti reported that he had accepted a similar 1914 offer from the ruler of Cochin only to have the Government of Madras refuse his secondment, another reason he was now sounding out Bray privately.

Rather than reply, Bray immediately contacted Madras whose officials again learned of a Galletti initiative from someone other than Galletti himself! Chief Secretary Campbell chastised Galletti early in 1929, then in April reported the Government of India would refuse any transfer request should the Travancore offer eventuate. The situation was clear. Even if the ruler agreed to Galletti's progressive terms, New Delhi and Madras would not

---

51   Galletti to Secretary (Political), GOI, 27 December 1928, Galletti Papers.

tolerate him transferring power in Travancore while British India resisted further constitutional reform. Galletti declared himself 'relieved' the opportunity had passed. He realized, however, that yet another opportunity was lost, mainly because of his own actions.[52]

For Arthur Galletti, the 1920s ended with frustration and disappointment at being passed over for yet another significant post. Late in 1929 his old friend Charles Souter was appointed as Second Member of the Board of Revenue, and Galletti genuinely believed himself wronged. He congratulated Souter, saying he had no quarrel with him personally: "it is the dull men in authority who are a trial."[53] Galletti reported that he had recently discussed the political situation with the Viceroy who toured Tinnevelly, assuring Lord Irwin that any new Congress political agitation posed no threat so long as government adopted a sensible policy. That sensible policy, of course, was Galletti's tolerant one. Following that conversation, Galletti believed he would attend the London Round Table Conference to keep "Gandhi and other cranks, my friends, in order by Soul Force."

Despite his friendship with Souter, Galletti protested the appointment with the Governor, his covering letter containing a Telugu phrase Galletti thought captured the situation:

> If a lustrous gem is set in brass, what harm is done to the gem?[54]

Galletti had saved this barb, modified from Entry 677 in his copy of Captain M.W. Carr's *A Selection of Telugu Proverbs*: "What does a ruby suffer by being set in brass?"[55] Carr's interpretation captured Galletti's sense of his career: "The disgrace of putting

---

52   Galletti to Campbell, 11 April 1929, Galletti Papers.

53   Galletti to Souter, 20 December 1929, Galletti Papers.

54   Galletti to Chief Secretary, 5 December 1930, GOM Public (Special) GO 270, 17 March 1931, TNA.

55   Carr M.W., *A selection of Telugu proverbs* (Madras, Sastrulu, 1922).

a talented man in a mean situation attaches to the employer not the employee." That summarised Galletti's prime theme, repeated to several colleagues: he was the obvious candidate for the Second member post, it was bad for government's reputation among Indians to keep passing him over, and the changing constitutional environment empowered liberals like him. Indian friends, he said, imputed malice to his treatment by government. It was bad politics for government "to pass over a man merely for his sympathy with Indian aspirations." It was his 'Duty with a big D' to allow government an opportunity to rectify its mistake.[56]

If not a mistake, there was certainly a weakness in government's position, as acknowledged indirectly during 1930. Galletti argued that selection protocols were ignored, that his seniority was overlooked. The government initially denied that seniority was paramount. However, it later very quietly changed the rules, retrospectively, to ensure that selection to the position of Second member, Board of Revenue, emphasized merit rather than seniority.[57] That was a moral victory, but Galletti's appeal was still denied.

Galletti's proverb and its allusions enraged Secretariat officials. Charles Cotton, by now Chief Secretary, wrote one of the strongest-ever Galletti criticisms, referring to his 'egotistical memorial':

> There is more than a hint of impertinence in the Telugu quotation introduced into Mr. Galletti's covering letter. It is his conviction, originating in overwhelming conceit, and sedulously encouraged by sycophants, that he is (a) the ablest and (b) the most popular District officer in the Presidency. His successors in the various Districts in which he has served could tell a different story. He

---

56 Galletti to C.W.E. Cotton, 18 November 1930; Galletti to Bhore, 5 December 1930, Galletti Papers.

57 See GOM, GO Public (Special) 948, 4 August 1930, TNA.

poses as the one malleable officer in the steel frame: the only white Civilian who really sympathises with Indian aspirations and who is immune to colour prejudice![58]

Most Fort St. George and Chepauk Palace senior officers shared Cotton's view and, indeed, Galletti was usually the only issue uniting the two power centres! Galletti's old foe A.Y.G. Campbell, now on the Board, noted in the same file that Galletti was shifted out of Guntur in 1922 because of his weak administration during non co-operation.

C. Deveraja Mudaliar was disappointed for Clara that the Travancore appointment did not eventuate, but also for Galletti whom he thought had a 'broad and liberal political outlook'. 'D', however, believed the ICS 'clique' would never accept Galletti's appointment to any senior position following his White Mutiny stand.[59] Galletti, however, retained support from many prominent Indians he served in his district. One Indian woman, on her way to Europe by ship in mid-1929, reported that:

Oh! Mr. Galletti, *our friend*—He is the best Collector we have. We like him very much. But the Government does not because he sympathises with us–I know it.[60]

Despite that local support, Galletti remained marginalised in Madras. Following his futile appeal against Souter's appointment Galletti wrote to the Chief Secretary, acknowledging the case closed as the Government of India had refused intervention. He sought information on whether "the endorsement of the local government [to the Government of India] contains any observations in disparagement of my work or character".[61] It was a wistful, sad inquiry. Even if Madras had disparaged

---

58 C.W.E. Cotton note, 15 January 1931, GOM, Public (Special) GO 270, 17 March 1931, TNA.

59 C. Deveraja Mudaliar to Clara, 28 October 1929, Galletti Papers.

60 Clara to Arthur, 18 August 1929, Galletti Papers.

61 Galletti to Chief Secretary, 5 December 1930, Galletti Papers.

him to Delhi, which they had, they were unlikely to tell him. Galletti knew that, and realised his now increasingly isolated professional position. His political views were also now isolated on the eve of new political instability.

Civil Disobedience, Gandhi's second mass action movement, began in 1930 with a symbolic attack on the Salt Tax. That tax contributed significantly to government income, and was increased substantially to help blunt the world economic depression's impact on India. Gandhi's great 'Salt March', during which he and his followers made salt illegally thereby avoiding the tax, gained worldwide attention and cast Raj officials as heartless economic exploiters caring more for the balance of payment than the welfare of their subjects. The march was emulated all over India, including Madras Presidency, governments responding with mass jailings.

Galletti's immediate response to the Salt March was logical if quixotic. As the march began, the *Hindu* newspaper printed an open letter to Gandhi from 'Romanus' that appeared first in the *Times of India*.[62] 'Romanus' had read the Tamil version of Gandhi's "excellent" little book entitled *Health*. In that work, Gandhi argued that salt was an insidious substance causing innumerable health problems, and suggested people reduce or eliminate salt from their diets. If Gandhi believed that, 'Romanus' commented, he should advocate a salt tax *rise* rather than a *reduction*. That is, a salt tax rebellion would *encourage* people to use salt when, in fact, the Mahatma wanted a salt boycott.

'Romanus' was Arthur Galletti. Right in principle, he vastly underestimated the symbolic effect of Gandhi's action. The Mahatma probably shared Galletti's view, but had a far sharper sense of symbols to which the broad population would respond. Galletti's fixed political position helped him lose touch with the very public and popular sentiment he revered and respected, and had fought to have heard for so long.

---

62   A copy of the *Hindu* reference is contained in the Galletti memoir.

He wrote to the Chief Minister of Madras from Porto San Giorgio in mid-1930, reporting the fight against Souter's Board appointment but also conveying views on possible constitutional reforms. He welcomed reform, Galletti wrote, because currently he was doomed professionally. Everywhere he went Indians declared: "You are our friend, therefore you are in the black books of the government'. He served happily as a Collector, he said, but bypassing men like him meant government's authority and credibility were undermined. It was nonsense to argue for the continued presence of nominated ICS members on the provincial council. The civil service should obey rather than be the government as he suggested directly to the Secretary of State for India, William Wedgwood Benn. The Madras ICS, though, was determined to maintain a Council presence. Galletti remained convinced the Round Table Conference would reject ICS representation, and his prospects would improve. His views were unpopular, he emphasised, and following the White Mutiny storm it was well known that "Galletti gets nothing" became Secretariat policy. He got on well personally with all ICS men, he suggested, but there was a fundamental principle. Consequently, "the next great step will be when the Round Table Conference agrees to turn the I.C.S. out of office."[63] The Chief Minister surely shared that letter with his ICS colleagues, Galletti's stocks falling even lower.

Galletti wrote directly to William Wedgwood Benn, the Secretary of State for India, seeking audience in London where he could convey his views personally. That meeting denied, he drafted notes for the Secretary of State's office.[64] Galletti returned to his 1907-08 battle with Sir Gabriel Stokes, arguing that Indians understood toleration even if the British did not. Toleration marked Indian life and culture, he argued, so Indians reacted badly to repression and lack of respect. The great Lombard liberator Visconti Venosta followed that principle in the struggle against

---

63   Galletti to Chief Minister, 23 July 1930, Galletti Papers.

64   "Interview with Secretary of State: note", second [letter sent 30 March 1932], Galletti Papers.

Austria, Galletti advised. Erecting a statue to commemorate General Radetzky was a good idea, because it angered then mobilised Lombards. The British should follow that example in India, as two excellent case examples demonstrated. When Mrs. Besant was freed early after her 1917 Home Rule imprisonment and then again when Gandhi was released early during Non Co-operation, Indian people responded positively and political agitation died quickly.

What he now feared, Galletti informed Benn, was Britain seizing too quickly the 'easy road' to repression to combat the new Gandhian campaign. The most sensible approach was to adopt 'infinite patience'. No doubt, he wrote, the intolerant approach came from the ICS overlords, Galletti's despised law and order men. The Viceroy, Lord Irwin, was well liked by the people, as Galletti knew from personal experience in Tinnevelly, but the ICS would demand his imminent replacement be a man with greater 'strength', a stronger supporter of repression. Galletti later claimed that Lord Irwin listened to his views so intently in 1929, and took so much to heart the idea of conciliation that it led directly to the Irwin-Gandhi Pact of 1931 that suspended Civil Disobedience. The "people do not love the I.C.S.', Galletti went on in his notes for Benn, so one sure way to snuff agitation was to announce that the ICS would play no part in any new government under revised constitutional arrangements.

Galletti's vision for that new government was conservative to the point of reactionary. A new ministry would be appointed directly by the Viceroy, without popular democratic contribution, at least half the members drawn from India's European community. That reflected Galletti's view of India needing long tutelage to prepare for full responsible government. He was confident the arrangement would satisfy Indian political Moderates whom he knew well. Gandhi and his acolytes were already lost to the British, Galletti declared, having made 'a religion of their patriotism', but they would be similarly lost to most Indians if Britain demonstrated tolerance. The best demonstration would be to banish the ICS from government and leave it in administration.

One of Clara's letters captured the household's contemporary political sense.[65] India was far too large and complex a country for people like Gandhi to run. In fact, Gandhi and his accomplices were the biggest fools in the world, as demonstrated recently in Bombay when he was released from prison. There was no organisation, Gandhi exercised no restraint, his followers showed none and the result was injury and death among the welcoming throng. It was respectable and acceptable for India to seek political independence, but the movement needed moderation and leadership. The 'silly politicians', for example, wanted Britain to quit India but leave its navy to be controlled by Congress! "Today's British India is England's creation—political atmosphere and all," Clara continued, so the only possible solution was for a federation to serve the interests of the princely states and help alleviate Hindu-Muslim tension as well as meet nationalist demands. Clara concluded that her 'respect' for Indians had decreased as a result of her long residence in and experience of the country. Arthur added to her comments, noting he 'created' the federal idea but that it would not work if directed by 'extremists' like Gandhi. All the political brains sat on the Moderate side of Indian politics, Galletti argued, and they sought Dominion Status rather than independence.

What Wedgwood Benn and his senior advisors made of these views is not known, but Galletti's ideas were certainly conveyed back to Delhi and Madras. A few years later, after he retired, Galletti sent a copy of his views to the Earl of Halifax as Lord Irwin had then become. The documents provoked a reaction that might have tempted Benn's people, because Halifax's Private Secretary replied apologizing that the papers were 'torn across' [that is, in half] 'by accident', but had been repaired! [66] A senior official, angered by the contents, ripped up the papers. Galletti

---

65   Clara to Cynthia, 29 January 1930, Galletti Papers.

66   Private Secretary for the Earl of Halifax to Galletti, 1 April 1936, Galletti Papers.

was renowned by now for his antagonism towards the service of which he was a member, for his disdain for its senior members, and for the extremes to which his views took him.

Galletti knew that, as he indicated in another later letter. By 1937 he was still trying to publish an account of the Guntur campaign, the latest version of which contained his political views. He approached G.A. Natesan, his longtime acquaintance and publisher of the *Indian Review*. Galletti said the new version had necessarily awaited passage of the new constitutional legislation that saw Congress take political office in Madras that year. That was because his old sparring partners "Souter and Bracken would not have liked the article to appear under their regime."[67]

That did not stop Galletti giving senior officers the benefit of his views. He informed the Chief Secretary, Charles Cotton, that he would contest Souter's Board appointment because government should always have opportunity to rectify its glaring mistakes. Government needed to know that Indian opinion saw malice in its approach to him, so reconsideration would be wise and beneficial. [68] He continued that line throughout 1931. He claimed that a subsequent letter to Secretary of State Benn recommended total abolition of the ICS. The service was now clearly unable to deal with alternative views like his. It was bad for government "to pass a man over merely for his sympathy for Indian aspirations." He mentioned that Monahan, the Bengal civilian he nominated to survey Madras ICS opinion back in 1919, suffered the same fate.[69]

Much later in the Civil Disobedience campaign, in a Berhampore speech, he revealed how distant he now was from Congress aspirations as distinct from those he thought held by 'everyday' Indians. The speech marked the retirement of the

---

67   Galletti to Natesan, 10 April 1937, Galletti Papers.

68   Galletti to Chief Secretary, 18 November 1930, Galletti Papers.

69   Galletti to Bhore, 5 December 1930, Galletti Papers.

Ganjam District Board Chairman whom Galletti supported and liked. The Chairman, Galletti said, improved things practically, and always considered the welfare of the people before his own future or position. People like the Chairman would achieve most for India, Galletti said, people like the current Chief Minister who chaired the Chittoor District Board while Galletti was there and the current Minister for Education who chaired the Tinnevelly Board during Galletti's tenure. Dyarchy enabled local development and growth, he said, providing an excellent platform from which India could reach self-government. Shared responsibility under sensible and enlightened British direction provided the best development model.

They had all worked for over 30 years, Galletti continued, to achieve the responsible self-government now imminent, and these new political conditions could produce the same good results as dyarchy. That would only occur, however, if power went to men like the Chairman who worked at local level and understood his constituents. Power would be wasted on the self-serving, the self-promoting and the self-interested, clear reference to Congress leaders with whom Galletti was by now completely disillusioned. He warned the audience that Andhra for the Andhras and Orissa for the Oriyas, his great federal scheme, would finally happen and their life's work be vindicated, but the new order would fail them if delivered into the hands of an unworthy Congress.

A heartfelt, sad and disillusioned speech, it ignored the fact that Congress had long placed its people in local boards and agencies all over the Presidency and India, building a powerbase and gaining support from the population while the Raj tried to maintain the political status quo. Galletti himself, sympathetic to India and its people and their wishes, now looked part of the very British camp he had fought from within for so long.

8

Bellary

When Civil Disobedience appeared early in 1930 Galletti was Collector in Tinnevelly, a politically-charged district with a several decades history of Congress activism including the 1911 murder of an ICS predecessor, R.W.D. Ashe. Senior Government of Madras officials were uneasy having the sensitive district directed by someone they did not trust, who in their view performed badly in Guntur 10 years earlier, and who had a self-professed sympathy with Indian political aspirations. Galletti was immediately "sent on leave" for several months to remove, as he admitted later, any possibility of his handling the new Congress campaign and embarrassing government. His well-known views did not favour let alone please government. As Clara recorded, an Indian friend telling the Governor of Madras that Galletti was 'The People's Collector' confirmed government's worst fears.[1] Clara's diaries depict Arthur as 'very angry' during April and May 1930, confirming he went on leave against his will having expected to handle the campaign in Tinnevelly. Being ordered to go on leave in that way helps explain the subsequent sharpening of Galletti's political attitudes, and his writing to senior English political figures.

Their European leave was as stressful for Arthur and Clara Galletti as remaining in India might have been, with daughter Beatrice the main cause. A few years earlier she announced her intention to become a nun and her parents were horrified. They pleaded with her to complete architecture studies, but Beatrice was set on entering the Church. She now met her parents in London, announcing she had taken the final step and was about to leave for

---

1   Clara Galletti Diary, 5 February 1930, Galletti Papers.

France to begin novitiate training. Clara thought the move would occur later, but Arthur decided it better to let Beatrice go sooner given her determination. Just after this, Clara wrote to Arthur's sister declaring "there is an emptiness in my heart."[2] It was a wrench for Clara. She did not want Beatrice to enter the Church, thinking her daughter immature and limited in social outlook and experience. The rift between the two never really healed, and Clara never recovered from the pain of this separation. The day after Beatrice departed Galletti insisted on taking Clara to Lords to watch K.S. Duleepsinjhi, another Cheltenham man, score his maiden test century for England against Australia, but even that fine innings could not cheer Clara who normally appreciated the game.

Once back in India Galletti was sent to Bellary district, recognised within the service as a 'punishment' posting for the incompetent, major blunderers or those seriously out of favour with Secretariat bosses. In a climatically hot Presidency Bellary was a very hot district: its average maximum March to May temperature was over 100F with the annual average 93F.[3] The average annual district rainfall of 22 inches was the lowest in the Presidency, and Bellary town itself averaged only 19. That rainfall was unpredictable, too, making the district more than usually liable to disastrous seasons—that is, highly susceptible to famine. In the terrible 1876-78 famine, Bellary lost 400,000 people, approximately one third of its total population. Agriculture (growing grain and herding sheep, cattle and goats) occupied 75 per cent of the workforce with the rest in spinning and weaving or service industries including, as Francis put it:

> The doctors and astrologers, priests and school-masters who see to their bodily, spiritual and mental welfare; the musicians, jugglers and players who amuse their idler moments; and the parasites (thieves and beggars, religious and other) who live upon them.[4]

---

2   Clara to Cynthia, 11 June 1930.

3   W. Francis, *Bellary* (Madras, Government Press, 1916) details the district.

4   *Ibid.*, p.106.

Bellary had fewer people than almost every other Presidency district, its population density half that of more fertile districts. Telugu was the official district court system language, but only one third of district people had it as a mother tongue with Canarese and Hindusthani the two other main languages, along with Marathi. The population was under-educated even by Presidency standards, only five per cent of people could read and write with Canarese-speakers most literate and Telugu-speakers least. Bellary was a dry, treeless, hot, impoverished district whose main claim to fame was Hampi, the ruins of the great 14th to 16th century Telugu Vijayanagar empire. Clara confirmed headquarters as a cheerless place with their official bungalow full of shabby and inadequate furniture but the Collector's Club was excellent, she added, and several Europeans lived in town.[5]

The Secretariat posted Galletti there anticipating little scope for him to cause trouble. They were wrong, again, beginning with Civil Disobedience. While Galletti's enforced leave meant he missed the initial 1930 phase of Gandhi's new campaign, he was in Bellary for much of the rest of it, especially during the late 1931-early 1932 recrudescence. By his own admission, his approach challenged Government of Madras policy.[6] Shortly after their arrival, Clara informed her family that government was eyeing Arthur suspiciously because of his 'unprovoking' attitude. There was little political agitation in Bellary, she argued, despite a profusion of the fashionable Gandhi caps, simply because Arthur would not be goaded by Congress.[7]

When government gathered Collectors' reports on Civil Disobedience experiences early in 1931 Galletti's response was relaxed and folksy, to say the least.[8] He recapped the story

---

5   Clara to Cynthia, 27 November 1930, Galletti Papers.

6   Galletti to John Collier, 21 January 1932.

7   Clara to Cynthia, nd, Galletti Papers.

8   See the section on Bellary in *The Civil Disobedience Movement—Madras 1930-1931* in GOI Home Political 14/21/1932, NAI.

until his arrival in November 1931, suggesting most local Congress leaders hid behind others initially, then abandoned the movement when Congress declared for independence early in 1930. That suited his view that most politically-minded Indians desired moderate progress under British tutelage. He overlooked or ignored the obvious emerging growth of Telugu-speaking peasant movements that would create several Communist organizations, and the growing demands for Britain to leave India entirely. Galletti rapped official policy, suggesting the release of innumerable political prisoners from three major district jails housing Civil Disobedience activists from all over the Presidency and India caused all local problems. Political meetings grew in number and size after their release, he reported, hinting mischieviously that had his 'Soul Force' approach been used then none of this would have happened. As it was, a District Congress Secretary and released notables toured Bellary promoting demonstrations, inciting strikes and cutting down date palms, finally leading the previous Collector to action. However, Galletti noted, all was quiet since his arrival on 17 November 1930 because of his calming influence:

> There is no want of patriotic feeling and Gandhi caps are commonly worn but I find the wearers of these caps just as friendly and respectful as anyone else and am received cordially everywhere.

The People's Collector was in control and telling government so. Government was unamused, however, because Galletti might have a 'quiet' district but his sympathies could see "control" take a direction other than the one desired.

Early in 1932, senior Government of Madras officials informed Galletti they were concerned that "the attitude which you appear to be adopting appears to the government to be lacking in firmness." All District Magistrates and/or Collectors must follow government policy exactly for it to be fully effective. Galletti replied that he followed the 1921-22 Willingdon policy so successful in Guntur. He was tolerant, he said, and people responded positively. There was *no* Civil Disobedience in Bellary, no matter how often government inquired nor how many concerned telegrams it sent him. He was 'a person of immense Influence and Popularity' whom people respected, so there was no agitation. In fact, Galletti claimed, Congress was so concerned by the lack of activity resulting from his approach that it sent a radical emissary to stir up events. The campaign failed. Galletti called the man in, inviting him to tennis with some local Indian friends. The man refused, but Galletti allowed him to address club members who simply ignored the 'agitator'.[9] Clara, too, spoke to the man, R.K. Gupta from Calcutta, telling him that Congress demands were unreasonable.[10] Galletti's idiosyncratic approach aggravated government officials but, for once, they neither transferred nor placed him on leave, as Galletti noted gleefully.

Galletti's attitude towards Civil Disobedience and Congress bordered on patronising, and suggested to government that he did not take the situation seriously. In April 1932, for example, there was a Presidency-wide attempt to resurrect a campaign whereby Congress volunteers would picket foreign cloth shops and liquor outlets. Galletti reported very small numbers involved, with key ringleaders being Brahmins who enjoyed little local support. Cloth shop and toddy stall proprietors told Galletti they did not fear the picketers. He reported 23 picketers jailed: a doctor, some lawyers with little or no practice, a journalist's wife, a few petty shopkeepers. In Galletti's view, that confirmed the movement's flimsiness.[11] Yet he worried Madras because he argued that lower level government servants were passively sympathetic towards Congress, as were local Muslims which was even more worrying. Secretariat men wondered what

---

9   Galletti to Sir John Collier, 21 January 1932, Galletti Papers.

10   Clara Galletti Diary, 17 January 1932, Galletti Papers.

11   Galletti to Chief Secretary, 30 April 1932, District reports, Bellary, TNA.

Galletti was doing about this state of affairs. To them he looked 'soft' on trouble-makers, and that was ironic because by now he had no time for Gandhi and the nationalist cause.

Clara, too, had no love for either Gandhi or the Viceroy because, in her view, neither demonstrated willingness to compromise. She admired Gandhi's goals and principles if not his limitations and extreme views. How could he, for example, expect Britain to simply hand over control of the army? The problem, she thought, was that unlike Lord Irwin the new Viceroy, Lord Willingdon, did not keep Gandhi in good humour so Gandhi became frustrated. Her close Muslim friend Mrs Bajlullah, with whom she spent considerable time in Madras, thought the Mahatma should be jailed for the duration.[12] This reflected Arthur's sympathy for India and its people but disdain for radical, impatient political leaders who ignored the need for serious, prolonged political tutelage. Clara loved India, too, and would ideally 'kick out' all Europeans who did not. Indians were always friendly towards English officials who were friendly to them, she thought. Unfortunately, too many Indians were swayed by the unqualified admiration given Gandhi by American and other uninformed journalists. Gandhi was simply full of 'humbug and cant', because he preached non-violence but tolerated violence.[13]

Clara supported *Swaraj*, but thought most *Swarajists* 'very stupid' and duplicitous.[14] The Galletti family view advocated greater freedom for India led by Moderates, not by Gandhi and Congress. Removing diehard British officials and non-officials would help, a federal scheme elevating sympathetic officials like Galletti and so facilitating full independence. The proof of their position, Arthur and Clara believed, lay in their rousing

---

12 Clara to family, 14 January 1931, Galletti Papers.
13 Clara to Cynthia, 13 March 1931, 26 March 1931, 23 April 1931, Galletti Papers.
14 Clara to Cynthia, 3 June 1931, Galletti Papers.

reception from local Bellary people, the true Indians sincere British officials wished to serve: "no amount of Civil Disobedience or Round Table Conference seems to make any difference to the people's attitudes towards us."[15] Their troubles lay more with the Secretariat than the masses.

One of Arthur Galletti's long-term career activities, for example, provided ex-prisoners with social support following their release from jail. In every district where he served as Collector, he established a Discharged Prisoners Society using local notables to identify and provide employment opportunities, social support, essential supplies and services for ex-prisoners. In Tinnevelly, Galletti claimed to have created the most successful branch in India. The organizations were well supported by local communities and considered a genuine contribution to social development.

Galletti established a Bellary branch, but the district police chief reported to Madras that activities included staging a play inside the main Bellary prison where many political prisoners were held. The police chief thought the play overtly political, favouring Congress, and that Galletti showed poor judgment in allowing it to proceed. Government immediately took the same view, until Galletti pointed out several inconsistencies in the report and that led subsequently to the police chief having to apologise.[16] The pair despised each other. Inevitably, government officials believed Galletti had escaped on a technicality, again, and that his political loyalties were definitely suspect. For that reason, and his history, senior government members constantly sought opportunities to discipline their Bellary man who, of course, did his best to upset them.

Late in 1931 the Government of Madras censured Galletti severely over a salary and income tax issue.[17] Earlier that year,

15 Clara to Cynthia, 21 October 1931, Galletti Papers.

16 Galletti to Chief Secretary, 17 January 1933, Galletti Papers.

17 GOM, GO Public 1181, 20 November 1931 and extended in GO 276 Public, 18 February 1932, Galletti Papers.

Madras argued, Galletti drew his April salary in March, thereby avoiding an additional Rs. 203 in income tax under a new rate implemented from 1 April. government faced severe financial shortfalls and rising costs because of policing Gandhi's campaign, so raised tax rates. Senior government members were incensed, charged Galletti and found him guilty. Board Member Sir Archibald Campbell, keen to pin Galletti on at least one charge, argued he should be censured for "abusing his position". Government consequently felt "constrained to express their grave displeasure at the action of Mr Galletti in abusing his position."[18]

As always, it was not that simple and Galletti reacted: "I am a man of straightforward character incapable of any such intention."[19] He rebutted the censure order with a classic Galletti mix of logic, sarcasm, arrogance and sardonic humour. The Board and its Secretary, he claimed, 'appear not to be aware' of what he considered 'elementary' aspects of tax law that reflected complete legal clarity. He was aggrieved: "I have saved government money for many years by conveying *peons* and government effects in my private lorry without charge." However:

> My feelings are not hurt because I recognise that it is a case of sheer ignorance; but the Board and the government will, I respectfully submit, feel that it as due to themselves, if not to me to express regret for mistaken reflections on the honour of an officer with an unblemished reputation for integrity. Or, to put the same thing with less rodomontade: Government thought I had been dishonest over my income-tax; I was not; will government please withdraw?

He wrote subsequently to the Chief Secretary suggesting the censure showed "a want of affection and esteem for me and

---

18   GOM, GO (Public Special) 1181 Ms Confl., 20 November 1931, TNA.

19   GOM GO (Public Special) 276 Ms Confl., 18 February 1932, TNA—the following section is drawn from this file.

wounds my feelings."[20] Senior officials like Campbell rejected his view of having an unblemished record, disliked his lectures and his open ridiculing of their abilities.

Galletti argued that, since 1922, he had used an Indian Income Tax Act provision utilized by few if any other officers, the ability to declare their own income tax 'end of year'.[21] Galletti chose 31 March, and based all his income tax returns accordingly. It was not clear how that related to the charge he faced, but he made one excellent point. Given that the new tax regime was not announced until after the April pay was issued, then presumably all officers and not only Galletti contravened the new arrangements and gained a technical windfall. The government maintained Galletti conspired with his Treasury head and local bank manager to lodge his April pay claim at the last moment possible in March, thereby avoiding the additional Rs. 203.

Galletti was livid. The government had already ordered a 10 per cent salary cut as an austerity measure. Not only did he accept that, he protested, but voluntarily gave up a further Rs. 116 per month. (It is not clear what Clara thought of that). As reward, he was now accused of creating an elaborate ruse to make a paltry, one-off Rs. 203 'profit'. The accusation affronted his honour, his long service and his performance, he protested. Between November 1931 and March 1932 he wrote several long and technical letters, gathered evidence from several people to clear his name and faced the usual interview to discuss his performance, but the censure remained.

Typically, Galletti thought the affair ended in 'complete victory' for him.[22] He suggested Campbell should back down because the Board of Revenue man had become 'a trifle above himself'. Galletti was more sinned against than sinning in this

---

20   GOM, GO (Public Special) 447 Ms Confl 19 March 1932.

21   Galletti to Chief Secretary, 7 March 1932, Galletti Papers.

22   Galletti to Clara and Sir John Collier, 23 March 1932, Galletti Papers.

tax matter, but his long record of constantly irritating superior officers worked against him, as did the timing. The confrontations arose during considerable political stress for the Secretariat. Gandhi's Civil Disobedience campaign continued, heading towards significant resurgence in late 1932. Daily, Campbell and his colleagues orchestrated the provincial response to match Government of India policy, even though they disagreed with the Delhi strategy. Given his history and views, Galletti was completely unhelpful to them. For example, government planned an orchestrated district propaganda campaign, trying to restore loyalist confidence and deflect support from Congress. One proposal envisaged a series of leaflets issued in English and the local language. Collectors' opinions were sought, back from Bellary came a surly Galletti note: "I have no faith in leaflets."[23] Given he responded thus amidst a series of fights with his superiors suggests he had little or no understanding of just how seriously placed he was at this point. On the contrary, he took every opportunity to lampoon his superiors.

During these battles between Galletti and his bosses the Chief Secretary, now Geoffrey Bracken, observed there must be serious doubts as to Galletti's 'mental stability and capacity to be in charge of a Collector's office."[24] The comment reveals how close Galletti was to being dismissed from his position, if not from the service entirely. It also raises the possibility that Galletti was suffering a serious medical condition, because for years now he had endured his untreated thyroid problem.

Bracken's observation concerned what became known as the 'Hospet sugarcane farm' affair in which Galletti was again charged with insubordination. As with so many of his 'scrapes' the conflict's origins became secondary to a fight over procedural interpretation and precedent. Late in 1931 A.R. Cox,

---

23   Galletti to Campbell, 22 February 1932, GOM GO (Public) 555 Confl, 11 April 1932, TNA.

24   GOM GO Public (Special) 596 (S-1) Ms Confl 21 April 1932, TNA.

a Board of Revenue Member, visited Bellary and Galletti invited him to join the inspection of a government-run sugar farm. According to Galletti, "It declined, saying it wanted to see Hampi, not Sugarcane Farms".[25] Returning to Madras, Cox reported that Galletti had not inspected the farm regularly enough! The Board seized this and admonished Galletti's poor performance. As usual, Galletti contested the charge but challenged Board procedures rather than deal with facts. The letter to the Secretary of the Board of Revenue was vintage Galletti:

> I am right. I request you to move the Board to so inform you and to reprimand you for your neglect of the correct procedure even if you are excused for inexperience.

He regarded the Secretary "with that affection and esteem that I have for all members of the service," he said, and wrote as he did solely to ensure that procedural principles were observed so the Secretary might learn from the experience.

The letter was referred to the Chief Secretary who promptly charged Galletti with insubordination. Galletti responded that it was a private joke. He would never attack the Board:

> I have a great respect for it; it has done and continues to do excellent work; but *quando que bonus dormitat Homerus* [Even good Homer nods, sometimes; the wisest make mistakes] and the Senior Collector may without offence refer to mistakes it has made in a private chit to a member who is his junior.

The 'Senior Collector' reference was to remind Board members and others that, despite his service and ability, Galletti was regularly overlooked for promotion. In private, Galletti wrote he was 'going' not for 'the Board but for Cox', his junior who was 'mean' in approach, and 'had no business to... overrule me'. This letter invoked the insubordination charge. Galletti declared he hated "wrangles with the venerable Board," but

---

25   Galletti to Charles Souter, 1 February 1932, Galletti Papers.

such fights would soon disappear because the Board would be abolished under impending constitutional changes. Abolition was welcome, he said. The 'better men below' could concentrate on their work and not have to 'make the Board look silly'.

There was envy in here, too. Alexander Ranken Cox, educated at Clifton then Emmanuel College, Cambridge was yet another of those Galletti watched arrive after yet be promoted before him. Two years younger than Galletti, Cox joined late in 1902 and established a strong early reputation while on secondment to the princely state of Mysore. Having served in the military towards the end of World War I, Cox returned to Madras and became Collector before a Secretariat appointment then elevation to Second Member in 1931. It was a textbook career, unmarked by controversy and, to Galletti's mind dull, time-serving and self interested. By terming the Board 'It', Galletti confirmed his disdain for people like Cox who unquestionably sharpened his enmity.

In attacking Cox, though, Galletti upset one of his oldest acquaintances and strongest supporters. By now Charles Alexander Souter was the leading Member on the Board, soon to be knighted and appointed to the Governor's Council. Slightly younger than Galletti and joining a year later, in 1901, the Scot was educated at Arbroath High School then the University of Edinburgh before Caius College, Cambridge. He and Galletti served together in the Secretariat for several years during their early careers, and lived in the Club for two years sharing dinner most nights. After the Secretariat Souter became administrator in Coorg for several years before returning as a Collector, then a posting back into Madras as Secretary to the Public Works Department. By 1930 he was on the Board of Revenue, the very appointment against which Galletti appealed.

Souter was used to Galletti's outbursts, but this was one too many. Charged with insubordination, Galletti wrote immediately to his old friend under the guise of a "private" communication, complaining about Cox and sundry other matters. It was in this diatribe that Galletti anticipated the Board's demise and made his famous reference to 'better men below'. To Galletti's surprise, Souter declared the letter an official communication, deemed it improper and referred it to the Chief Secretary who promptly charged the Collector. When Galletti asked 'how on earth' the Chief Secretary came by the 'chit' Souter replied that it was no 'chit', and he had referred it as unacceptable.

The episode reveals just how much Galletti now worried Secretariat officials even though they were preoccupied with major political concerns, severe economic pressures, imminent constitutional change, anxiety about the changing nature of the ICS, and differences of opinion with Delhi. As the Secretary to the Board of Revenue commented, this was "an example of Galletti's extraordinary conception of his position as a Collector."[26] The last thing the Secretariat needed was a Collector running personal vendettas, behaving oddly, causing trouble, undermining government's authority locally, wasting time in futile game-playing to score points against ICS adversaries imagined and real. Souter pleaded with Galletti to cease antagonising superior officers and concentrate on his work. Otherwise his antics wasted time, caused friction, and did his personal reputation no good whatsoever.[27] Galletti would soon need and appreciate Souter's support.

While these serious matters followed their tortuous paths Galletti added yet another strand. During 1931 the Chief Secretary's position fell vacant when Charles Cotton died suddenly and prematurely from pneumonia. For some reason, despite being embroiled in the income tax and insubordination proceedings, Galletti decided he was the logical and unquestioned replacement. He even suggested that to Geoffrey Bracken

---

26 Secretary Board of Revenue to Secretary Revenue, 8 February 1932, GOM GO Public (Special) 596(S-1) Confl, 21 April 1932, TNA.

27 Souter to Galletti, 12 April 1932, Galletti Papers.

who was appointed to act temporarily in the position.[28] In an ill-considered, pompous, pleading, self-serving and entirely destructive submission Galletti argued that the Governor, the Council, the Secretariat and the ICS collectively would surely "not leave an old and faithful servant of the state to retire under the slur of unwarranted suspension." It would be "only just to transfer me to a post on higher pay and with a better climate at the end of my career." Naturally, there was "no question of my fitness" for the role having done the work easily on earlier occasions, and having for the previous 15 years "borne the burden and the heat of the day in the plains as Collector of one great district after another". He was always 'extra efficient' as the Governor himself had witnessed on a recent visit to Tinnevelly. Galletti's popularity with those Indians already or about to be provincial Ministers under the coming reforms made him a prime candidate to oversee constitutional transition. Naturally, if appointed he would want eight months leave before taking up the position.

It is impossible to assess accurately what he was thinking, but Arthur Galletti was almost certainly deep into what he described as one of his 'manias', aggravated by his medical condition. Throughout his life he endured frequent bouts of compulsive behaviour that defied explanation, especially given his acute intelligence. In these phases he always went too far, whether goading his wife and family or taunting superiors and peers. At this point, with a series of serious charges arrayed against him, it appears he was not thinking rationally. As a result, he was genuinely shocked and disappointed when Bracken was appointed Chief Secretary permanently, considering it yet another slight from reactionary forces in Madras. That hurt, disappointment and alienation now escalated into the final and most serious rebellion, a furious row about the possibility of famine in Bellary.

---

28   Galletti to Bracken, 17 March 1931, Galletti Papers.

Both before and after 1857, famine was the natural disaster feared most by British administrators in India and at 'Home'. The reasons were simple. No-one wanted to see thousands of people die slowly and in agony. As part of their ICS covenant, officers like Galletti accepted a duty to protect and serve local populations, to improve their welfare and living conditions. Serious famine was the single most symbolic indication of that duty having failed. Monsoon flooding could be anticipated as could hurricanes, like the 1917 Tinnevelly one Galletti experienced when his railway carriage was blown off the track. Natural elements would always prevail, officials comfortable in the knowledge that they had taken all possible steps to serve their people. Technically, famine was similar. Psychologically it was not, however, because there was always a nagging sense that more might have been done to prevent tragedy.

The terrible 1877 famine hit Madras Presidency hard, especially Bellary, the subsequent inquiry producing a revised procedural code for implementation where and once famine was declared. The administrative balancing act was difficult. People had to be protected and saved wherever possible, but the financial cost was considerable. Ever alert to possible famine Secretariat officials worried about moving too slowly, but also avoided acting too quickly and incurring unnecessary cost. That caution intensified during economically fragile periods like the 1920s and 1930s. Provincial, All-India and British governments had to balance cautious action against risking a public relations disaster created by famine outbreak. World newspaper headlines proclaiming the death of tens of thousands of Indians because of food shortages experienced under British rule would be problematic, to say the least. If those headlines appeared at politically sensitive moments, like during a Gandhian Civil Disobedience campaign, the negative impact deepened.

Bellary was prone to food shortages because vital seasonal rains failed periodically. During the 19th century scarcities/

famines occurred almost every decade, rainfall being both light and "capricious and uncertain'.[29] In the 1866 famine, death rates were possibly as high four per cent of the population, despite massive relief works being implemented. Ten years later, almost 400,000 people died in Bellary. Over the course of a century or so, then, the district experienced famine periodically, the Madras Government routinely declaring official famine conditions so that complex government-funded relief programmes might start. Galletti's arrival in Bellary coincided with just the sort of dry spell that on earlier occasions preceded famine.

Galletti, now almost 55, did extremely well initially. Crop failure appeared towards the end of 1931, coinciding with Congress Civil Disobedience campaigning, and he identified the signs early, convincing government a relief programme was needed then energetically organizing several projects. The Famine Commissioner praised Galletti alone for 'exceptionally' good work in the early phases. Even his Board of Revenue adversaries endorsed officially 'the unceasing vigilance shown by Mr. Galletti during the earlier stages'.[30] Given Galletti's views concerning the Board and successive Members' views about him, that comment was designed as an armistice to help a longstanding irritant leave the service on a high note, given his retirement was imminent. Galletti ignored the peace signs, however and, really, the positive reporting left much unsaid because during 1932 and 1933 Galletti's Bellary actions saw him almost sacked again.

The struggle began late in 1931. Unilaterally and without reference to the Board, Galletti decided economic conditions in one Bellary area were so bad he would not collect kist, the annual land revenue tax on which government based its budget. Board Members were appalled. Amidst an economic and political crisis,

---

29 W. Francis, *Bellary* (Madras, Government Press, 1916 edn), p.127. The following section is drawn from Ch. VIII.

30 Board of Revenue Proceedings, 4, Press, 14 January 1933, P. 12000, IOR.

here was a Collector foregoing revenue. Galletti was censured for acting on inaccurate information, exceeding his authority, and ignoring the rules by which he was bound as an ICS officer. Galletti declared hostilities, the intensity of which was conveyed in a prose poem he wrote about the episode. Galletti describes a Board Member (A.Y.G. Campbell) speaking:

> Bitterly of the Collector of Bellar and his proud ways and his contempt for the Rule of Account and for the Rule of the Channel whereby no Collector may approach a God of Tin save through the Commissioners of Chepauk and the Great Bureau in the Fort.[31]

These were his favourite subjects, of course, the 'Tin Gods' of the Board of Revenue in the Chepauk Palace and the "Great Bureuacrats' of the Secretariat in Fort St. George. They were heartless, rule-bound bureaucrats while he was the sensitive and knowing man on the ground.

By now, government had each Collector reporting fortnightly on district political and economic activity. In his first 1932 report, Galletti challenged the Board.[32] He lectured government about his excellent handling of Congress political campaigning. There were few agitators, he claimed, because he engaged and reasoned with local leaders who all agreed with his approach and views. There were some troublemakers, certainly, but after he spoke with them and conveyed his firm policies they withdrew leaving behind peace and quiet. He made tolerance and reconciliation work. Tolerance and reconciliation failed elsewhere in India because others lacked his ability, he declared, but it would still work if tried. The Secretary of State and the Prime Minister both realised that, he thought, so should be informed about his Bellary success and be encouraged to continue negotiating

---

31 "Mr X.Y. of the Tribe of the Philistines", Galletti Papers.
32 Galletti to Chief Secretary, 25 January 1932, Galletti Papers.

with Gandhi! At the very least, the Governments of Madras and India should publicly congratulate Bellary on its behaviour to encourage development of the same approach elsewhere.

Government, Galletti wrote, especially 'our kind and easy-going British government', should honour and reward those bowing to its wishes. He won loyalty in Bellary, acted kindly and with toleration, and won even more co-operation. Government should follow that model. His leadership ensured Bellary had no 'racial feeling': why, he and his daughters were playing mixed doubles tennis with Indians at the Cosmopolitan Club!

This was defiant criticism of government policy, Galletti linking it to his work on what he argued were famine conditions. A famine, he said, was no time for a frustrated Collector to await orders issued at leisure from Madras by an unknowing Board. Action was required. Inaction cost over 50,000 lives in Mysore during the 1877 famine, and must not be tolerated. The Board and the government should read its own rules and historical reports before censuring decisive men like him. His 'plain duty' was to use his initiative and take all necessary action to prevent famine. Analyse results later and impose penalties on him if necessary, but do not treat as 'felonies' actions taken to prevent Bellary famine deaths. Government should not undermine and discredit the Collector's authority because that eroded public confidence and caused further trouble, like reviving the political disturbances he had done so much to quell.

That open attack challenged government directly at a time of political uncertainty and difficulty, at a time when his own future required him getting his full pension because he was facing substantial economic costs, and at a time when the government was of little mind to tolerate further Galletti eccentricities.

Galletti received from Chief Secretary Bracken as sharp a letter as could be mustered within the polite prose of official correspondence. Bracken commented that the report was "improper and savours of impertinence."[33] Further, it contained material and commentary unsuitable in an official report. Government was well aware of Bellary's political quiescence, because it resembled the situation in other districts where Collectors did not trumpet their success. Bellary was a district with low potential for trouble (which was why Galletti was posted there, of course). In future, Galletti should "refrain from long disquisitions that serve no useful purpose and waste your own time and that of the Government."

The message was clear. As his famine diary shows, however, Galletti persisted because he believed genuinely that Bellary faced substantial famine.[34] From early December 1931 until his removal from the district in mid-1932 Galletti covered hundreds of miles by car, horse, bicycle and foot, observing and despairing about the conditions experienced by villagers. Crop failure was partial rather than total, he reported, but conditions in most villages necessitated tax remission. Where crops appeared, they were much poorer than normal so price returns would slip markedly. Elsewhere, crops were hit with disease caused by water shortage. Even in irrigated areas, less water than normal was available because of rain failure, so crops there promised lower prices. As 1932 deepened, Galletti reported substantial tracts where crops failed completely. Government-funded famine works, usually road building, were needed to employ hundreds of peasants so they could buy increasingly expensive food.

On 9 December 1931 he sent the Board a special Bellary condition report. A few days later he recorded a 12 mile inspection tour conducted on foot and bicycle, during which he received numerous representations from village groups reporting their plight and seeking assistance. Charles Souter, the long-standing

33　The following details are drawn from "Collector's Famine Diary" reports, Galletti Papers.

34　Chief Secretary to Galletti, 15 February 1932, Galletti Papers.

but recently offended friend and also the Famine Commissioner, visited Galletti in mid-January 1932. On their first day they travelled 67 miles inspecting villages, crops, irrigation systems and talking with local district board members. On 11 January, before Souter arrived, Galletti had already suspended even more tax collections, effectively defying Bracken's late-December censure. On 30 January Galletti rode 30 miles on horseback, confirming his views that Bellary villagers faced imminent disaster. Over subsequent weeks he developed the famine relief works system and pressed government for more assistance. By May he was hounding Madras for an additional eight staff members and Rs. 20,000 to deal with the crisis—'Souter of course agrees', he added, implicating the Famine Commissioner in his quest.[35]

This was an almost theatrically symbolic clash between the man on the ground seeing local conditions and applying his experience to predict likely outcomes, and his Secretariat superiors trying to balance politics, Presidency-wide strategy and economics as well as government's public image. Had it been anyone other than Galletti in Bellary the matter would have been resolved quietly and a compromise position reached. The problem was that government had 'parked' Galletti in Bellary, only to have him become the centre of attention representing local economic and political interests.

Galletti was hauled to Madras to appear personally before and explain his conduct to Geoffrey Bracken. Robert Galletti, Arthur's son now serving under him in Bellary, thought his father in 'really serious' trouble this time. Clara reported that, unlike her, Arthur seemed unworried. She hoped he might pass the new trial with flying colours, commenting nonetheless:

---

35 Galletti to Campbell, 10 May 1932, Galletti Papers. Souter certainly took much of Galletti's view: Famine Commissioner Report, 25 May 1932, GOI, EHL, 55-2/32, L&O, 1095, 25 May 1932, NAI.

But, honestly, he hardly deserves it because the imp of mischief which animates him is really getting far too much the upper hand! [36]

Galletti returned from the interview without reprimand, but was warned again about over-testing his superiors' patience.

Galletti remained unruffled, however, and the increasingly shrill interchange persisted through the first half of 1932. Then Galletti sent to the Revenue Member, his old sparring target A.Y.G. (nicknamed XYZ) Campbell, the first of several memoranda that exacerbated matters dramatically.[37] Galletti announced he had initiated five roadwork camps employing labour paid for by the famine relief funds. There was some difficulty with landholders but 'I do not compromise'. While Galletti simply informed those owners their land was resumed for government purposes, he claimed to have persuaded rather than compelled them to accept his view for the common good. Repeating his favourite *mantra* for government, he advised it was always 'better to convince than compel'.

This constant criticism of government's ill-advised policies heightened senior officials' irritation. Pressing on, Galletti suggested government was misinformed and misguided on basic Bellary facts. Rather than 200 square miles being famine-effected there were 1600 and, worse, government thought relief workers were paid over-generous wages. In Galletti's view, 'Soviet' workers were paid more than his, and it was disgraceful that peasants were 'sweated' for want of new funding. If need be, Madras should ask Delhi for new relief pay guidelines because workers were deserting British India for the princely states where they were better treated.

---

36 Clara to family, 26 April 1932, Galletti Papers.

37 Galletti to Second Member, Board of Revenue, 12 June 1932, Famine: Very Urgent–Memorandum No 1, Galletti Papers.

Galletti ran a complex, confrontational, conspiratorial campaign. In early June 1932, the Secretary for Local Self government in Madras received a letter purportedly from the President of the Bellary District Board. The letter suggested Government had "completely ignored the local conditions and opinions of local authority." Surely "Government was for the people and not the people for the Government." This was not the time to simply follow and enforce the "rigour of an anachronic antediluvian famine code."[38] That letter remains among Galletti's own papers suggesting, as does the language, that he was the author. Galletti claimed to have received the letter from the President and simply referred it to government. In so doing he observed that invoking Famine Code provisions would give him authority, and he preferred 'direct control'.

Galletti and his superiors became increasingly alienated at a time of intense political and economic difficulty. The Collector argued he and his staff risked assault, so intense was public discontent with government policy, and he ordered police guards to all famine stations. He again lectured Campbell: "famine is no time for references, consultations and proper channels'. That was disrespectful enough but he followed it with:

> The honourable member may have difficulty in making up his mind quickly at Ootacamund without these consultations...

But perhaps he might gain authority to act from his august colleagues, come down from the cool hills to the hot plains to look for himself then make sensible directives![39] The following day Galletti wrote again to Campbell, suggesting the Governor take control of famine operations just as the-then Governor, the Duke of Buckingham, did in 1877.[40]

---

38 President Bellary District Board to Secretary Local Self Government Department, Government of Madras, 2 June 1932. Galletti Papers.

39 Galletti to Campbell, 18 June 1932, Galletti Papers.

40 Galletti to Campbell, 19 June 1932.

That was enough for Board members. On 22 June 1932 Galletti was ordered to suspend all famine operations. Separately, he learned he was being transferred out of Bellary.[41]

Undeterred and unbending, Galletti escalated the row with a Minute of Remonstrance to Campbell.[42] He must, he said, seek reconsideration of the order halting support, because his people had no resources on which to fall back. According to the Famine Code enacted after the 1877 disaster, one of few government policy documents Galletti admired, the Collector must control action because he was on the ground and could move quickly to avoid unnecessary deaths. In Galletti's opinion, rapid action was now needed to avoid famine deaths. If there was any question about that, he continued, Madras should request the Government of India to provide a definitive ruling.

Galletti sent that Minute directly and in copy to the Secretary of Education, Health and Lands in the Government of India. That deliberately provoked his Madras superiors. As so often before, Galletti was testing the principle that all communication with Delhi go via the local chain of command. Not content, Galletti provided a "Sixth And Last Minute Before I leave The District" to Campbell.[43] The matter was simple, he argued. There were 250,000 agriculturalists spread over 1600 square miles in Bellary who, after several bad years, now faced a crop failure approximating 150 lakhs [Rs. 15million] of produce on which they depended for sustenance and income. The relief scheme costs represented just 1/3000th of the total loss but would see peasants through and save lives, so why was government reluctant to approve the additional works? The government should at least give his successor, F.W. Stewart, the powers and support denied to Galletti.

---

41   Clara Galletti Diary, 16 June and 24 June 1932, Galletti Papers.

42   Galletti to Campbell, 26 June 1932, Galletti Papers.

43   Galletti to Campbell, 23 June 1932, Galletti Papers.

With that Galletti returned to Ganjam, his favourite posting, thankful to be not consigned to a punishment station like Cuddapah but apprehensive about what might happen next. He prepared his defences in typical style. Before leaving Bellary he wrote to his old friend Sir C.P. Ramaswami Iyer, now in New Delhi serving at All-India level.[44] He would not contest the transfer, Galletti wrote, but would appeal to the Government of India on the famine matter. He bore animus towards none in Madras, he said, but was driven by logic, reason and compassion for the people he served. "The dreadful mistakes made in previous famines must not be repeated". Arguing he was 'responsible to my people', Galletti maintained he should not be charged with insubordination for doing his duty. However, if Madras did proceed against him, he expected Sir C.P. to speak with their other old friend, Viceroy Lord Willingdon, and see off the threat. Willingdon and Sir C.P. were both full of 'humanity', as he was, and would understand why he had acted decisively in Bellary.

Galletti wrote similarly to Campbell in his last Fortnightly Report from Bellary.[45] Recalling wryly the earlier rebuke for the tone of his reports, Galletti apologised if anything in the ` famine communications was offensive. He did not want to cause offence, simply do his duty: "I care for nothing but the interests of the State.". Campbell he considered a personal friend, and he hoped that feeling was reciprocated. However, Galletti "felt very strongly about the right and the wrong way to deal with Civil Disobedience and the Famine". Given the conflict, he realised transfer was inevitable and was grateful for not being sent to Cuddapah, that was kind. Galletti was not completely subservient, though. For Campbell's information, Galletti enclosed one of many letters he received during the massive public support given him when the transfer news emerged. Galletti claimed to have argued against public demonstrations and the anti-government

44   Galletti to Sir C.P. Ramaswami Iyer, 2nd, Galletti Papers.

45   Galletti to Campbell, 25 June 1932, Galletti Papers.

newspaper campaign waged on his behalf. Inevitably, though, Galletti went on, he was compared locally with Sir Thomas Munro, the great 19th century administrator. He rejected such flattery because government knew he was 'straight', saying and doing what he thought best for his people.

Just before Galletti left Bellary, he was farewelled officially by a large group of local notables at the Cosmopolitan Club, then at the railway station the next morning by hundreds of people who appreciated his efforts for them.[46] Clara recorded that he was garlanded 'up to his eyes' but never stopped talking through the mass of flowers.[47]

Galletti was not entirely "straight" with Campbell, though: privately he pilloried the man. Two days after the peace offering, he wrote to his old friend Sir Frank Noyce in New Delhi.[48] It was ridiculous, he commented, that Campbell, Hopetoun Stokes and Thomas Moir were all elevated to the Board and the Council ahead of him. He claimed his old boss, Sir George Forbes, was astonished to discover in 1930 that Galletti was still only a Collector with distinctly lesser men promoted above him. Galletti remained a Collector by choice, he claimed, rejecting a Board appointment in 1926 and telling senior officials he preferred to await a direct Council appointment. There is no evidence to support that claim. His time was coming, though, Galletti thought, with the imminent reforms. As Chief Secretary to the Governor with a place in Cabinet, he would be "a most useful liaison officer between the British Government and the Swaraj Government in Madras." That was simply because his "popularity with the Indian public has always been great and is increasing." That was in the future, he suggested, but for the moment Stokes and Campbell opposed declaring a state of famine in Bellary so he was transferred. What Noyce made of this is unknown, but he

---

46   *Justice*, 30 June 1932.

47   Clara Galletti Diary, 28 June 1932, Galletti Papers.

48   Galletti to Noyce, 27 June 1932, Galletti Papers.

did openly reply that Campbell was a 'hide-bound Bureaucrat', so he and Galletti clearly shared Montagu's earlier low opinion of the Madras hierarchy.

Shortly afterwards, another despised person, G.T.H. Bracken, wrote to Galletti asking if the Minute copied to New Delhi was, in fact, sent.[49] Galletti knew what that meant, and immediately replied he had copied the letter to the Government of India for information but as a 'private' matter. After all, according to the rules, the Government of India was the appellant authority with the right to be informed. Galletti told Bracken 'no disobedience or disrespect was intended', and he obeyed the instruction to cease relief works even though he considered it incorrect. "Innocent blood might have been on my head," so he acted in the best interests of the district's population throughout the affair.[50]

Bracken responded quickly, formally charging Galletti with insubordination for having gone directly to the Government of India and contravening procedural rules.[51]

The People's Collector was in deep trouble. The specific issue was significant enough in its own right. Galletti had defied his superior officers, cast doubt on their abilities, and questioned their actions with the Government of India. Effectively, he challenged their authority, and invited intervention from New Delhi. No senior official could tolerate that, any more than in the past when he tried similar attacks. That was bad enough but it followed the income tax and Board disrespect affairs, so Galletti's tactical objective was to quarantine those skirmishes from this one. He realized that any 'grouping' of his behavioural indiscretions would be professionally fatal.

---

49   Bracken to Galletti, 27 July 1932, Galletti Papers.

50   Galletti to Bracken, 29 July 1932, Galletti Papers.

51   Bracken to Galletti, 8 August 1932, Galletti Papers.

Given that, Galletti's choice of strategy was critical. He could either offer himself up to his superiors, take a sharp reprimand and nullify the problem he had created, or he could contest the issue, risking more damage and further alienation from his colleagues. Naturally, he chose the latter course.

His first defence was that the charge lacked substance.[52] Clear and longstanding precedent practice, he protested, required that the appellant authority be 'informed' on such matters, and that was all he had done. He had acted similarly in his earlier career without consequence. In Chittoor, for example, an Indian officer came to work for him having been demoted by the Government of Madras. Galletti investigated the case, found the decision faulty, reported that to New Delhi and had the demotion overturned. No-one in Madras minded, claimed Galletti.

Then Galletti stepped up the attack. The charge required that he appear before Bracken to defend his actions. Galletti noted that the Chief Secretary (using the third person to refer to Bracken) was his 'junior' so he should appear before the appropriate member of the Board (Campbell) and the Governor. That was a clear snub to Bracken, and further inflamed opinion against Galletti.

He compounded matters with two long follow-up submissions. The first outlined a series of precedents where the appellant authority was informed, with no consequences like those now levelled at Galletti. The second argued the case from a legal standpoint, Galletti concluding the charge was unconstitutional.

The usual question arises: why did he do this when he was bound to lose? First, he certainly felt great responsibility for the Bellary people, seeing what they faced, fearing the worst, and acting to prevent distress. In that respect, he risked his career

---

52   Galletti to Bracken, 17 August 1932, Galletti Papers.

for their welfare. Second, while claiming to have no ambition he was galled that men he considered inferior and junior gained executive positions from which they might direct his actions. Third, his sense of infallibility was highly developed. While he accused Secretariat officials of inflexibility, his own responses were often moreso. Finally, his wicked sense of mischief and his 'mania' remained sharp, even after so many occasions when it threatened his future and his family's security.

Just after receiving the charge Galletti wrote provocatively to the Governor's Private Secretary.[53] He was never against government, he suggested, 'only against the Machine'. The Machine was an army of clerks and a clutch of junior Madras Secretaries so bound by rules and regulations they eschewed decisive action, even when facing catastrophic famine. The Famine Code mandated action against the Machine, so he wrote "begging and praying' that Campbell be ordered to tackle the famine problem directly by giving Galletti 'orders direct and eliminate the Machine'. That, of course, did not happen, but the letter suggests Galletti's deep concern and his efforts to gain direct action from Madras.

Simultaneously, though, he had a curious and unworldly approach, best illustrated in his musings to Noyce. After all that had happened and now facing a formal insubordination charge, Galletti imagined that some enlightened and far-seeing senior official would recognise his qualities, and pick him out to guide Madras into the great new world of transferred government. Given he had alienated everyone of influence in Madras and had serious critics in New Delhi, it is unclear who he imagined the saviour or saviours might be. His optimism was either naïve, or defence against the disappointments waiting at the end of a once promising career.

---

53 Galletti to A.D. Crombie, 15 August 1932, Galletti Papers.

His search for support widened. He wrote again to Campbell.[54] What would you have done, he asked the Board of Revenue man? People would have died had he not acted. As the responsible man on the ground, what else might he have done? He apologised, again, if his actions and representations had offended. He sought not to offend, but he wanted to ensure tragedy did not emerge from the most desperate situation. Clara and the Galletti sons disliked this 'abjectly humble' letter.[55] Galletti explained to the Governor's Private Secretary that he acted because he feared what might befall the Bellary people. He wanted to forestall a calamity, not just get his own way[56]

Already charged with ignoring procedural rules, Galletti aggravated matters by writing directly to two old non-European Madras Council friends. Sir Muhamad Usman and Sir M. Krishnan Nair were prominent conservative leaders with whom Galletti had worked earlier, and he now attempted to set them against ICS members of Council. Those ICS men, Galletti wrote, thought an Indian could live on seven *pies* a day, the relief wage rate set by government and ignored by Galletti. Usman and Nair knew better than that, and so would understand why Galletti acted. The pair should talk to the Governor and ensure Galletti be treated fairly. Predictably, Bracken and colleagues learned about the letters and Galletti was admonished for writing directly to individual Council members. Even then, Galletti would not repent. He contested Bracken's ruling, claiming the right to approach Council members.[57]

Galletti prepared for the hearing before Bracken. Predictably, the Secretariat did not embarrass its man by granting Galletti's request for a meeting with the Governor and Board. The formal interview early in September 1932 was a difficult, searching

54   Galletti to Campbell, 15 August 1932, Galletti Papers.

55   Clara Galletti Diary, 22 August 1932, Galletti Papers.

56   Galletti to A.D. Crombie, 15 August 1932, Galletti Papers.

57   Bracken to Galletti, 30 August 1932, Galletti Papers.

and humbling one for Galletti. Even so, he would not repent. Afterwards, he wrote immediately to Bracken, contesting comments and observations passed about his professional performance.[58] Galletti was upset especially by references to the other disciplinary and inquiry cases in which he was involved. That possibility had worried him from the outset because while one case was awkward, several cases considered together was positively dangerous. No matter how much he protested, however, the Secretariat was always going to consider this specific charge in the context of his overall performance even if he claimed to have been cleared on every charge. Galletti thought his record unblemished, an odd and myopic view.

Bracken had none of that.[59] Galletti's apologies were not accepted. He was censured severely and reported to the Government of India, a serious and rare action in ICS terms. Bracken pointed out that while no action was taken against Galletti on earlier charges he had been condemned, not cleared on all counts. For the third time in a short period he was guilty of impertinent behaviour towards senior officers, breaching protocols and procedures, causing serious damage to the standing of the ICS: "It is not for him [Galletti] to argue about precedents but to obey orders." Bracken concluded ominously: "any further act of insubordination will entail the most serious consequences." Decoded, that meant any further incidents would see Galletti sacked.

Arthur Galletti was fortunate not to be sacked immediately. He was spared, probably, only because of the intersecting political and economic circumstances. Staring down serious political unrest stimulated by economic weakness, the Government of Madras could ill-afford a public demonstration of internal dissension. Had Galletti been sacked there would have been intense media speculation, and Galletti himself would

---

58   Galletti to Bracken, 12 September 1932, Galletti Papers.

59   Bracken to Galletti, 13 October 1932, Galletti Papers.

have contributed to that. A show of unity was required, at least, and even Galletti had to be accommodated. Galletti realised the gravity of his position, however, and sought to mollify Bracken in two personal meetings in Madras. The first went badly, the second much better.[60]

His friends knew how lucky he was, and even Galletti conceded the Government of Madras was 'very angry'. [61] Bishop Weller of Madras, for example, was with Galletti in Bellary the night the order halting relief had arrived and, seeing his host's distress, intervened with Campbell on the Collector's behalf. Now, though, Weller ruled out further 'butting in' because it would inflame rather than alleviate the situation.[62] Earlier Charles Souter, who still supported Galletti despite their earlier disagreements, asked why Galletti acted as he did because it caused offence and further weakened his overall position.[63]

There were deeper personal twists in all this. Inexplicably, the Government of Madras had met Galletti's request that his son Robert (Berto) be posted to Bellary as his Assistant Collector. Galletti argued his newly married son faced great costs, so living with his father in the Collector's house would provide both a personal saving and a boost to good district governance. Berto topped his ICS entrant year following an excellent academic career at Balliol College, Oxford after earlier education at Breek's School in Ootacamund then Cheltenham. He married Eda Upshon, an Anglo-Indian whose family were long time Malabar residents and whose father was the jailer for the 1921 Moplah uprising prisoners.

Galletti and son soon fell out seriously over financial matters and did not speak for several years, but for the moment Berto was in the awkward position of reporting Bellary events unofficially

---

60   Clara Galletti Diary, 14 September 1932, Galletti Papers.

61   Galletti to Noyce, 19 October 1932, Galletti Papers.

62   Weller to Galletti, 23 October 1932, Galletti Papers.

63   Souter to Galletti, 27 August 1932, Galletti Papers.

to his father following the latter's departure. Among other things, Berto gained 'insider' reports about a visit to the district by Campbell and the Governor. There was a widespread view that the Governor was prevented from seeing the worst of things. 'Onlooker' soon after wrote to a local newspaper suggesting the visit was stage-managed, that there were no consultations with anyone who knew the conditions, and that the visit was used to justify increasing relief wages when the need for that was clear all along.[64] Galletti was 'Onlooker', because the contents of the letter to the editor resembled strongly those sent to him by Berto.

The other personal twist was that while Galletti went to Ganjam, his family stayed behind in Bellary for a double wedding set around the time Galletti appeared before Bracken. He travelled from Ganjam to Bellary for the wedding of his son, Arthur and of his youngest daughter, Isabella, then returned via Madras for the hearing. Isabella's wedding had its own drama because she was found in bed with the man set to marry her sister, Emma. Galletti ordered that the pair marry. Emma was sent off to London to study medicine but on the ship over met Jack Ricketts whom she soon married. Photographs of the double wedding show Galletti looking tired, and ageing. That was hardly surprising because, as Clara's diary reveals, his private life was as chaotic as his professional one. The pressure of events bore in on him, and he erupted around the time of his transfer to Ganjam in June.[65]

Clara was about to take a short trip to England and Italy where her cousin Max had been jailed by the Fascists. Galletti himself wrote to the Fascist authorities arguing Max's case. Clara and Arthur had several arguments about expenses for the trip. On 24 June 1932 Galletti received a registered letter

---

64 This appears in the Galletti Papers, and most likely appeared in *Justice*.

65 The following section from June entries in Clara Galletti Diary, 1932, Galletti Papers.

from the government in Ootacamund informing him he was being transferred because government was dissatisfied with his handling of the 'famine'. Appallingly, the Gallettis had already learned of the transfer from the *Madras Mail* a few days earlier. Clara recorded her extreme unhappiness with the government's wickedness. The very next day, 'despondent, almost despairing', Clara typed a letter to Campbell from Galletti, "one of his grandiloquent ones". During the dictation, Galletti again attacked Clara's trip expenses his attitude, posture and face so aggressive that Clara hit him, then 'screamed the house down'. These strong minded people were both under severe stress.

Galletti's response was odd, even by his standards. He had to leave for Ganjam, and he intended taking Rerto's wife Eda with him. She refused, mainly because of yet another family dispute. Berto and Eda wanted to live out of the Collector's house, but Galletti said if they moved out he would not support them financially. The couple did not speak to him for several years afterwards. Galletti tied Eda's refusal to accompany him to Clara's attitudes and jealousies.[66] He then proceeded to give 'My Advice To Clara'. If Clara could smile at life, he wrote, then life would smile back. It would be a tragedy if in her old age Clara became like her mother, 'a thoroughly bad old woman' with vices she called 'nerves'. Screaming the house down over packing duties was simply ridiculous:

> I love Clara and do not despair of her, but let her exercise
> a little self-control.

He also revealed just how serious was this family moment, and how insensitive he was to Clara's emotions.

> The pretence that you want to separate is also just a silly
> piece of vulgarity.

The separation did not eventuate and husband and wife were soon reconciled, as they had been many times over the

---

66 This section drawn from Arthur to Clara, 5 July 1932, Galletti Papers.

years because of their deep emotional attachment to each other. Clara had to watch her husband almost terminate his career and her security without accepting any of her advice. They and the family survived and Clara made clear her affection for her husband, but at mid-1932 Galletti's marriage was on the verge of collapse, he was alienated from at least two of his children, and he was barely hanging onto his career. The man was scarcely in control of himself let alone being able to command a district.

That helps explain one of his most famous escapades. Just after Galletti arrived in Ganjam, stressed by recent events, his Indian Deputy Collector consigned a cook to prison for a night for having burned the evening meal. Galletti was outraged, called the Deputy, put a label entitled 'Ass' around the man's neck, and had him committed to the town's animal pound for a day! The man's family then had to pay to retrieve him, just as for a straying dog. The family was furious, and yet another complaint about Galletti reached Madras.[67] Galletti claimed it was a trivial matter blown out of proportion and that he was distracted by several murder cases. Geoffrey Bracken replied that the government considered Galletti's action totally inappropriate, displaying "levity and a lack of a proper sense of responsibility."[68]

Professionally wounded, Galletti withdrew from Bellary but not from combat. Over the next several months he compiled and printed up his version of the famine events.[69] He pointed out where he anticipated government approval to sanction relief work, and the difficulties under which he worked. The District Board President, he suggested, had threatened a No-Tax campaign if relief was not forthcoming, so connecting the famine with latent political discontent. Galletti, of course, had reasoned with the President and the crisis was avoided. In

---

67 A version of this story appears in S.K. Chettur, *The steel frame and I:life in the I.C.S.* (Bombay, Asia, 1962), pp. 68-69.

68 Bracken to Galletti, 26 January 1933, Galletti Papers.

69 "A brief account of the Bellary famine 1931-1932", Galletti Papers.

the end, government suspended the relief and was fortunate that the rains broke soon after because otherwise a disaster would have occurred. He concluded that bureaucracy was obviously incapable of dealing with such events. The governor should always take control to avoid endless bureaucratic manoeuvring.

Galletti sent this account to the Governor. Through his Private Secretary, the Governor rejected Galletti's view that he was "not supported by the organs of government and wrongly blamed for taking matters into his own hands."[70] Nonetheless, Galletti still believed he was right, that the Board had ignored the gravity of the situation, and that his decisions and actions were justified. It was a defiant if sad response to a major professional rebuff.

During late 1932-early 1933 another senior promotion possibility arose in the service, yet again on the Board of Revenue. Galletti was not so much overlooked as ignored, apart from Secretariat speculation about how his case might best be handled. Seniority was still a prime factor in selection even if his behaviour ruled him out. Galletti appealed against his non-selection in an official Memorial to the Government of India that began by quoting Oliver Cromwell: a man's opinions should not be held against him if it was clear he could do the work required of a good civil servant. In his covering letter, Galletti slyly suggested the Government of India could always appoint him as Resident in Hyderabad or Mysore if they did not overturn the Madras decision![71]

Then, towards the end of 1934, two vacancies for ICS men arose on the Madras Executive Council, just as the 1935 Government of India Act was about to empower locally-elected provincial governments. All provincial governments were extremely sensitive about such appointments. The Madras Governor, Lord

---

70 A.D. Crombie to Galletti, 1 July 1933, Galletti Papers.

71 Galletti to Secretary Home Dept GOI, 5 April 1933 enclosing Memorial Against Supersession, 5 April 1933, Galletti Papers.

Erskine, took great care over the two positions, mindful of the role the occupants would play in the transition and afterwards. He proposed putting in Souter and C.F. Brackenbury, indicating that both privately and personally to the Secretary of State whom he knew personally. The reason for his care was obvious. Putting in Souter and Brackenbury meant overriding the seniority claims of Cox and Galletti. However, he said, the detailed grounds on which their claims had previously been rejected for positions as Chief Secretary and on the Board of Revenue still held good.[72]

Despite several years of constant combat with his superiors and perennial rejection for senior posts, in 1934 Galletti decided it would be in everyone's best interests if he stayed on in the service. ICS rules rigidly insisted that officers retire after 35 years service, and it was unknown for any officer to stay on unless transferred to the Princely States or given some special out-of-service posting. Among those of Galletti's era in the first category were H.D.C. Reilly who moved to Mysore and ended up staying in India almost 50 years; and Loftus Tottenham who moved to Pudukottai where he died in service, leaving most of his wealth to fund an annual mass feeding of the poor. The most famous special posting was Sir Frederick Nicholson, a legendary Madras ICS man who stayed on many years after his 1904 formal retirement. Their records were all far more impeccable than Galletti's, however.

Galletti argued that with imminent and substantial constitutional reform allowing Indians to run provincial governments, sympathetic and experienced men like him were needed to ensure smooth transition.[73] He was well suited to high office, he suggested, even if serially passed over for juniors. He

72 Erskine to Secretary of State, Private, 3 December 1934, MSS Eur D 596/7, IOR; the same messages are contained in L/PJ/7/782, IOR and L/PO/8/65 (i), IOR- Erskine was taking no chances.

73 See his Memorial to the Secretary of State Seeking An Extension of Service, nd [mid-1934], Galletti Papers.

was intelligent, experienced, had deep understanding of south India, sympathy for Indian aspirations, great drive and vision, and was well liked by the politicians about to take office. Given that, the rules should be waived so that he could contribute to the new order.

It was a weak, unconvincing petition and even he seemed to know that. He brought the case clearly under the disappointment of being rejected for the Council posts, because he opened the Memorial by stating he had again been superseded by a junior. He now saw more junior men even than Souter elevated, and it hurt. When the Memorial arrived in Madras, the Government immediately collated at least eight Secret Files relating to Galletti's recent activities. They included the Gandhi tour; the 'Deputy Collector in the pound' incident; improper reporting to government, and a very large file concerning some recent prosecutions that Government was concerned about but had yet to raise with him.[74] Inevitably, the rejection of his plea was swift, even brutal. Government saw no need whatsoever to have Galletti remain in India. The letter came from Acting Chief Secretary Edward Francis Thomas. He joined Madras three years after Galletti yet was posted to the Board in 1931 and would become First member in early 1935. He was almost the perfect symbol of what Galletti thought he was up against.

After serving in Ganjam for just six months Galletti took eight months leave early in 1933, arriving back in November that year to a posting in Anantapur, a district renowned in the service and publicly regarded as perhaps *the* punishment station. Dry, arid and hot, it was not the district given normally to senior officers about to retire. The Madras establishment was giving Galletti one final message. While there for just over a year before taking retirement leave in December 1934, Galletti still caused his superiors considerable disquiet.

---

74 GOM GO Public (Special) Confl 934, 5 September 1934, TNA–unfortunately, the prosecution files have not been traceable.

Almost immediately, Mahatma Gandhi visited Anantapur as part of a southern tour. By now it was well-known that Galletti had earlier corresponded with Gandhi, because the latter boasted about it to several service colleagues and members of the public. Gandhi called him 'Dear Friend', Galletti was fond of saying.[75] Given that, having posted Galletti to this out of the way place, the Secretariat was now alarmed by events and, inevitably, trouble ensued.

Galletti's report of Gandhi's visit was almost but not quite innocuous.[76] Gandhi spent two days in the district addressing public meetings, collecting funds, emphasising the need to improve the lot of untouchables, and attracting crowds up to 5,000 people. According to Galletti, Gandhi's 'personal popularity' among the people remained 'undiminished', not something Madras wanted to hear. Gandhi spent little time advocating temple entry for untouchables, according to Galletti, because it was an unpopular issue in the south where the masses were unenthusiastic about uplifting untouchables. All arrangements made for the visit were satisfactory, "especially at Anantapur where I supervised them personally." Again, senior officials considered that Galletti puffed his work and achievements. Galletti concluded that "the tour did not attract as much notice as might have been expected".

The Government of officials, however, were deeply concerned about this tour and thought Galletti considerably underplayed the seriousness of the situation.

By now he was truculent rather than spirited, curmudgeonly rather than creative, bitter rather than indomitable. The world had changed for him, and not for the better. Towards the end of 1934 the Government of Madras made significant changes to the conduct rules under which ICS officers worked. That was

---

75   Gandhi to Galletti letter, nd [1926], Galletti Papers.

76   Galletti to Chief Secretary, 9 January 1934, GOM, Secret File 877, 1 March 1934, TNA.

in preparation for the new political order and mainly involved procedural issues around reporting. Galletti's response was wistful and resentful:

> We already have too many rules, too little discretion, too little personal intercourse, too little sympathy with the small official. [77]

It was time for him to go.

As his final act in the service, however, and before proceeding on final leave before retirement Galletti wrote to A.D. Crombie, the Private Secretary to the Governor, announcing that he was organizing famine relief arrangements before he left Anantapur. He was assailed by everyone to stay on, he said, but government refused so he must leave.[78] However, he was confident his arrangements would serve the district well. He had informed C.F. Brackenbury, now the Famine Commissioner, about the Anantapur situation and what had to be done. Brackenbury, he declared, had "grasped the situation and will not be indulging in any sycophantic optimism." Sir Hopetoun Stokes was amused, thinking it "satisfactory to note that Mr G. approves of his superior officer, the Famine Commissioner!" Sir Geoffrey Bracken, however, was angry, because Galletti was suggesting Board Members reported what Council wanted to hear rather than the facts.

As his parting gift from India, in Memorandum 29381-1 dated 7 December 1934 from Bracken, Galletti was censured for one final time about his tone of address and his comments concerning the conduct of the Board and its members. His 'Board Must Go' campaign had failed, and the Tin Gods had won out. With that he left India, never to return but never to forget, either.

---

77 Galletti to Secretary Board of Revenue, 14 October 1934, Galletti Papers.

78 GOM Public (Special) GO 1257 Confl, 11 December 1934, TNA.

9

India After

Arthur Galletti did not want to retire, for two interlocked reasons, one philosophical and the other personal. The latter concerned his finances. During his career he took several long periods of 'special' leave that were, effectively, unpaid. That hit both his income and his pension accumulation. Added to that were his extensive and expensive travel costs, and repayments to the uncles who had supported his education. His own children's education in India, Italy and England over several years added to the burden. Although he was not bereft Galletti could almost not afford to retire, were it not for Clara's owning the *Cassace* and its lands back in Italy.

His imminent ICS pension allocation, then, became especially important but, as Galletti and other ICS officers had said for over 10 years, what once was comfortable was no longer so. On average, an ICS retiree could anticipate approximately £1,000 a year pension, and the figure had stuck at that level now for many years. Before the war its beneficiaries were well off, but through the 1920s retirees reported finding things difficult. The ICS associations formed just after the war debated the issue constantly and service frustration grew, despite the arrival of the economic depression that should theoretically have improved things for those on fixed incomes.

Even though Arthur and Clara were returning to Italy where their costs might predictably be lower than in England, Galletti's grand plans for the *Cassace* suggested even more expense would undermine their income, and Clara was especially worried. That financial pressure, in turn, fed the more substantial reason for Galletti wanting to stay on.

He enjoyed playing the "People's Collector' despite the troubles it brought him, his family and the few colleagues who still retained affection for him. He loved India and its people, especially the Telugus. But important though that Collector role was in south India, it was far from what he had always imagined his career grade might be. He and many others thought he would reach the top: Chief Secretary, Board of Revenue, Council member, probably an All-India role. That was why he resented the rise of those he considered inferior men, and that heightened his antagonistic behavior. To finish up as Collector of a remote Madras Presidency 'punishment' station after those grand initial prospects was a resounding blow to a proud, even arrogant man reckoned among the most intelligent to have ever entered the ICS. It was embarrassing, humiliating even, and he needed another chance to reconcile his self-image with the reality of his professional standing, and to prove his many detractors wrong.

His frustration was exacerbated by the Indian political transformation he confronted daily. From his arrival in Madras Galletti regarded himself as a liberal in the purest sense of that word. He supported political change, but on his terms. While his earlier efforts were radical in the contemporary ICS, they also contained the harbingers of his disappointment. Galletti believed it would be a long time before Indians were ready for self-rule that should arrive gradually and in careful stages. That helps explain his doubts about the Morley-Minto reforms and the Montagu-Chelmsford ones that followed: he supported reform in principle, but these seemed to move too fast for him, a simplistic response to momentary crises. As he now struggled to stay on, he also doubted the wisdom of the 1935 Government of India Bill that would transfer provincial responsibility to elected majorities.

At the heart of this conflict lay Galletti's belief in the political pre-eminence of the local educated elites and the so-called 'natural leaders' of the people, even though this group's strongest days were well behind them. These people, like Sir P.S. Sivaswami Iyer, sat mainly with what were identified as the 'moderates' but around World War I some began showing up in Indian National Congress ranks. Galletti initially believed he could work with local Congressmen, and that was why the Guntur nightmare changed him irrevocably—it proved he could not communicate with the new Congress as he had imagined. In Madras, too, as added complication, the moderates were swamped by the Government of Madras-sponsored non-Brahmin movement designed to counter Brahmin leadership in Congress. Galletti neither understood nor approved these shifts, because they threatened orderly progress towards fitness for rule. For Galletti, this represented the worst possible result of British rule, a struggle for power between groups driven by specific self-interest.

From there his political compass went increasingly awry, as demonstrated by what happened in his beloved Andhra. Many local leaders he supported there were big *ryotwari* or *zamindari* landowners who dominated local self-government boards and the main political associations. From Galletti's standpoint, it became increasingly obvious that these leaders were not interested in welfare of 'the people', and certainly not in land reform. It was not that Galletti sought sweeping land reform, but he did want a better deal for those who worked the soil. Throughout the 1920s and into the 1930s, three conditions interacted to change Andhra dramatically.[1]

First, the Russian Revolution created great interest among the Andhra reading classes that had grown substantially since the later 19th century. Oddly, that fed into the Gandhian revolution because the Mahatma, too, emphasised the needs of "the people". During the 1920s there appeared throughout Andhra numerous local leaders who were well educated, now

---

1   Brian Stoddart, *Land, Water, Language and Politics in Andhra: the Evolution of an Indian Region From 1850* (Delhi, Routledge, 2011).

followed Gandhi at the expense of their careers and incomes, and focused on improving conditions for the lower social orders. That change was then accelerated by the onset of the depression that had a huge impact on lives and livelihoods in coastal Andhra. This was a perfect breeding ground for a new political movement.

By the time Galletti was about to leave India, the Socialist Party wing of the Congress was emerging rapidly, with coastal Andhra its heartland. Spearheaded by the Oxford-educated economist-turned-peasant-leader Dr. N.G. Ranga, the Congress Socialist Party movement turned into a crusade for landless labourers. By the mid-1930s momentum was such that a CSP split saw one wing become a full Communist movement led by P. Sundarayya. Andhra was swept by socialists and Communists who rivaled the influence of the traditional Congress leadership. The speed and spread of transformation was astonishing, vastly different from the political evolution Arthur Galletti had imagined.

That simply reinforced his long-held view that India needed intelligent, insightful, sympathetic officials like him to help avoid coming catastrophes if people like Ranga and Sundarayya gained further sway. It was not just that Galletti wanted to stay on. In his mind India needed him to stay on to guarantee an ordered and prosperous future.

Unfortunately for him, his Government of Madras Secretariat superiors took a very different view of Galletti's indispensability. As many subordinates, colleagues and bosses had commented over the years, the wonder was that his career went full term. At any number of points he might well have been dismissed. He openly questioned government policy and defied instructions, belittled and ridiculed senior officers, had questions raised about his loyalty, extolled his own intellectual powers and dismissed those of others. For many senior officers, Galletti's 'People's Collector' image was irritating on two counts. First, he used it to suggest that he alone in the ICS sympathized with the cause of ordinary Indian people. Second, he extended the idea directly into the policy field to play the role of 'voice of the people' when, in fact, many senior officers felt he was oblivious to challenges the service now confronted.

There was scarcely a precedent for officers staying on beyond their full term. Sir Frederick Nicholson was appointed to consultancy roles at the end of his distinguished career, and one or two judges transferred into the princely states at the end of their regular service. There was no instance, however, of a district officer being appointed to continue past normal retirement age. Given that, and Galletti's record, there was no possibility he could continue. He likely knew that, because he began looking around the world for possible posts in places like Eritrea. That was desperate and sad for him, and for Clara who was ready to return to Italy.

So Arthur Galletti officially retired from the ICS at age 57 and left Madras on 10 December 1934, exactly 34 years after he first arrived there. He proceeded on one month and six days of fully paid leave, followed by nine months and 14 days on half pay, then a further special allowance of one month and 10 days on further half pay, so he had a year's income before his pension entitlements set in. He never again set foot in India.

The country still interested him, and he still believed he had wisdom to dispense there but he was now a spectator, not a participant. Like most people leaving influential positions he found it difficult to separate and to adjust. He had been the 'King of Khondisthan', as Clara had declared. Now he was to be a very large *sahib* in a very small *commune*. The 1935 Government of India Act was enacted a few months after his departure, with Congress and the Justice Party then battling out the 1937 provincial elections that resulted in a Congress victory. Galletti took a dim view of the prospects. C. Rajagopalachariar, Rajaji as he was known and a prominent Tamil leader, become Chief

Minister supported by figures known to Arthur and Clara like S. Satyamurthy and especially Tangaturi Prakasam, the Guntur activist now both an Andhra movement leader and Congress notable. He would become Chief Minister of the Madras Presidency in the run-up to Independence in 1947, then of the new Andhra province when it was finally created in 1953. These were not the people to whom Galletti had anticipated power being transferred, and the long wait for the creation of Andhra that he had pressed for first all those years ago was agonizing.

His frustration was heightened by knowing several of his old ICS adversaries were now inaugurating the political change. Principal among them was G.T.H. now Sir Geoffrey Bracken. After the spell as Chief Secretary during which Galletti took up so much of his time, Bracken was promoted to the Executive Council and became Governor Lord Erskine's chief adviser leading into to the 1937 elections. Erskine became increasingly impressed by Congress and Rajagopalachariar, in particular, and Bracken supported him.[2] The result was that many Madras ICS members formerly skeptical about India's preparedness for self-rule were won over. Just five years earlier they supported suppression of Congress and Galletti looked like a radical. Now they believed they could work with Congress and Galletti looked like a reactionary. It was a swift transformation that Galletti neither comprehended nor appreciated.

Immediately upon retirement Galletti sailed for Auckland, New Zealand to undergo thyroid surgery, believing an eminent surgeon there was among the world's best. Clara was left to supervise one final Indian house packing, shipping their belongings from Anantapur to Italy and farewelling her few friends before setting off alone.

---

2   David Arnold, *The Congress in Tamil Nadu: nationalist politics in South India, 1919-1937* (Delhi, Manohar, 1977), p.179.

Galletti's surgery is an important part of his story, because it adds considerable insight to his performance and behavior through much of his Indian career. As with any medical condition thyroid symptoms are case-specific, but Galletti had the condition for at least 10 years before it was treated, as revealed in Clara's diaries. Commonly, thyroid-related problems and especially hyperthyroid ones produce anxiety, irritability and even depression, while changes to facial muscle conditions often cause eye problems including double vision accompanied by strong pain. Given Clara's accounts of Arthur's headaches, his frequent rests in a darkened room, and his routine wearing of dark glasses, he certainly suffered the condition throughout the period of his most litigious behaviour. From 1930 onwards, when he was most intransigent, his medical condition undoubtedly influenced his behaviour.

Even that, however, does not fully explain his earlier behaviour patterns. It is highly likely the thyroid conditions were predated by depression and/or a more specific condition such as Aspergers syndrome. Galletti's behaviours bear strong similarity to Aspergers that was first diagnosed only in 1944, well after he retired. Those afflicted generally lack empathy with or for anyone around them, along with an under-developed ability to express emotion. Sufferers commonly exhibit extreme verbosity, strong preoccupation with a single subject, exaggerated concern for detailed patterns, inflexible routines, high levels of pedantry, literal interpretations of materials and conditions, failure to place conversations in context, and an inability to pick up disapproving signals from people caught amidst a one-sided conversation.

Galletti's personal and professional relationships demonstrated all these characteristics before, throughout, and after his time in India. Clara, for example, constantly sought stronger emotional commitment from him. She frequently referred to his intransigent 'theories' and views as unbending and uninformed by any arguments she and others put up. ICS colleagues and superiors lamented his ability to prolong discussions and debates well beyond their useful life, and to shroud his arguments in pedantic detail. Galletti frequently focused intensely on one subject for a prolonged period, such as his preoccupation with the similarities he drew between Italian farming practice and Indian rice paddy production. His end-of-career obsession with the Bellary 'famine' was an excellent example. Similarly, he demonstrated an unwillingness to change, even though outwardly he supported 'progress'.

One good example concerns camping and being on tour. Up until World War I, touring dominated life for ICS officers and their memoirs are replete with stories on the subject. They went on horseback, were away for weeks at a time, hunted, met the locals and communed with nature. As motor vehicles and road conditions improved substantially from World War I onwards, though, officers more commonly completed inspections in one day. Camping and being on tour changed. Right until the end of his career, however, Galletti prided himself on the amount of traditional camping he did. For him it was the mark of a good officer and befitted his ideal of the 'People's Collector', a man who lived among his subjects. His commitment can equally be read as resistance to change and insistence upon an habitual routine.

Galletti was certainly verbose, too, as family and colleagues alike commented frequently. Intense and lengthy monologues often overwhelmed audiences without his noticing. Clara's diaries and letters record his tendency to talk non-stop, and be oblivious to the effect he had on others. The precedents, arguments and objections he raised against specific orders infuriated superiors who thought his pedantic, antiquarian approach a straightforward challenge to authority.

Early in 1939, Clara wrote to her son Robert revealing her most direct-ever view of Arthur Galletti. Berto sought advice on resolving the rift with his father. Why ask her, she replied?

She had no influence over Arthur at any point in their lives, nor had anyone else in either personal or professional spheres. He considered himself right in every matter, and rode roughshod over the views of anyone else, she reported. She and Arthur had always had "disagreements" throughout their life together. In spite of that, however, and in spite of the 'fierce gusts of angry passion' that occurred frequently, she had and would always love Arthur because, deep down, he had 'sterling goodness'.[3] In many ways, his ICS colleagues would have agreed. They all reckoned him able, intelligent, committed—but also obdurate, obsessive and myopic.

Galletti most likely suffered an undiagnosed behavioural condition aggravated by the thyroid onset. For a man in his senior administrative position that created an enormous burden he dealt with by sheer force of will. He drove himself to keep working, to keep challenging his superiors despite the major problems that created for him, his family and his professional relationships. The ICS had enormous difficulty dealing with 'oddity' such as Galletti's behaviour, mental illness generally, alcoholism, divorce, financial stress, cultural isolation, family difficulties and other social problems. One of Galletti's own junior officers in Bellary, for example, was clearly an alcoholic. There was no attempt at treatment or intervention, he was simply shipped 'Home' where he died not long after arriving. The service provided no help to any officer facing such difficulties. It was sink or swim.

So it was that Galletti sought a thyroid cure only at the end of his service days. While in Auckland, though, he wrote home to say he had spent an afternoon with a newspaper editor whom he had given the benefit of his wisdom about India. The New Zealand public, Galletti thought, was now infinitely better informed about what was happening in the subcontinent!

---

3   Clara to Roberto, 15 March 1939 [contained in a letter Emma to Beatrice, 2 November 1966], Galletti Papers.

There is no evidence, unfortunately, that the editor in question published those views. Had they appeared, however, they would almost certainly have doubted the wisdom of the 1935 reforms and been pessimistic about India's future despite the strength and qualities of its 'real people'.

Arthur Galletti's subsequent focus on India was blurred by events in his own life as well as his professional frustration. For example, while in New Zealand he gave Clara one last personal torment. He wrote of a young Scots woman named Jessie and her mother he met on the ship and continued to see in New Zealand. One of his letters reported he had kissed the young woman in front of her mother; another that they were planning to meet in Palmerston North (a most unlikely tourist destination) and at the hot springs in Rotorua. Clara immediately suspected the worst, naturally. Because it coincided with her worries about leaving India and her anxiety about Arthur undergoing a serious operation, the 'Jessie' episode caused Clara as much torment as had the abiding 'Nancy' one. She wrote to Arthur: "Leave me for good or *never* leave me again for so long and go so far."

To the last, their lives together as two very strong-willed people created passion and friction in equal measure, as it had in India. Unfortunately, they did not have all that much time left together. Life in India was hard for Clara physically, and from at least the 1920s on she was frequently ill, losing weight and energy, especially after the operations she underwent in the late 1920s. After their return to Italy she improved with a more settled lifestyle, despite Arthur's building plans and renovations stretching financial resources yet again.

There were further family anxieties. Beatrice remained in Europe as a nun, her father still challenging her beliefs and her mother still regretting them. The India connection remained strong through the other children. Arthur junior was still serving in the artillery there, Emma lived in the south with her planter industry husband, and Bella through the 1930s maintained a strained relationship with her engineer husband there. Robert remained in the Madras ICS and corresponded a little with his father, but a deep personal gulf remained between them for several years. Through all those sources Arthur senior still gained some impression of what was happening politically, and was not encouraged.

In mid-1939, sadly, Clara was referred to a Perugia clinic where she was diagnosed with advanced stomach cancer. Arthur junior and Robert both visited her that month, but neither Beatrice nor Emma could travel to Italy. After several weeks of pain, Clara Salvadori Galletti died on 26 November 1939 at the age of 59, just two months after the beginning of World War II and six before Italy joined against the allies.

Arthur was devastated. Photographs show a gaunt, bent figure dressed in formal clothes following the horse-drawn hearse at Clara's funeral in Porto San Giorgio. He later published privately a series of poems written for her over the years, and some written in grief leading up to and at the time of her death.[4] Expressed in English, Italian, German and Telugu, the poems were for Clara but also revealed the difficult and dominant character that Clara, their friends and colleagues had struggled with over the years:

> Hope that you will see my view, Know I never loved but you And if our days are now but few, Give them all to me: See that I was always right, That I glowed with holy light, Like a start serene and bright, Shining on the sea.[5]

In that he reasserted his belief in the moderate, "Sacred" love he championed for so long and against Clara's wish for a more passionate commitment from him. But there was despair, too. He still believed he was right, but wished he had been able

---

4   Arturo Galletti, *Versi A Mia Moglie: Negli Ultimi Anni Della Sua Vita-In Memoriam*, Galletti Papers.

5   "*LÁmore Moderato, 19 luglio 1939-XVIII*, Galletti Papers.

to convince Clara, first, that he really did love her and, second, that he had been better able to convince her about his views. The same could be said of his views on politics in India.

By then Arthur Galletti had developed local friendships, worked sporadically on his Italian-English dictionary, maintained his religious dispute with Beatrice and read widely. His immediate triumph after retirement was the publication by Oxford University Press of his Telugu-English dictionary, a symbolic demonstration of his love for Andhra and its people but also, as we have seen, containing some delightful barbs against his superiors. At first Galletti maintained contact with the few former colleagues he had not alienated. Hilton Brown was the main one, because they were of similar liberal disposition, as the Scot demonstrated in his 1920s novels set in India. Brown retired to become a fulltime writer and, after a spell back in England, returned to India to live because he felt more comfortable there, so contact with him became less easy especially after the war began.

By early 1939, though, Galletti had abandoned his attempts to publish his Guntur accounts. Even his strongest former public supporters, like the Madras publisher G.A. Natesan, thought the caravan had moved on so far there was little point in trying to rectify misconceptions about a now distant political *frisson*. Galletti did reprise some of his earlier historical interests, and in 1939 contributed a little piece on the San Thome Church in Madras to the 400th anniversary celebrations of the city's formation.[6] Galletti's library shows little sign of his having added much if any serious Indian political or constitutional materials following his retirement, mirroring his strong view that things were moving far too quickly. He was making a new life, effectively an Italian one even though no longer an Italian citizen following his renunciation struggles through and just after World War I.

---

6   A. Galletti, "San Thome (Mypalore) in Dutch and English Records" in *The Madras tercentenary commemoration volume* (Madras, Tercentenary Committee, 1939).

Because of that, his interest in Indian developments and politics was deflected by his growing concern with those in Italy. The rise of Italian Fascism alarmed Arthur and Clara, as did its divisive effect on their wider families. Clara's uncle Mario was a prominent regional Fascist. Conversely, Arthur's brother-in-law, Willy Salvadori was a prominent anti-Fascist in exile, as was Willy's son Max Salvadori who was later decorated for his work in the Resistance. Clara and Arthur's daughter Isabella, by now back in Italy, was outspoken against Mussolini and also joined the Resistance, so the family was conflicted, like many others. Galletti and Clara themselves were strongly anti-Fascist, but circumspect about expressing those views publicly. Years later Max Salvadori's daughter, Cynthia, observed that her father had a strong affection for Galletti and certainly would not have done so had Arthur leaned towards Fascism. Similarly, Max's wife would not have countenanced Clara had she shown anything but contempt for Mussolini and the blackshirts.

Family lore has Arthur keeping a photograph of *Il Duce* at hand in case of visitation by local *Fascisti* leaders, but for the most part that photograph faced the wall with a piece of art on its reverse side stared out at more benign callers.

A few months after Clara's death, Arthur's odd citizenship status caught up with him. He was arrested by the Fascists and interned until early in 1942 because he was a British citizen, not technically having regained his Italian citizenship. It was a considerable price to pay for a stand on principle taken over 20 years earlier. Being the man he was, Arthur Galletti would have seen the black humour in this—forced to give up being an Italian because the British feared his dual nationality, the Fascists now rounded on him because he was not Italian but British! He was eventually repatriated to England by the Red Cross but no records survive to indicate how that happened.[7]

---

7   Communication from the Red Cross Archives in Geneva.

Galletti then stayed with his daughter-in-law Rachel, Arthur junior's wife and her children David and Antoinette. Arthur junior was serving with the Royal Field Artillery in the Middle East. The children loved their grandfather, and recall now someone who played with them incessantly and prompted their love for learning. For Rachel, however, he was a trial. After a lifetime of service in India with juniors and servants to support his every need followed by a comfortable if expensive life in Italy, he was ready to resume his old ways after the privations of internment. This was wartime and rationed England, however, where things were very difficult. The household became tense. During 1943 Rachel and Arthur learned that their loved husband and son had died as a result of wounds in the desert. They were devastated, and the death placed greater pressure on their relationship. Arthur returned to Italy.

During this period the British in India faced the often violent rebellions of the Quit India movement, while in Andhra the communists exerted huge influence over large areas and populations. In less than 10 years, India had become a place Arthur Galletti would not recognize even if not burdened by his own trials and those of his family. The political forces he feared most and even despised were now in the ascendant. The 'natural leaders' had disappeared and, clearly, the days of the 'enlightened' administrators (let alone the unenlightened ones) were numbered. India would become independent far sooner than he had ever imagined.

Dismayed by developments in India and Italy alike, in 1949 Galletti created his own political party to promote liberal views that still reflected much of what he had believed. The *Partito Decentramento Radicale's* published programme advocated that Italy abolish as many levels of government and government agencies as possible; eliminate all Ministries bar internal affairs, international affairs, and defence; dispense with the President of the Republic; and send 'government' back to community level as closely as possible.[8] This bore strong resemblance to his earlier schemes for India where "Board Must Go" so that enlightened leaders like him could oversee the affairs of local people with little interference. The Party gained as little support as had his efforts in India, and soon disappeared.

Galletti still played to his India and ICS connections, however, and early in 1952 there appeared in *The Times* an advertisement seeking interest from Paying Guests. It announced that an "Italian country gentleman, I.C.S. (retired) will Let Rooms in his Castle on the Umbrian Hills". A chef was in attendance. The charge would be five guineas a day, with an extra half guinea for a room with a bath, and hot and cold running water was freely available. Shooting, tennis, swimming and squash was available along with a chapel and a library containing 2000 volumes. *The Times* airmail edition was taken daily.[9] Arthur Galletti was now running a country house aimed at attracting the well-off from England with a penchant for Italy, and an affection for Raj connections following India's bloody Independence in 1947.

Among those who responded was the Honourable L.E. Jones who, fortunately, left an account of his visit that, again, reveals how Galletti approached his work in India[10] An establishment figure, like many with whom Galletti worked, Jones (1885-1969) was the fifth Baronet from Cranmer Hall in Norfolk. His grandfather was a distinguished Peninsular War general, another family member became the Suffragan Bishop of Lewes. Sir Lawrence was a writer who, among other things, collaborated on a work with J.M. Barrie. Jones married Lady Evelyn, daughter of the fourth Earl Grey, and their daughter later married the son

---

8   "Programme ossia Meta da raggiungere eventualemente del Partito Decentramento Radicale." Galletti Papers.

9   *The Times*, 7 March 1952—I am indebted to Ian Galletti for the reference.

10 L.E. Jones, "An Eccentric In Italy" in his *I Forgot to tell you* (London, Hart-Davis, 1959).

of Herbert Asquith. Sir Lawrence Jones was a well-connected and influential social figure whose support might have done Galletti considerable financial good. Galletti, however, was true only to himself, as ever.

Jones and party were greeted by a "grey-headed man in his 70s, not undistinguished [who] limped forward to introduce himself as the Count." The walk up the hill took an hour and a half because Galletti was still recovering from a broken leg but, as Jones described, that gave the Count an excellent opportunity to talk:

> His theme was himself, and a good theme, too, had there been less of it... by the time we had arrived at the lighted doorway of the Castello, crowded with the welcoming faces of his staff, we had lived with our host through his English public school and college, his 30 years as an Indian Civil Servant, his clashes with Curzon, his decisive influence on Indian affairs as *eminence grise* to Gandhi on the one side and to a series of Viceroys on the other.

Galletti's English was 'faultless and idiomatic', but Jones could never interrupt the Count for long enough to discover why an Italian citizen had served in the ICS.

Dinners became the place where guests listened to Galletti— he was shocked when Jones attempted conversation with a neighbour: 'That man keeps talking!' Conversations ranged from Galletti's reincarnation as, among other people, Erasmus, and church doctrine. He was extremely well read in Jones' view, had an acute mind and knew his texts. Logic and rational argument marked his attack on the Catholic church. His staff loved him, because they were relaxed in his company, as were the numerous share-croppers who occupied the Galletti lands. He was the *padrone* in the best sense.

The food was excellent, the scenery marvellous, the house comfortable, but Galletti inescapable and relentless. Late in the week Galletti announced, as he had done throughout his life: "Never in my life...have I known what it is to be in love." Jones denied that, rejoining: "You have been in love with yourself all your life". The party left, but Jones admitted there was "good fun to be had from such fanatical egoism." It was the perfect mirror of Galletti's approach and behavior in India, demonstrating why so many of his superiors found him so irritating, and why his political views that looked so progressive early became an anachronism later.

He might not have followed Indian affairs closely up until Independence in 1947, but in later years seized every opportunity to remind people just how important he was in helping India gain independence, and in determining what happened in Madras.

In May 1952 he wrote an article for his old outlet *The Indian Review*, entitled "Have the British Done Well to Leave India?"[11] Galletti suggested that while 'Imperialists' like Churchill, following in Kipling's footsteps, resisted independence until the very last, the work of reformers like him rendered their position impossible. As early as 1906 he had advocated that India become the federated republic it now was, and while working as Chief Secretary advised that India be liberated immediately. Liberals like Morley took up the cause, Gandhi was an ally, and Congress men in his districts always looked to Galletti for ideas that would deliver independence. It was the Indian equivalent of the *Risorgimento*, and Galletti became widely known in the south as 'Our Friend'. Diehards considered him a traitor, but he pushed India to the point where the British government convinced itself that Indians could now run their own affairs.

This was a telling rendition of his personal view on his Indian mission, and an inevitable reconstruction of how his views had changed. Unquestionably, he was amongst the most liberal ICS thinkers when he first arrived in Madras. Galletti's family background and his own reflections convinced him that some aspects of British rule in India were injurious, and that some

---

11   *The Indian review*, 53, 5 (May 1952).

form of self-rule was necessary. That view remained intact until Guntur, at which point he lost faith in newer generation Congress politicians whom he considered driven by self-interest rather than national and/or liberal zeal. He retained that view until he left India, believing firmly that "real" India needed men like him to protect its interests. The 'real people' were abandoned by the British and left at the mercy of the professional politicians. There was just one area where he thought there was a positive result, the adoption of linguistically-based states.

In 1953 he recalled his role in creating Andhra Pradesh.[12] The idea for a Telugu-based state came to him in Bezwada in 1901, he wrote, while Assistant Collector there. He organized the local political elite, linking the drive for Andhra with his political scheme for India's political independence. He even had Government buy land in Bezwada on which would stand the new Andhra provincial capital. The movement spread like 'wildfire', Galletti stoking it in his submissions to the 1909 and 1919 reform commissions.

This was another telling recollection. Unquestionably, he was an early supporter of a separate administrative region for Telugu-speakers, arguing a strong and logical case. His own interest in 'everyday' Telugu language as distinct from the more literary form fuelled his view. In turn, that linked to his views on the need for social reform as depicted by Kandukuri Veerasalingam. Galletti's post-Independence view, however, linked that language-based state idea far more directly to political reform than he did at the time, at least according to the available evidence. The linking of language and liberation came essentially from organizations led principally by Tanguturi Prakasam and Konda Venkatapayya. Galletti tolerated them before Guntur because of their support for the Telugu state idea, but after Guntur their political allegiance to and leadership of Congress ruined matters for him. Because of that, his call for a Telugu-based state was considerably quieter between 1922 and 1934 than earlier.

---

12   *The Indian review*, 54, 6 (June 1953).

Over the last years of his life Arthur Galletti still worked daily in his library at the *Cassace*. His main project was the Italian-English dictionary that was to match the Telugu-English one he had produced in 1935. Pascal Ricketts, Galletti's grandson, recalls the work affectionately. It was based, he remembers his grandfather saying, on the works of three great thinkers: Shakespeare, Dante, and Arthur Galletti of whom the last was the most important! Despite their estrangement his daily religious debate with daughter Beatrice continued, while Emma returned to look after her father and the property. Isabella built on her wartime experiences and became involved in Italy's international relations, spending considerable time in Australia as Consul-General in Melbourne then later in Ireland. According to her daughter Elizabeth Skinner, Isabella never had a strong affinity with Galletti. That stemmed from the Bellary shotgun wedding days when Arthur declared his daughter 'amoral'. Estranged son Robert Galletti, meanwhile, went on to a distinguished career in the Foreign and Commonwealth Office following his departure from the ICS.

Several grandchildren loved and were inspired by their most unusual grandfather, most recalling him as a warm and encouraging figure but one who could be tough, obstinate and even rigid. Elizabeth Skinner spent several years growing up with Galletti, and recalls receiving little sympathy when she told him she was seeking a divorce. For him, he said, there was only ever one woman, and that was Clara. If his own written recollections are true then that was not necessarily so, but in his later mind that was what he believed.

Arthur Galletti died on 23 February 1967, having been cared for by Emma and reconciled with Beatrice in his final days. "Daddy's death has taken away the central force of the family. For me he was always a dominant factor and even if you did not agree with him it was fun to argue with him."[13] Coming as it did

---

13   Bella to Beatrice, 22 March 1967, Galletti Papers.

from Isabella whose relationship with her father was so difficult for so long, the comment revealed just how strong a focal point Arthur Galletti was in the lives of so many who knew him. He was an intellectual force, an advocate for 'doing things', the provider of impulsive ideas in search of change, and the centre of a constant whirlwind.

Arthur Galletti did much in his life, but India remained the dominant force as reflected in the words he chose for his grave marker in Torre San Patrizio where he grew up in *Our Home by the Adriatic:*

> Who half his life toiled for the Good, the True in India
> Then in age retired to rest in Italy and there at Gubbio
> gave his body to that pleasant country's earth and his
> pure soul unto his Captain Christ under whose colours
> he had fought so long.[14]

He had, in his own distinctive way, certainly toiled for the Good and True in India. But his Good and True differed considerably from those of his masters with whom he was in conflict for so long and so often. He had a vision for India that never really transpired, but he was remembered long and well by many of the 'true' Indians he admired and sought to serve.

---

14   Galletti, Self-*epitaph,* 16 June 1966.

Bibliography

Private Papers

HELD PRIVATELY

Galletti Family Papers

Sir John Thorne memoir manuscript

INDIA OFFICE RECORDS, BRITISH LIBRARY

Earl of Birkenhead Papers Mss Eur D703 [also in microfilm at National Archives of India]

Lord Erskine Papers Mss Eur D596 [also in microfilm at National Archives of India]

Earl of Halifax (Lord Irwin) Papers Mss Eur C152 [also in microfilm copy at the Nehru Memorial Museum and Library]

Earl of Templewood (Sir Samuel Hoare) Mss Eur E240 Papers [also in microfilm at Reid Library, University of Western Australia]

PUBLIC RECORDS OFFICE OF NORTHERN IRELAND

H.F. MacDonald-Tyler Papers

NATIONAL ARCHIVES OF INDIA

M. R. Jayakar Papers

NEHRU MEMORIAL LIBRARY

C. R. Reddy Papers

G.A. Natesan Papers

STATE ARCHIVES OF ANDHRA PRADESH

T. Prakasam Papers

CAMBRIDGE CENTRE FOR SOUTH ASIA ARCHIVES

A. Ewing Papers

J.T. Gwynn Papers

Sir Christopher Masterman Papers

Stokes Family Papers

G.R.F. Tottenham Papers

A.R.C. Westlake Papers

BODLEIEAN LIBRARY, OXFORD UNIVERSITY

E.S. Montagu Papers

H.D.C. Reilly Papers

Archival Material

INDIA OFFICE RECORDS, BRITISH LIBRARY

L/P&J	Public & Judicial, 1900-1940
L/H	Home Miscellaneous, 1900-1940
L/PO	Secretary of State, Private Office Papers
L/S&G	Services and General, 1920-1940
P	Proceedings, Madras, 1850-1930

NATIONAL ARCHIVES OF INDIA

Home Department, branch files: Political, 1923-45 (these include
The Madras Fortnightly Reports)
Public, 1923-45
Police, 1923-37
Special, 1927-30

Education, Health and Lands, branch files: Lands, 1924-33
Lands and Overseas
1933-38

Reforms Office, branch files: Special, 1927-29
Reforms, 1930-37
General, 1919-21; 1937-40

Central Board of Revenue branch files: Salt-I, 1929-35
Salt-II, 1929-35

Finance Department branch files: Finance, 1925-35
Budget, 1930-35
General, 1925-37

Commerce Department branch files: Commerce, 1925-35
General, 1925-35

NEHRU MEMORIAL LIBRARY

All-India Congress Committee files. 1919-47

STATE ARCHIVES OF ANDHRA PRADESH

Public Department files,   1900-51

Revenue Department files,   1900-39

Law Department files,   1900-51

Under Secretary's Safe files,   1921-48

"Material Gathered for the History of the Freedom Struggle in Andhra Project". This collection runs to well over 100 volumes of material gathered from various government and public sources

"Material Gathered by the Committee for the History of the Andhra Movement". This three-volume collection consists of Telugu and English material relating to the drive for a separate Telugu-speaking state.

TAMILNADU ARCHIVES

Public Department files,   1900-51

Revenue Department files,   1900-39

Law Department files,   1900-51

Under Secretary's Safe files   1921-48

Finance Department files   1900-39

Commissioner for the Northern Circars Proceedings, 1850-1900

NOTE:

When India's state boundaries were redrawn along linguistic lines in 1956, files held by the government of Madras were divided in that files relating to the Telugu-speaking region were largely but not entirely transferred to the new government of Andhra Pradesh.

Official Government Publications

GOVERNMENT OF GREAT BRITAIN

Report of the Royal Commission on the Public Services in India. London: HMSO, 1914

Report of the Royal Commission on the Superior Civil Services in India. London: HMSO, 1924

Report of the Indian Statutory Commission. London: HMSO, 1930. Volumes I-VI, XV-XVII

Report of the Indian Franchise Committee 1932. London and Calcutta: HMSO/Government of India, 1932

Report of the Joint Committee on Indian Constitutional Reform. (Session 1933-34). London: HMSO, 1934

East India (Progress and Condition): Statement Exhibiting the Moral and Material Progress and Condition of India During the Year...... London: HMSO, yearly 1925-37

GOVERNMENT OF INDIA

Report of the Sedition Committee. Calcutta: Government of India, 1918

Report on Indian Constitutional Reforms. Calcutta: Government of India, 1919

Report of the Reforms Enquiry Committee 1924. Calcutta: Government of India, 1929

Report of the Royal Commission on Agriculture in India. Calcutta: Government of India, 1927. Vol. III relates to Madras

Reports on the Working of the Reformed Constitution. Calcutta: Government of India, 1928

Report of the Indian Delimitation Committee. Delhi: Government of India, 1936

Statistical Abstract for British India with Statistics, Where Available, Relating to Certain Indian States. Calcutta: Government of India, annually

Reports on the Census of India. Calcutta/Delhi, Government of India, decennially, Madras vols. For 1911, 1921 and 1931

Land Revenue Policy of the Indian Government. Calcutta: Government of India, 1920 reprint

India in.... Calcutta/Delhi, Government of India, annually,1922-1935

The Imperial Gazetteer of India. London, Clarendon Press, 1931 edition, (authorised by the Government of India), vols. IV-XXIV contain references to many areas of the Madras Presidency, and vol. XXVI some maps.

Report of the Linguistic Provinces Commission. New Delhi, Government of India, 1948

White Paper on Hyderabad. Delhi, Government of India, 1948

GOVERNMENT OF MADRAS

Godavary, Kristna and Cauvery Delta and the Penner Anicut System. Madras: Government of Madras, 1883

Memorandum on the Progress of the Madras Presidency During the Last Forty Years of British Administration (compiled by S. Srinivasa Raghavaiyangar). Madras: Government of Madras, 1892 Report Regarding the Possibility of Introducing Land and Agricultural Banks into the Madras Presidency. Madras: Government of Madras, 1897

Alphabetical list of Villages in Taluks and Districts of the Madras Presidency. Madra:, Government of Madras, 1924

Report of the Committee on Co-operation in Madras, 1927-28. Madras: Government of Madras, 1928

The Working of the System of Government. Madras: Government of Madras, 1928

Madras Provincial Banking Enquiry Committee. Madras:Government of Madras, 1930

The Madras Presidency, 1881-1931 (compiled by G.T. Boag). Madras,: Government of Madras, 1931

Report on Agricultural Indebtedness (compiled by W.R.S. Sathyanathan). Madras: Government of Madras, 1935

Report of the Madras Estate Lands Act Committee. Madras: Government of Madras, 1938

Handbook of Information on the Administration of the Presidency of Madras. Madras: Government of Madras, 1939

Note on the Permanent Settlement. Madras: Government of Madras, 1940

Land Revenue Reforms Committee: First Report. Madras: Government of Madras, 1951

A Statistical Atlas of the Madras Presidency: Revised and Brought Up to the end of Fasli 1350 (1940-41). Madras, Government of Madras, 1949

Report on the Administration of the Madras Presidency for the Year... Madras: Government of Madras, annually. 1900-36

History of the Services of Gazetted Officers. Madras: Government of Madras, quarterly, 1900-47

Fort St. George Gazettes. Madras: Government of Madras, 1900-35

Madras Legislative Council Debates, 1923-36

Madras Presidency District Gazetteers. Madras: Government of Madras, 1868-

Indian Civil Service Manual: Madras. Madras: Government of Madras, 1895

Indian Civil Service Manual: Madras. Madras: Government of Madras, 1912

Indian Civil Service Manual. Madras,:Government of Madras, 1941

GOVERNMENT OF ANDHRA PRADESH

Select Documents on Telangana (second edition). Hyderabad:Government of Andhra Pradesh, 1972

White Paper on Official Language (Telugu). Hyderabad: Government of Andhra Pradesh, 1963

CONTEMPORARY NEWSPAPERS AND JOURNALS

Hindu,	1900-40
Madras Mail,	1900-37
Madras Times	1900-30
Civil & Military Gazette	1920-30
New India,	1927-28
Harijan,	1933-34
Indian Review,	1910-35
South of India Observer	1918-20
Asiatic Review,	1925-40
Indian General Register,	1923-35
The Times,	1890-1980

Native Newspaper Reports, 1917-37 (I include these in this section for they are now a well-known government collection. The Madras volumes may be consulted in the National Archives of India or the Tamilnadu Archives; the Australian National Library has a microfilm copy)

Oral Sources

I benefited greatly from discussions with the following people:
Emma Galletti Ricketts Brofferio
Pascal and Sally Ricketts

Ian Galletti

David Galletti

Antoinette and John Moat

Elizabeth Skinner

William de Bruyn

Anna Ricketts

Beatrice Ricketts

Simon Gooch

B. Shiva Rao

P.G. Sundararajan

N.S. Varadachari

Professor M. Venkatarangaiya

Secondary Sources

1921 movement: reminiscences. New Delhi: Publications Division, Ministry of Information and Broadcasting, Government of India, 1971.

1928, All Parties Conference. *Report of the committe appointed by the conference to determine the principles of the constitution for India.* Allahabad: All-India Congress Committee, 1928.

Alexander, H.M.L. "Discarding the 'steel frame': changing images among Indian civil servants in the early twentieth century", *South Asia,* 5, 2 (December 1982).

Andhra Pradesh Congress Committee souvenir: A.I.C.C. session, October 1958. Hyderabad: Andhra Pradesh Congress Committee, 1958.

Andhra through ages. Guntur: Maruthi Book Depot, 1958.

Annaji. *Congress ditties and other rhymes.* Bombay, 1928.

Arnold, David. *Police power and colonial rule: Madras, 1859-1947.* Delhi: Oxford University Press, 1987.

—. *The Congress in Tamilnad: nationalist politics in South India, 1919-1937.* Canberra: Australian National University, 1977.

Arunachalam, *K. Khadi economics: a few aspects.* Madurai: Koodal Publishers, 1974.

Asher, R.E. "Dravidian separateness: invention or reality?" *South Review,* 6, 1 (October, 1972).

Asylum press almanack and directory of Madras and Southern India. Madras: Asylum Press, 1870-1930.

Awasthi, D. *Administrative history of modern India: Sir Spencer Harcourt Butler's idea, policies, and activities in the United Provinces of Agra and Awadh, 1918-1922.* Delhi: Publishing House, 1973.

Baden-Powell, B.H. *The Indian village community.* London: Longmans Green, 1896.

—.*The land systems of British India.* Oxford: Oxford University Press, 1892.

—.*The spirit's pilgrimage.* London: Longman's, 1960.

Bailey, F.G. *Stratagems and spoils: a social anthropology of politics.* Oxford: Basil Blackwell, 1969.

—."The peasant view of the bad Life." *The advancement of Science* (University of Sussex joint Report, No. 7) 23, 114 (December 1966): 399-409.

—.*Gifts and poison: the politics of reputation.* Oxford: Basil Blackwell, 1971.

Baker, C.J. *The politics of South India, 1919-1939.* Cambridge: Cambridge University Press, 1976.

Bakshi, S.R. "Simon Commission and political awakening in India." *Journal of Indian history.* LII, II and III (August-December. 1974).

—."Simon Commission—A case study of its appointment." *Journal of Indian History* Vol. L No. II (August 1972).

Balagopal, K. "Andhra Pradesh: beyond media images." *Economic and Political, Weekly,* 12 June 2004

—."Land unrest in Andhra Pradesh-1: ceiling surpluses and public lands." *Economic & Political, weekly,* 22 September 2007)

Baliga, B.S. *Studies in Madras administration.* 2 Vols. Madras: Madras University, 1957.

Barker, Ernest. *The future government of India and the Indian civil service.* London: Methuen, 1919.

Barnes, Margaritha. *The Indian press: a history of the growth of public opinion in India.* London: Allen and Unwin, 1940.

Bayley, C.A. "Local control in Indian towns-Allahabad, 1880-1920." *Modern Asian studies,* 5, 4 (October. 1971)

Beals, Alan, R. Gopalpur. *a south Indian village.* New York, Holt: Rinehart and Winston, 1962.

Beauchamp, Joan. *British imperialism in India: prepared for the labour research department.* London: Martin Lawrence, 1935.

Bernays, Robert. *Naked fakir.* London: Victor Gallancz, 1930.

Bernstorff, Dagmar and Hugh Gray. *The kingmakers: politicians and politics in Andhra Pradesh.* New Delhi: Har-Anand, 1998.

Beteille, Andre. Caste, *class, and power: changing patterns of stratification in a Tanjore village.* Berkeley: University of California Press, 1965.

—. *Castes: old and new; essays in social structure and social stratification.* London: Asia Publishing House, 1969.

—. *Studies in agrarian social structure.* Delhi: Oxford University Press, 1974.

Bhatia, B.M. *Famines in India: a study in some aspects of the economic history of India, 1860-1965.* 2nd edition. Bombay: Asia Publishing House, 1967.

Bhattacharya, S. *Southern Indian economy: agrarian change, industrial structure and state policy 1914-1947.* Delhi: Oxford University Press, 1991.

Birkenhead, *Earl of. Halifax:* the life of Lord Halifax. London: Hamish Hamilton, 1965.

Blunt, Sir Edward. *The I.C.S.: the Indian civil service.* London: Faber, 1937.

Bondurant, Joan V. *Regionalism versus provincialism: a study in problems of Indian national unity.* Berkeley: University of California press, 1958.

Bose, Subhas Chandra. *The Indian struggle, 1920-1942.* London: Asia Publishing House, 1964.

Braibanti, Ralph and Joseph J. Spengler. *Administration and economic development in India.* Durham: Duke University Press, 1963.

Brailsford, H.N. *Subject India.* Bombay: Vora, 1946.

Brass, Paul R. and Marcus Franda (eds). *Radical politics in South Asia.* Cambridge, Massachusetts, and London: MIT Press, 1973.

Brass, Paul R. *Factional politics in an Indian state: the Congress party in Uttar Pradesh.* Berkeley: University of California Press, 1965.

Brockway, A. Fenner. *The Indian crisis.* London: Victor Gollancz, 1930.

Broomfield, J.H. *Elite conflict in a plural society: twentieth-century Bengal.* Berkeley: University of California Press, 1968.

Brown, C.P. *English Telugu dictionary.* Delhi: Oscar, 2007 edition.

—. *Essay on the language and literature of the Telugus.* Delhi: Asian Educational, 1997edition.

Brown, Hilton (ed.). *The sahibs: the life and ways of the British in India as recorded by themselves.* London: William Hodge, 1948.

—. *Asylum Island.* London: Methuen, 1950.

—. *Both sides of Suez.* London: Douglas, 1930.

—. *Dictators* limited. London: Allen and Unwin, 1923.

—. *Dismiss.* London: Methuen, 1923.

—. *Humbug hall.* London, Bles, 1939.

—. *Locust food.* London, Bles, 1935.

—. *Maya.* Calcutta: Arts Press, 1933.

—. *Ostrich eyes.* London: Allen and Unwin, 1928.

—. *Parry's of Madras.* Madras: Parry's, 1954.

—. *The gold and the grey.* Blackwell: Oxford, 1936.

—. *The hare of cloud.* London, Bles, 1937.

Brown, Judith M. *Gandhi and civil disobedience: the Mahatma in Indian politics 1928-1934.* Cambridge: Cambridge University Press, 2008.

—. *Gandhi's rise to power: Indian politics 1915-1922.* Cambridge: Cambridge University Press, 1972.

Buettner, Elizabeth. *Empire families:* Britons and late imperial India. Oxford: Oxford University Press, 2004.

Burns, W. *Sons of the soil: studies of the Indian cultivator.* Delhi: Government of India Press, 1941.

Butler, Sir Harcourt. *India insistent.* London: Heinemann, 1931.

Butterworth, A. and V. Chetty. Venugopala. *Copper-plate and stone inscriptions of south India.* Madras: Government of Madras, 1905.

Butterworth, A. *The southlands of Siva.* London, John Lane, 1923.

—. *The substance of Indian faith.* Camberley, Hickmott, 1932.

—. *The Formation of Madras.* Camberley: Hickmott & Co, 1932.

Cadogan, Edward. *The India we saw.* London: John Murray, 1933.

Candy, Margaret. "Relating feminisms, nationalisms and imperialisms: Ireland, India and Margaret Cousins' sexual politics." *Women's history review.* 3, 4 December 1994.

Carr, M.W. *A collection of Telugu proverbs.* Madras: Sastrulu, 1922.

Catanach, I.J. *Rural credit in western India: rural credit and the co-operative movement in the Bombay Presidency.* Berkeley: University of California Press, 1970.

Chakrabarty, Dipesh. *Habitations of modernity: essays in the wake of subaltern studies.* Chicago: University of Chicago Press, 2002.

Chandra, Bipan. *The rise and growth of economic nationalism in India: economic policies of Indian national leadership, 1880-1905.* New Delhi: People's Publishing House, 1966.

Chenchiah, P. *Problems of linguistic states in India.* Calcutta: YMCA, 1954.

Chettur, S.K. *The steel frame and I: life in the I.C.S.* Bombay: Asia Publishing House, 1962.

Chirol, Valentine. *India old and new.* London: Macmillan, 1921.

Chowdari, G. Rudrayya. *Prakasam:* a political study. Madras: Orient Longman, 1971.

"Chronicler". *"The crisis and the truce: a survey of Indian politics from the Simon Commission to the Irwin-Gandhi Pact.* Madras: New Epoch Publishers, 1931.

"Civilian" [J.C. Molony]. *The civilian's south India.* London, John Lane, 1921.

Cohn, Bernard S. *India: the social anthropology of a civilization.* Englewood Cliffs, New Jersey: Prentice-Hall, 1971.

—. *The development and impact of British administration in India.* New Delhi: Indian Institute of Public Administration, 1961.

—. "Society and social change under the Raj." *Indo-British review Vol.* III, No. 3.

—. The Initial British Impact on India: a Case Study of the Benares Region", *Journal of Asian Studies,* XIX, 4 (Aug. 1960)

Condition of India: *being the report of the delegation sent to India by the India League in 1932.* London: Essential News, 1932.

Coupland, R. *the constitutional problem in India.* London: Oxford University press, 1943.

Cousins, James H. and Margaret E. *We two together.* Madras: Ganesh and Co., 1950.

Cousins, Margaret. *The awakening of Asian womanhood.* Madras: Ganesh, 1922.

Crawley, W.F. "Kisan Sabhas and agrarian revolt: the United Provinces, 1920-21." *Modern Asian studies* 5, 2 (April 1971).

Cronin, Richard P. *British policy and administration in Bengal, 1905-1912.* Calcutta: Firma, 1977.

Croome, A.C.M. *Fifty years of sport at Oxford, Cambridge and the great public schools.* London: Southwood, 1913.

Cumming, Sir John. *Political India, 1832-1932. A co-operative survey of a century.* London: Oxford University Press, 1932.

Curtis, L. *Papers relating to the application of the principle of dyarchy to the Government of India.* Oxford: Clarendon Press, 1920.

Darling, Malcolm Lyall. *The Punjab peasant in prosperity and debt.* London: Oxford University Press, 1928.

—. *At freedom's door.* London: Oxford University Press, 1949.

Das, C.R. *The way to Swaraj: speeches in Madras.* Madras: Tamil-Nadu Swarajya Party, 1923.

Das, M.N. *India under Morley and Minto.* London: Allen and Unwin, 1964.

Desai, A.R. *Social background of Indian nationalism.* Bombay: Popular Prakashan, 1966.

Desai, Mahadev. *The story of Bardoli: being a history of the Bardoli Satyagraha of the 1928 and its sequel.* Ahmedabad: Navajivan, 1957.

Dewey, Clive. *Anglo-Indian attitudes: the mind of the Indian Civil Service.* London: Hambledon, 1993.

Dhanagre, D.N. *Peasant movements in India.* Delhi: OUP, 1983.

Diwakar, R.R. *Satyagraha: its technique and history.* Bombay: Hind Kitabs, 1946.

Dodwell, H. Henry. *The nabobs of Madras.* London: Williams and Norgate, 1926.

—. (ed). *The Cambridge history of India. Vol. 6, the Indian Empire 1858-1918.* Cambridge: Cambridge University Press, 1932.

Duncan, Arthur. *"White flag" or "British villainy" in India?* London, Adelphi: 1933.

Dutt, R.C. *Land problems in India.* Madras: G. A. Natesan, n.d.

Elliott, Carolyn M. "Caste and faction among the dominant caste: the Reddis and Kammas of Andhra", in Rajni Kothari (ed.). *Caste in Indian Politics.* New Delhi: Orient Longman, 1970.

Fischer-Tine, Harald. *Low and licentious Europeans: race, class, and "White subalternity" in colonial India.* New Delhi: BlackSwan, 2009.

Forbes, Gordon S. *Wild life in Canara and Ganjam.* London: Swan Sonnenschein, 1885.

Frykenberg, Robert E. *Guntur district, 1788-1848; a history of local influence and central authority in South India.* Oxford: Clarendon Press, 1965.

—. *Land control and social structure in Indian history.* Madison: University of Wisconsin Press, 1969.

—. "British society in Guntur during the early nineteenth century." *Comparative studies in society and history.* IV, 1 (January. 1962).

Fuller, J.F.C. *India in revolt.* London: Eyre and Spottiswoode, 1931.

Gallagher, John, and Gordon Johnson and Anil Seal. *Locality, province and nation: essays on Indian politics, 1870-1940.* Cambridge: Cambridge University Press, 1973.

Galletti, A.M.A.C. *Galletti's Telugu dictionary.* Oxford: Oxford University Press, 1935.

—. *The Madras lunacy manual for Magistrates.* Madras: Government of Madras, 1906.

—. *The vinodha tharangini.* Rajahmundry: Viveka Varthani Press, 1902.

—. *The Dutch in Malabar.* Madras: Government of Madras, 1911.

—. *Il Decentramento.* Gubbio: Tipografia Bagnoli, 1950.

—. *In Memoria Di Mis Figlia Beatrice.* Gubbio: Tipografia Bagnoli, 1951.

—. *Poems and Plagiariasms.* Gubbio: Private, 1935.

—. *Poems and plagiarisms.* Bellary: Privately printed, 1934.

—. *Poesie.* Private.

—. *Paddy and Pasture.* Madras: Addison, 1926.

—. *Sahacarula parapati.* Sanghamalu: Private.

—. *Selections From the records of the Madras government: papers relating to the history of the Banganapalle state.* Madras: Government of Madras, 1912.

—. *Sermons of the pure concept.* Tinnevelly: Hilal, 1928.

—. *Versi A Mia Moglie.* Private, 1939.

—. *The Madras ecclesiastical manual.* Madras: Government of Madras, 1906.

—. "San Thome Church" in *The Madras tercentenary commemoration volume.* Madras: Tercentenary Committee, 1939.

—. *Traduzioni Inglesi.* Gubbio: Tipografia Bagnoli, 1953.

—. *The true religion of Christ: Indian parallels.* Gubbio: Tipografia Bagnoli, 1931.

Galletti, Margaret Collier. *Babel.* Edinburgh: Blackwood, 1887.

—. *Our home by the Adriatic.* London: Bentley, 1886.

—. *Prince Peerless.* London: Fisher Unwin, 1887.

—. *Rachel and Maurice.* London: Chapman Hall, 1892.

—. *The Camorristi.* London: Remington, 1882.

Gangulee, N. *The Indian peasant and his environment. (The Linlithgow Commission and after).* London: Oxford University Press, 1935.

Ghosh, Durba. *Sex and the family in colonial India.* Delhi: CUP, 2006.

Ghosh, Papiya. *The civil disobedience movement in Bihar, 1930-1934.* Delhi: Manak Publications, 2008.

Ghosh, S.K. *Riots: prevention and control.* Calcutta: Eastern Law House, 1971.

Gilmour, David. *Curzon: imperial statesman.* New York: Farrar, Straus and Giroux, 2003.

—. *The ruling caste: imperial lives in the Victorian Raj.* New York: Farrar, Straus and Giroux, 2007.

Girija, S. *Freedom movement in India: Nellore district.* Delhi: Discovery Publishing House, 1990.

Godavari District Association Selections from the proceedings of the Godavari District Association in 1914. Cocanada: Godavari District Association, 1915.

Gooch, Simon. *The Collier family.* Private, 2007.

—. *The de Bruyn Ouboter Family.* Private, 2008.

Gopal, Ram. *British rule in India, an assessment.* New York: Asia Publishing House, 1963.

Gopal, S. *The viceroyalty of Lord Irwin, 1926-1931.* Oxford: Oxford University Press, 1957.

Goschen, Lord. "The working of the reforms in Madras." *Asiatic review,* XXVI, 86 (April 1930).

Gowri, C.M. and M. Venkata Ramaiah. "Land reforms and agrarian conditions in Andhra Pradesh during post-independence era." http:ssm.com/abstract=304527, 20 November 2008.

Greenberger, Allen J. *The British image of India: a study in the literature of imperialism.* London: Oxford University Press, 1969.

Guha, Ranajit. *Elementary aspects of peasant insurgency in colonial India.* Delhi: Oxford University Press.

—. *Subaltern studies: writings on south Asian history and society.* Delhi: Oxford University Press, 1982.

—. "Neel-Darpan: the image of a peasant revolt in a liberal mirror." *journal of peasant studies Vol. 2,* No. 1 (October, 1974).

Gwynn, J.T. *Indian politics. a survey.* London: Nisbet and Co., 1924.

Hale, H.W. *Political trouble in India, 1917-1937.* Allahabad: Chugh Publications, 1974.

Hardgrave, Robert L. *The Dravidian movement.* Bombay: Popular Prakashan, 1965.

—. *The Nadars of Tamilnad: the political culture of a community in change.* Berkeley: University of California Press, 1969.

Has Congress failed? a historical survey of the years 1918-1939 by a student of public affairs. Bombay: The Time of India Press, 1943.

Hemingway, F.R. *Madras district gazetteers: Nellore.* Madras: Government of Madras, 1907.

Higginbotham's guide to Madras. Madras: Asylum Press, 1900.

Hobsbawm, E.J. and George Rude. *Captain Swing.* London: Lawrence and Wishart, 1969.

Hobsbawm, E.J. *Bandits.* London: Weidenfeld and Nicholson, 1969.

Hopkins, Clare. *Trinity: 450 years of an Oxford college community.* Oxford: Oxford University Press, 2005.

Horne, W.O. *Work and sport in the old ICS.* London: William Blackwood, 1928.

Houghton, Bernard. *Bureaucratic government.* Madras: S. Ganesan, nd.

Hoyland, John S. *Indian crisis.* London: Allen and Unwin, 1943.

Hunt, Roland and John Harrison. *The district officer in India, 1935-1947.* London: Scolar Press, 1985.

Indian, An *Bridging the Gulf: a study of the background of the Indian situation with some suggestions.* London: P.S. King and Son, 1930.

Irschick, Eugene F. *Politics and social conflict in South India: the non-Brahman movement and Tamil separatism, 1916-1929.* Berkeley: University of California Press, 1969.

Irwin, Lord. *Indian problems.* London: Allen and Unwin, 1932.

Iyer, C.S. Ranga. *India in the crucible.* London: Selwyn and Blount, 1928.

Jayakar, M.R. *The story of my life.* 2 vols. Bombay: Asia Publishing House, 1959.

Jha, Manoranjan. *Civil disobedience and after: the American reaction to political developments in India during 1930-1935.* Delhi: Meenakshi Prakashan, 1973.

Johnson, Alan Campbell. *Viscount Halifax. A biography.* London: Robert Hart, 1941.

Johnson, Gordon. *Provincial politics and Indian nationalism:* Bombay and the Indian National Congress, 1880-1915. Cambridge: Cambridge University Press, 1973.

Justice Party *golden jubilee souvenir.* Madras: Justice Party, 1968.

Justice year book 1929 (Being a detailed account of all that the Justice Party stood for, worked for, and achieved during the year 1929). Madras: Justice Printing Works, 1929.

Kaushik, P.D. *The Congress ideology and programme, 1920-1947: ideological foundations of Indian Nationalism during the Gandhian era.* Bombay: Allied Publishers, 1964.

Kelsall, John. *Manual of the Bellary district.* Madras: Government of Madras, 1872.

Kincaid, Dennis. *British social life in India, 1608-1937.* 1938: George Routledge and Sons, London.

Koss, Stephen E. *John Morley at the India office, 1905-1910.* New Haven: Yale University Press, 1969.

Kumar, Kapil. *Congress and classes: nationalism, workers, and peasants.* Delhi: Manohar Publications, 1988.

Kumar, Ravinder. *Essays on Gandhian politics: the Rowlatt Satyagraha of 1919.* Oxford: Oxford University Press, 1971.

—. *Western India in the nineteenth century: a study in the social history of Maharashtra.* Canberra: Australian National University Press, 1968.

Lawson, Sir Charles. Memories of madras. London: Swan Sonnenschein, 1905.

Leach, Edmund and S.N. Mukherjee (eds). *Elites in South Asia.* Cambridge: Cambridge University Press, 1970.

Leonard, J.G. "Politics and social change in south India: a study of the Andhra Movement." *Journal of commonwealth political studies.* 5, 1 (March 1967): 60-77.

—. "Urban government under the Raj: a case study of municipal Administration in nineteenth century South India." *Modern Asian studies.* 7, 2 (April 1973).

Lewandoski, Susan. "Urban growth and municipal development in the colonial city of Madras, 1860-1900." *Journal of Asian studies.* XXXIV, 2 (Feb. 1975).

Low, D.A. (ed.). *Soundings in modern South Asian history.* Canberra: Australian National University Press, 1968.

—. *Congress and the Raj: facets of the Indian struggle, 1917-1947.* London: Heinemann, 1977.

Ludden, David. *An agrarian history of South Asia.* Cambridge: Cambridge University Press, 1999.

Macleod, R.D. *Impressions of an Indian civil servant.* London: Witherby Ltd, 1938.

Macmillan, Allister (ed.). *Seaports of India and Ceylon; historical and descriptive, commercial and industrial, facts, figures, and resources.* London: W.H. and L. Collingridge, 1923.

Macmillan, Margaret. *Women of the Raj.* London: Random House, 2007.

Macnicol, Nicol. *India in the dark wood.* London: Edinburgh House Press, 1930.

MacNunn, Lieut-General Sir George. *Turmoil and tragedy in India, 1914 and after.* London: Jarrolds, 1935.

Maconochie, Evan. *Life in the Indian civil service.* London: Chapman and Hall, 1926.

Mallik, B.K. *The individual and the group; an Indian study in conflict.* London: Allen and Unwin, 1939.

Manikumar, K.A. *A colonial economy in the Great Depression, Madras (1929-1937).* Chennai: Orient Longman, 2003.

Mason, Philip. *The men who ruled India.* London: Jonathan Cape, 1954.

Masters, John. *Bhowani junction.* Harmondsworth: Penguin, 1954.

Metcalf, Thomas R. *Ideologies of the Raj.* Cambridge: Cambridge University Press, 1995.

Mills, C. Wright. *The sociological imagination.* New York: Oxford University Press, 1959.

Minney, R.J. *India marches past.* London: Jarrolds, 1933.

Misra, B.B. *The administrative history of India* 1834-1947. Delhi: Oxford University Press, 1991

Mitchell, Tony. *High art in a foreign tongue: Adelaide Ristori's 1875 Australian tour.* Brisbane: Australasian Drama Studies Association, 1995.

Moat, Antoinette. *On two fronts: a soldier's life of travel, love and war.* London: Long Riders Guild, 2008.

Montagu, Edwin S. *An Indian diary.* London: William Heinemann, 1930.

Moon, Penderel. *Divide and quit.* London: Chatto and Windus, 1962.

Moore, Barrington. *Social origins of dictatorship and democracy: lord and peasant in the making of the modern world.* Harmondsworth: Penguin, 1969.

Moore, R.J. *The crisis of Indian unity, 1917-1940.* Oxford: Oxford University Press, 1974.

Morgan, Michael. C. *Cheltenham college: the first one hundred years.* Cheltenham: Sadler, 1968.

Morris, H. *Godavari district manual.* Madras: Government of Madras, 1878.

Mosse, David. *The rule of water: statecraft, ecology and collective action in south India.* Delhi: Oxford University Press, 2003.

Mukerjee, Radhakamal. *Land problems of India.* London: Longmans, Green & Co., 1933.

Mukherjee, Nilmani. *The Ryotwari system in Madras.* Calcutta: Firma K.L. Mukhopadhyay, 1967.

Muller, Gregor. *Colonial Cambodia's 'bad Frenchmen'.* London: Routledge, 2006.

Muthiah, S. *Madras rediscovered.* Chennai: East West Books, 2008.

Naidu, Ch.M. *Salt satyagraha in the coastal Andhra.* Delhi: Mittal Publications, 1986.

Nair, Janaki. "Beyond exceptionalism: south India and the modern historical imagination." *Indian economic and social history review.* 43, 3(September, 2006).

Nair, Sir C. Sankaran. *Gandhi and anarchy.* Madras: Tagore, 1922.

Nanda, B.R. *Socialism in India.* Delhi: Vikas Publications, 1972.

Narain, Brij. *India in the crisis.* Allahabad: The Indian Press, 1934.

Narayan, R.K. *Lawley road and other stories.* Delhi: Orient Paperbacks.

Naidu, B.V. Narayanswami *The Madras Agriculturalists' Relief Act-a study.* Annamalai: Annamalai University Press, 1939.

Natesan, G.A. (Ed.). *All about the war: the Indian review war book.* Madras: G.A. Natesan & Co., 1915.

Nethercot, Arthur H. *The first five lives of Annie Besant.* London: Rupert Hart-Davis, 1961.

—. *The last four lives of Annie Besant.* London: Rupert Hart-Davis, 1963.

Nikku, Bala Raju and Irna van der Molen. "Conflict, resistance and alliances in a multi-governance setting: reshaping realities in the Andhra Pradesh Irrigation Reforms." *Energy and Environment,* 19, 6 (November, 2008).

O'Malley, L.S.S. *The Indian civil service.* 2nd edition. London: Frank Cass, 1965.

Orwell, George. *Burmese days.* Harmondsworth: Penguin, 1972.

Pandey, Gyanendra. *The ascendancy of the Congress in Uttar Pradesh: class, community and nation in northern India.* London: Anthem Press, 2003.

Panjabi, K.L. *The civil servant in India.* Bombay: Bharatiya Vidya Bhavan, 1965.

Parthasarathy, G. and Rao B. *Implementation of land reforms in Andhra Pradesh.* Calcutta: Scientific Book Agency., 1969.

Perumal, Nikan. K. *Nageswara Rao.* Madras: R.J. Ram, 1937.

—. *Two important men: a biographical record.* Madras: R.J. Ram, 1938.

Playne, Somerset. *Southern India.* London: Unwin, 1915.

Pole, D. Graham. *India in transition.* London: Hogarth Press, 1932.

Police raj under the Emergency Ordinance. Madura: Printed by the Satyagraha Press, 1932.

Potter, David C. *Government in rural India: an introduction to contemporary district administration.* London: G. Bell & Sons, 1964.

Prakasam, Tangaturi. *Na jivita yatra,* (Telugu). Hyderabad: M. Sechachalam and Co., 1972.

Raju, P. Yanadi. *Rayalaseema during colonial times.* Delhi: Northern Book Centre, 2003.

Ramakrishnan, K.C. and Thomas P.J. *Some South Indian villages: a resurvey.* Madras: University of Madras, 1940.

Ramanadham, V.V. *The economy of Andhra Pradesh.* Bombay: Asia Publishing House, 1959.

Ramaiah, V. *Independent India of plenty; what Congress government ought to do.* Madras: Andhra Publishing House, 1946.

Ranga, N.G. *Economic conditions of the zamindari ryots (the report of the Economic Enquiry Committee, 1933).* Bezwada: Peasants Protection Committee, 1933.

—. *Economic organization of Indian villages.* Bombay: D.B. Taraporevala, 1929.

—. *Fight for freedom.* Delhi: S. Chand, 1968.

Ranson, C.W. *A city in transition: studies in the social life of Madras.* Madras: Christian Literature Society for India, 1938.

Rao, B. Seshagiri. *History of the freedom movement: Guntur district 1921-1947.* Ongole: Prasanna, nd

Rao, G.V. Krishna. *The Chirala-Perala tragedy: an episode of voluntary exile.* Madras: Ganesh, 1922.

Rao, K. Rama. *The pen as my sword: memoirs of a journalist.* Bombay: Bharatiya Vidya Bhavan, 1965.

—. *Economic development of Andhra Pradesh.* Bombay: Asia Publishing House, 1959.

Rao, K. Sreeranjani Subba. *Struggle for freedom: case study of the east Godavari district, 1905-1947.* New Delhi: Mittal Publications, 1989.

Rao, K.R. Seshagiri. *Studies in the history of Telugu journalism.* Delhi: Narla Shashtyabdapurti Celebration Committee, 1968.

Rao, K.V. Narayana. *The emergence of Andhra Pradesh.* Bombay: Popular Prakashan, 1973.

Rao, P.R. *History of modern Andhra.* Delhi: Sterling Publishers, 2009.

Rao, Rajeswara *P. T. Prakasam.* New Delhi: National Book Trust, 1972.

Rau, Khasa Subba. *Sidelights on Rajaji.* Madras: Vyasa Publications, 1961.

Ray, Lajpat. *Ideals of non-co-operation.* Madras: S. Ganesan, 1924.

Reddy, N.B.K. "Urban evolution, growth pattern and urbanization trends in the Krishna and Godavari Deltas." *National Geographical Journal of India.* XVI, 3-4 (Sep-Dec, 1970)

Reddy, Palle Sivasankara. *Civil disobedience movement in Andhra.* New Delhi: Classical Pub. Co., 2001.

Reed, Sir. Stanley. *The India I knew, 1897-1947.* London: Odhams Press, 1952.

Reeves, P.D. "The politics of order: anti-non-co-operation in the United Provinces, 1921." *Journal of Asian studies* XXV, No. 2 (Feb, 1966).

Regani, Sarojini. *Highlights of the freedom movement in Andhra Pradesh.* Hyderabad: Government of Andhra Pradesh, 1972.

Robb, Peter and David Taylor. *Rule, protest, identity: aspects of modern South Asia.* London: Curzon Press, 1978.

Rude, George. *The crowd in the French Revolution.* Oxford: Oxford University Press, 1959.

Sandford, Charles. *India: land of regrets.* London: Fenland Press, 1934.

Santhanam, K. *British imperialism and Indian nationalism*. Bombay: Bharatiya Vidya Bhavan, 1972.

—. *Satyagraha and the state*. Bombay: Asia Publishing House, 1959.

Sarkar, Sumit. *A critique of colonial India*. Calcutta: Papyrus, 2000.

—. *Modern India, 1885-1947*. Delhi: South Asia, 2005.

—. *Writing social history*. Delhi: Oxford University Press, 1997.

Sastri, Alladi Jagannatha. *A family history of Venkatagiri Rajas*. Madras: Addison Press, 1922.

Satabhisha. *Rashtrapathi Dr. Pattabhi*. Madras: Jateeya Jnana Mandir, 1948.

Sathyanathan, W.R.S. *Report on agricultural indebtedness*. Madras: Government of Madras, 1935.

Satyanarayana, A. *Dalits and upper castes: essays in social history*. New Delhi: Kanishka Publishers, Distributors, 2005.

—. *Society, economy, and polity in modern Andhra*. New Delhi: Kanishka Publishers Distributors, 2007.

Sayana, V.V. *The agrarian problems of Madras Province*. Madras: Business Week Press, 1949.

Seal, Anil. *The emergence of Indian nationalism: competition and collaboration in the later nineteenth century*. London: Cambridge University Press, 1968.

Sen, S.P. (ed.). *Dictionary of national biography*. 4 vols. Calcutta: Institute of Historical Studies, 1972.

Seshadri, K. *Politics and society in changing India*. Jaipur: Mangal Deep Publications, 2004.

Sharp, Henry Sir. *Good-bye India*. London: Oxford University Press, 1946.

Shaw, George Bernard. *The irrational knot*. London: Constable, 1905.

Simon, Viscount. *Retrospect: the memoirs of the Rt. Hon. Viscount Simon*. London: Hutchinson, 1952.

Singh, B.A. *Summary of Anglo-Indian fiction*. Delhi: Orient, 1934.

Sinha, Lalan Prasad. *The left-wing in India, 1919-47.* Muzaffarpur: New Publishers, 1965.

Sitapati, G.V. *History of Telugu literature.* New Delhi: Sahitya Akademi, 1968.

Sitaramayya, Pattabhi. *Feathers and stones.* Bombay: Padma Publication, 1946.

—. *History of the Indian National Congress.* 2 vols. Delhi: S. Chand, 1969.

Slater, Gilbert. *Southern India: its political and economic problems.* London: Allen and Unwin, 1936.

Slater, Gilbert. (ed.). *Some south Indian villages.* Madras: Oxford University Press, 1918.

Somasekhara, G. "Satyagrahi: moulding public opinion in the early twentieth century." *Economic and political weekly 38, 9* (1 March 2003).

Spangenberg, Bradford. *British bureaucracy in India.* Columbia: Mo., South Asia Books, 1976.

Speeches by the Rt. Hon. Sir Samuel Hoare, 1ᶜ 1935. London: Eyre and Spottiswoode, 1935.

Stoddart, Brian. "The unwanted commission: national agitation and local politics in Madras city, 1928." *South Asia,* 5, (December 1975).

—. "The structure of Congress Politics in Coastal Andhra, 1925-1937" in D.A.Low (ed), *Congress and the Raj* London: Heinemann, 1977.

—. *Land, Water, Language and Politics in Andhra: Regional Evolution in India Since 1850.* New Delhi and London: Routledge, 2011-05-04

Stokes, E. "The first century of British colonial Rule in India: Social Revolution or social stagnation?" *Past and present No.* 58, (Feb. 1973).

Subbarau, Gummidithala Venkata. *Andhraratna D. Gopalakrishnayya: Life and Message.* Bezwada: Goshti Book-House.

Suntharalingam, R. *Politics and nationalist awakening in South India, 1852-189.* Tucson: University of Arizona Press, 1974.

Templewood, Viscount. *Nine troubled years.* London: Collins, 1954.

The Andhra Movement. Guntur: Radha Press, 1915.

The black regime at Dharasana. A brief survey of the "Dharasana Raid". Ahmedabad: Gujarat Provincial Congress Committee, 1930.

The collected works of Mahatma Gandhi. Delhi: Publications Division, 1958.

Thomas, P.J. *Commodity prices in South India.* Madras: Diocesan Press, 1940.

—. *The problem of rural indebtedness.* Madras: Printed at the Diocesan Press, 1934.

Thompson, Edward. *An Indian day.* Harmondsworth: Penguin, 1927.

Thorne, J.A. *Verses.* Private. Nd.

Thurston, Edgar. *Castes and tribes of southern India.* Madras: Government of Madras Press, 1909.

—. *Ethnographic notes in southern India.* Madras: Government Press, 1906.

Trench, Victor. *Lord Willingdon in India.* Bombay: S.A. Ezekiel, 1934.

Trevelyan, Humphrey. *The India we left.* London: Macmillan, 1972.

Two years of Congress rule in Madras. Madras: Madras Legislature Congress Party, 1939.

Upadhya, Carol. "Social and cultural strategies of class formation in Coastal Andhra." *Contributions to Indian sociology.* 31.2, (1997).

—. "The farmer-capitalists of Coastal Andhra Pradesh." *Economic and political weekly,* 2 July 1988.

Vaikuntham, Y. *Studies in socio-cultural and political history: modern Andhra.* Hyderabad: Manohar, 2004.

Van Tyne, Claude H. *India in ferment.* New York: Appleton and Co, 1923.

Venkatappaya, Konda. *The Andhra movement.* Madras: Andhra Maha Sabha Publication, 1938.

Venkatarangaiya, M. (ed.). *Desabhakta centenary souvenir* (Desabhakta Konda Vekatappayya Pantulu Centenary Celebration Committee), 1966.

—. *The freedom struggle in Andhra Pradesh. 4 vols.* Hyderabad: The Andhra Pradesh state committee, 1965.

—. *The Development of local boards in the Madras Presidency.* Bombay: Local Self-Governing Institute, 1938.

Verma, B.R. and Unnikrishnan. K. *Encyclopaedic biography of Indian freedom fighters.* New Delhi: Commonwealth, 2004.

Vishwanath, V.T. *Mahatma Gandhi and the civil disobedience movement: a study in the dynamics of the mass movement.* Delhi: Eastern, 1988.

Washbrook, D.A. *The emergence of provincial politics: the Madras Presidency, 1870-1920.* Cambridge: Cambridge University Press, 1976.

Washbrook, D.A and C. J. Baker. *South India: political institutions and political change. 1880-1940.* Delhi: Macmillan, 1975.

Who's who in India. Lucknow: Newul Kishore Press, 1911.

Woolacott, J.E. *India on trial: a study of present conditions.* London: Macmillan, 1929.

Index

N

Images

Arthur Galletti and Clara Salvadori at their engagement, 1900

Clara and sisters with their Salvadori grandparents and cousin
Mario around 1905

Arthur, Clara, their three eldest children, Collector's Residence staff and local friends some time around World War I

Clara with her three daughters and local friends during the 1920s

Arthur Galletti on a snipe ground, 1930

The Collector's Residence in Tinnevelly where Arthur and
Clara lived in the late 1920s

Arthur and Clara on their final posting, with Collector's Residence staff—and a grandchild

Arthur Galletti and a family group during his long retirement in Gubbio

Arthur Galletti

Arthur, Clara and Arthur Junior around the time of Galletti's
retirement